NUTCA~

INTERNATIONA~

FIRST EDITION

by ELINA STEINERTE, LL.B. (Hons), LL.M., Ph.D
Research Associate, School of Law,
University of Bristol

REBECCA M.M. WALLACE, MA., LL.B., Ph.D
Professor of International Human Rights Law,
The Robert Gordon University, Aberdeen

London • Sweet & Maxwell • 2008

AUSTRALIA
Law Book Company
Sydney

CANADA and USA
Carswell
Toronto

HONG KONG
Sweet & Maxwell Asia

NEW ZEALAND
Brookers
Wellington

SINGAPORE and MALAYSIA
Sweet & Maxwell Asia
Singapore and Kuala Lumpur

NUTCASES

INTERNATIONAL LAW

Published in 2008 by Sweet & Maxwell Limited of
100 Avenue Road, London NW3 3PF
Typeset by YHT Ltd, London
Printed in the Netherlands by Krips.

No natural forests were destroyed to make this product.
Only farmed timber was used and re-planted.

A CIP catalogue record for this book is available
from the British Library.

ISBN 978-1-847-030177

CONTENTS

TABLE OF CASES

TABLE OF STATUTES

LATIN TERMS

Ad hoc	For this purpose (only).
Animus	Intention.
De facto	Existing as a matter of fact.
De jure	Existing as a matter of law.
Dolus specialis	Specific intent.
Ex aequo et bono	The ICJ has the power, if the parties to a contentious case agree, to take a decision, not on the basis of the sources limited to Art.38(1) of the ICJ Statute.
Fortiori	Adv. by the stronger; with better reason; all the more.
Forum prorogatum	Term, which describes the case where, by agreement of the parties, the case is submitted to a judge other than the judge ordinarily competent in the matter.
Hostis humani generis	An enemy of the human race.
Inter se	This doctrine is still acceptable to the extent that some aspects of *inter se* relationships are governed by the Conventions of the Commonwealth rather than international law.
Ipso facto	That very fact or act.
Jure imperii	Acts performed in a governmental or public capacity.
Jure gestionis	Acts performed in a commercial or private capacity.
Jus ad bellum	Refers to the right to make war.
Jus cogens	See Arts 53 and 64 of 1969 Vienna Convention on the Law of Treaties. Otherwise known as peremptory norms of international law. The term is founded in customary international law and is so fundamental it binds all states. No states can derogate from this and it can only be modified by a subsequent norm of international law with the same character.
Jus in bello	Relates to the laws and customs of war.
Locus standi	The right of a party to appear and be heard before a court.
Non liquet	Inability to decide due to lack of a legal source.

Obiter dicta	Something said by a judge in a decision that is not essential to the decision and does not form part of the *ratio decidendi.*
Obligations erga omnes	Obligations owed to the international legal community as a whole and obligations, which every state has an interest in having respected.
Opinio juris sive necessitatis	Is an essential element of custom. It requires that a state practice have legal obligations
Pacta sunt servanda	See Art.26 1969 Vienna Convention on the Law of Treaties. Agreements are binding upon parties to it and must be performed by them in good faith.
Pacta tertiis nec nocent nec prosunt	Third parties receive neither rights nor duties from contracts.
Par in parem non habat imperium	One cannot exercise authority over an equal.
Persona non grata	The process by which an ambassador or other diplomatic agent who is personally unacceptable to the receiving government is removed.
Ratio decedendi	The rule in a decision, crucial part of a judgment.
Ratione personae	This term relates to the person as opposed to the state.
Ratione temporis	This term relates to time.
Ratione materiae	The term refers to the nature of a dispute or subject matter of that dispute.
Rebus sic stantibus	Through a fundamental change of circumstance, international law recognises that treaties may cease to be binding upon the parties.
Stare decisis	The decisions of the ICJ have no binding force except between the parties and in respect of that particular case.
Terra nullius	Unclaimed land. The term is used in relation to discovery and is a method of acquiring territorial sovereignty.
Uta possedetis juris	Seen as a general principle of international law. The term is derived from the Spanish (South American), where the boundaries of former colonies were deemed to constitute the boundaries of newly independent successor states.

LIST OF ABBREVIATIONS

AC	Appeal Court
ACTA	Alien Claims Tort Act
AJIL	American Journal of International Law
ASIL	American Society of International Law
AYBIL	Australian Yearbook of International Law
BYIL	British Yearbook of International Law
CEDAW	Convention on the Elimination of all Forms of Discrimination against Women
CERD	Convention on the Elimination of Racial Discrimination
Co	Company
ECHR	European Court of Human Rights
ECOSOC	Economic and Social Committee
EEZ	Exclusive Economic Zone
EHRR	European Human Rights Reports
EU	European Union
FRY	Federal Republic of Yugoslavia
GA	General Assembly (UN)
HL	House of Lords
HRC	Human Rights Committee
ICC	International Criminal Court
ICCPR	International Covenant on Civil and Political Rights
ICESCR	International Covenant on Economic, Social and Cultural Rights
ICJ	International Court of Justice
ICJ Rep	International Court of Justice Reports
ICLQ	International and Comparative Law Quarterly
ICTR	International Criminal Tribunal for Rwanda
ICTY	International Criminal Tribunal for Yugoslavia
ILC	International Law Commission
ILM	International Law Materials
ILO	International Labour Organisation
Ltd	Limited
KB	Kings Bench
NGO	Non-Governmental Organisation

OAU	Organisation for African Unity (now known as the African Union)
Para	Paragraph
PCIJ	Permanent Court of International Justice
PIL	Public International Law
PLO	Palestine Liberation Organisation
QB	Queens Bench
RAPPORTEUR	A reporter who is appointed by the UN, normally to look into and report on specific topics
RIAA	Report of International Arbitral Awards
SC	Security Council (UN)
SIAC	Special Immigration Appeals Commission
UDHR	Universal Declaration on Human Rights
UK	United Kingdom
UN	United Nations
UNEP	United Nations Environment Programme
UNTS	United Nations Treaty Series
US	United States of America
USSR	United Soviet Socialist Republic
WHO	World Health Organisation
WTO	World Trade Organisation

1. SOURCES OF INTERNATIONAL LAW

Customary International Law

Key Principle: **Short passage of time is not necessarily a bar to the formation of customary international law.**

North Sea Continental Shelf cases (Federal Republic of Germany v Denmark); and (Federal Republic of Germany v Netherlands) 1969

Facts: Agreement was made between the Federal Republic of Germany (FRG) and the Netherlands in 1964, and the FRG and Denmark in 1965. These agreements were to the effect of drawing a lateral line between the Netherlands and the FRG, and Denmark and the FRG in respect of delimiting the North Sea Continental Shelf. These agreements only drew the dividing line for a short distance from the coast, namely in the immediate vicinity of their North Sea coast. Further agreement proved impossible and a special agreement was made referring the matter to the ICJ. The ICJ joined the two cases and addressed the question: "what principles and rules of international law are applicable to the delimitation as between the parties of the area with the Continental Shelf in the North Sea which appertain to them beyond the partial boundary as determined?"

Denmark and the Netherlands maintained that the appropriate principle to be applied in the drawing of the boundary line would be that of the "equidistance special circumstances principle" pursuant to Art.6(2) of the 1958 Geneva Convention on the Continental Shelf. FRG on the other hand favoured the doctrine of the just and equitable share. Denmark and the Netherlands were both parties to the 1958 Convention. The FRG, although a signatory, had not ratified the 1958 Convention. Denmark and the Netherlands contended that the method employed pursuant to Art.6(2), namely the equidistance principle was a reflection of contemporary customary international law. The matter had to be decided under customary international law as the relevant treaty, the 1958 Geneva Convention on the Continental Shelf was not yet in force for all parties to the dispute.

Held: See pp.52, 105, 110 and 199 for further discussion.

The ICJ held that in respect of time limits a short period of time is not necessarily or of itself a bar to the formation of a new rule of customary international law. However the Court noted that within the time period in question, the state practice, including that of states whose interests are specially affected, must be extensive and virtually uniform with regard to the provision and should moreover occur in such a way as to show a general recognition that a rule of law or legal obligation is involved.

The ICJ also held that the employment of the equidistance method of delimitation was not mandatory, and that no single method of delimitation was obligatory in all circumstances. The applicable rules of international law were that delimitation must be done by agreement in accordance with equitable principles and taking into account all relevant circumstances. This is to provide each party with all those parts of the Continental Shelf constituting a natural prolongation of its land, territory into and under the sea. In the event of an overlap, the parties involved should decide on a regime of joint use etc. The Court identified that in negotiations between parties such factors must be taken into account as the general configuration of the coasts of the parties; any special or unusual features; physical and geological structure; natural resources of the Continental Shelf areas involved; and the element of a reasonable degree of proportionality. 1969 ICJ Reports 3.

Commentary

This case indicates that the state practice must be accompanied by the relevant *opinio juris* so as to endorse that a rule of law or legal obligation has evolved. However the time element is of rather minimal importance and what is more relevant is that during the time period in question the state practice is uniform and extensive. The judgment shows that the Court paid special attention to the identity of the states concerned and their particular interest in the subject matter. The parties were under no obligation to apply either the 1958 Convention on the Continental Shelf or the equidistance method as a mandatory rule of customary international law.

The case was also instructive with regard to equitable principles.

It is worth noting that the parties used the ICJ's judgment as the basis of treaties for the delimitation of their respective Continental Shelf.

Key Principles: **The burden of proof lies with the party alleging the existence of the custom. An alleged regional custom demands greater uniformity in practice than a general custom.**

The Asylum case (Columbia v Peru) 1950

Facts: Following an unsuccessful rebellion in Peru in 1948 an arrest warrant was issued for one of the leaders of the rebellion (Haya de La Torre) a Peruvian national. He sought and was granted asylum by Columbia in its Peruvian Embassy in Lima. Columbia sought, but Peru refused, to provide a safe conduct for Haya de La Torre from the country.

Columbia requested the ICJ to rule that it (Columbia) as the state granting asylum was the country competent to characterise the offence as political for the purposes of the asylum. Columbia based its submission on treaty and "American international law in general" or regional or local custom peculiar to Latin American states.

Held: The ICJ held that the party relying on the custom must demonstrate that the custom relied upon was established in such a manner so as to become binding on the other party. Therefore it was incumbent on the Columbian government to demonstrate the rule it was seeking to rely on was in accordance with a constant and uniform usage practised by the states in question. This usage was the expression of a right appertaining to the state granting asylum and involved a duty on the territorial state. This, the ICJ maintained, flowed directly from Art.38 of the ICJ Statute and that article's reference to international custom "as evidence of a general practice accepted as law".

In spite of invoking a number of instances based on treaty, Columbia failed to show that the practice in question was followed because of a legal obligation rather than mere political expediency or courtesy. The ICJ considered that the instances put before it showed so much uncertainty, contradiction and fluctuation in the exercise of diplomatic asylum that there was no rule of customary international law formed. This was further reflected in a number of conventions on diplomatic asylum. Consequently in the judgment of the Court the Colombian government had failed to establish a rule of customary international law. The Court also took special note of the fact that Peru had not ratified the 1933 and 1939 Montevideo Conventions. 1950 ICJ Reports 266

Commentary
The case is illustrative as to how a regional rule of customary international law may be formed. The ICJ found against the existence of a regional custom because of a lack of evidence and put the burden of proof upon the party alleging the existence of a regional custom. However it should be noted that inconsistency per se does not prevent a rule from being accepted as customary international law. Nevertheless in respect of a regional custom the consistency should be more evident than with a general custom, because the development of a regional custom involves fewer participating states.

Key Principles: **General customary international law must be determined by the general practice of states and not just by the states party to the dispute before the ICJ.** *Opinio juris* **may be deduced from the attitude of the Parties concerned and that of states to certain General Assembly Resolutions.**

Nicaragua case (Nicaragua v United States (Military and Paramilitary Activities in and Against Nicaragua)) 1986

Facts: Following the overthrow of the right wing government in Nicaragua in 1979, the US in 1981 ceased economic aid on the ground that the left wing Sandinista government in Nicaragua had aided the gorillas fighting against the El Salvador government with which the US enjoyed good relations. Nicaragua claimed that the US had acted contrary to customary international law in doing so.

Among the activities complained of was the use of direct armed force against Nicaragua by virtue of laying mines in Nicaraguan internal and territorial waters, damage to both Nicaraguan and foreign merchant ships, the attacking and damaging of oil installations, Nicaraguan ports, naval bases, and provision of assistance to Nicaraguan gorillas (the Contras) who had been fighting to overthrow the Sandinista government. Nicaragua also claimed that the US had acted in breach of a bilateral Friendship, Commerce and Navigational Treaty (the US Nicaraguan Treaty 1956).

The US denied the ICJ had jurisdiction on the basis of a reservation to the jurisdiction of the Court submitted by the US excluding the matter from coming before the Court if it related to the application of a multilateral treaty. (Regarding the reservation and the Court's jurisdiction under Art.36(2) see section on Settlement of International Disputes.) The ICJ however established its jurisdiction and proceeded to hear the case on the merits, considering whether the US had infringed customary international law.

The relevant multilateral treaty was the UN Charter and in particular the provisions relating to the non-use of force, Art.2(4). Nicaragua contested that rules of customary international law, although similar in content to those of the UN Charter, had not been suspended by the UN Charter.

Held: See pp.55, 105, 110 and 182 for further discussion.

The ICJ held that even if a treaty norm and a customary norm were to have exactly the same content it did not necessarily follow that the treaty process was such to deprive the customary norm of its separate applicability.

The Court declared that the UN Charter Art.51 referred to pre-existing customary international law and found Art.51 did not subsume and "supervene" customary international law but it rather demonstrated that customary international law existed alongside treaty law.

The Court maintained that the two sources of law did not overlap exactly. However, even if the customary norm and the treaty norm were of exactly the same content, incorporation of the customary international law into treaty law was not such as to deprive the customary norm of its applicability as distinct from that of the treaty norm. In other words, reflection of customary international law in treaty law does not deny customary international law of its independent existence. The Court also held that it was necessary to maintain this independent existence from the stand-point of the applicability of the respective rules. The Court illustrated this by reference to an anticipated legal dispute affecting two states and the grounds whereby a state could exercise its right to terminate or suspend the operation of a treaty on the ground that the other party was in violation of a provision essential to the accomplishment of the object and purpose of the treaty. However if the rule also existed in customary international law the failure of one state to apply the other rule does not justify the other state declining to apply the other rule. The Court further maintained that rules identical in treaty law and in customary international law are distinguishable by reference to the methods employed for their interpretation and application.

In examining the existence of *opinio juris* necessary for the formation of a custom, the ICJ stated the existence of *opinio juris* must be confirmed by state practice. The Court acknowledged for a rule to be established as customary international law the corresponding practice did not require to be in "absolutely rigorous conformity with the rule". To deduce the existence of custom it is sufficient that the conduct of states should be generally consistent with the alleged custom. Inconsistencies to the given rule should generally be treated as breaches of that rule rather than indications of the recognition of a new rule.

As to how *opinio juris* may be deduced, the Court held that the attitude of the parties and states towards certain General Assembly Resolutions could be indicative of *opinio juris*. 1986 ICJ Reports 14.

Commentary

The Nicaragua case is an example of the ICJ dealing with a number of international law issues in one case. As far as the sources of international law are concerned and the formation of customary international law, the Nicaragua judgment makes it clear that treaty law and customary international law may have an independent existence and may have separate applications even in the case when the two bodies of law deal with the same subject matter.

The Court also made important clarifications about the formation of the crucial element of a custom, namely, *opinio juris*. It was stated this can be deduced from state practice, which does not need to be in absolute uniformity, but only of general consistency. The Court further noted that state practice can be deduced from the attitude of states towards UN General Assembly Declarations, see also *Legality of the Threat or Use of Nuclear Weapons case*, Advisory Opinion (below). However the Court warned that such *opinio juris* should be deduced with "due caution", given that politics may influence how states may vote in General Assembly Resolutions.

Key Principle: **General Assembly Resolutions may show the formation of** *opinio juris.*

Legality of the Threat or Use of Nuclear Weapons case Advisory Opinion 1996

Facts: The Advisory Opinion was requested by the General Assembly on the following question: "Is the threat or use of nuclear weapons in any circumstances permitted under international law?" The question was posed to the ICJ in the final paragraph of the Resolution 49/75K, adopted by the General Assembly on December 15, 1994.

Held: See pp.56, 193, 110 and 211 for further discussion.

The ICJ examined the Resolutions of the General Assembly and noted that these:

> "even if they are not legally binding, may sometimes have normative value. They can, in certain circumstances, provide evidence important for establishing the existence of a rule or emergence of an *opinio juris*. To establish whether this is true of a given General Assembly resolution, it is necessary to look at its content and the conditions of its adoption; it is also necessary to see whether *opinio juris* exists as to its normative character. Or a series of resolutions may show the gradual evolution of the *opinio juris* required for the establishment of a new rule" (para.70).

1996 ICJ Reports 226.

Commentary

In this Advisory Opinion the ICJ set out guidelines as to when General Assembly Resolutions may provide evidence of the formation of *opinio juris*. In this particular case, after having examined the formulation of the resolutions, their focus and whether they had been adopted with negative votes and abstentions being recorded, the ICJ concluded that *opinio juris* had as yet not been formed.

Key Principle: A local custom may exist between only two states.

Rights of Passage over Indian Territory case (Portugal v India) 1960

Facts: Portugal held a number of small territorial enclaves within India. One such enclave, Daman, was on the coast whereas the others were inland. Portugal claimed a right of passage to these enclaves and maintained that India had interfered with the exercise of that right.

Held: The ICJ rejected the claim by India that no local custom could be established between only two states. The Court ruled that it is difficult to see why the number of states between which a local custom may be established on the basis of long practice must necessarily be more than two. 1960 ICJ Reports 6.

Commentary
This case indicates that for a local custom to exist it is not necessary to have a prescribed number of states. Therefore a local custom may exist only between two states.

Key Principles: **International law governs the relations of states; rules of international law arise through the agreement of states; restrictions upon the independence of states cannot be presumed; jurisdiction is territorial but international law does not prohibit a state from exercising jurisdiction in its own territory over a case relating to acts which have taken place abroad; no rule of customary international law regarding collision cases; criminal proceedings fall within the exclusive jurisdiction of the flag state.**

SS Lotus case (France v Turkey) (1927)

Facts: A French steamer, the Lotus, and a Turkish steamer, the Boz-Kourti, collided on the high seas in the Mediterranean. The Turkish steamer was sunk and eight Turkish sailors died. On the arrival of the Lotus at Constantinople the officer on watch at the time of the collision was arrested and joint criminal proceedings instituted against him and the Captain of the Turkish steamer.

The matter was brought to the ICJ by special agreement and the question put to the Court was whether Turkey, by exercising jurisdiction over the French officer, was acting contrary to international law and in particular to Art.15 of the 1923 Convention of Lausanne. (Note: Article 15 provided that all questions of jurisdiction between Turkey and other Contracting Parties must be decided in accordance with the principles of international law.)

The contention of the French government was that the Turkish courts, in order to establish jurisdiction, should be able to point to some title of jurisdiction recognised by international law in favour of Turkey. France also maintained that the flag state had exclusive jurisdiction over all occurrences which took place on a merchant ship on the High Seas.

Held: See pp.55 and 134 for further discussion.

The Court ruled that apart from certain special cases defined by international law, the jurisdiction lay with the flag state over vessels on the high seas. However, the Court rejected the argument that a state in its own territory was precluded from exercising jurisdiction over acts which had occurred on board a foreign vessel on the high seas.

The Court concluded:

> "there was no rule of international law prohibiting the state to which the ship on which the effects of the offence have taken place belongs, from regarding the offence as having been committed in its territory and prosecuting, accordingly, the delinquent".

This could only be overcome if it could be demonstrated there was a rule of customary international law which gave exclusive jurisdiction to the flag state. The ICJ then looked at the evidence presented by France alleging the existence of such a rule but determined that it was not conclusively proven. (1927) PCIJ Series A No.10.

Commentary

What emerged from this case was that although there was evidence that states which, when in a similar situation as Turkey, would abstain from criminal proceedings, such abstention was not because of a conscious legal duty. Therefore the relevant *opinio juris* was not present. Thus the judgment demonstrates the importance of *opinio juris* and failure to prove its existence may be fatal to a case.

Key Principle: A state, that from the outset consistently objects to a particular practice, is not bound by any rule of alleged customary international law which may arise from the practice.

Anglo Norwegian Fisheries case 1951

Facts: See pp.106 and 136 for further discussion.

Held: The ICJ stated that:

> "although the ten-mile rule has been adopted by certain States both in their national law and in their treaties and conventions, and although certain arbitral decisions have applied it as between these States, other States have adopted a different limit. Consequently, the ten-mile rule has not acquired the authority of a general rule of international law. In any event the ten-mile rule would appear to be inapplicable as against Norway inasmuch as she has always opposed any attempt to apply it to the Norwegian coast".

1951 ICJ Reports 116.

Commentary
This case illustrates that a state which has consistently and constantly expressed its opposition to a practice will not be bound by any rule of customary international law, emerging from that practice.

Key Principle: Definition of *erga omnes*.

Barcelona Traction case (Belgium v Spain) (2nd Phase) 1970

Facts: Belgium brought a claim on behalf of Belgian nationals who held the majority of the shares in the *Barcelona Traction Light and Power Company Ltd*. The company, in addition to being declared bankrupt by a Spanish Court in 1948, sustained further adverse effects as a consequence of steps taken by the Spanish authorities.

Initially Canada intervened on behalf of the company but subsequently withdrew and following this, Belgium intervened. Spain objected to Belgium's intervention on the basis the injury was to the company and not to the shareholders. Accordingly Spain argued Belgium lacked the *locus standi* to bring the claim.

This preliminary objection of Spain was joined to the merits of the case.

Held: See pp.26, 171, and 220 for further discussion.

In making a distinction between different branches of international law, the ICJ stated that:

> "an essential distinction should be drawn between the obligations of a State towards the international community as a whole, and those arising *vis-à-vis* another State in the field of diplomatic protection. By their very nature the former are the concern of all States. In view of the importance of the rights involved, all States can be held to have a legal interest in their protection: they are obligations *erga omnes*" (para.33).

The ICJ enumerated instances of such *erga omnes* obligations and held that they arose from the outlawing of acts of aggression, and of genocide, as well as such basic human rights as protection from slavery and racial discrimination. 1970 ICJ Reports 3.

Commentary

This statement of the ICJ on the difference between a breach of international law and a breach of an *erga omnes* rule has become one of the most important and well-known statements of the Court on the issue of *erga omnes* rules. The instances of *erga omnes* obligations cited by the Court were only illustrative examples and the list was not intended to be exhaustive.

The statement is the most authoritative definition of *erga omnes* obligations and has been utilised by the ICJ on various occasions, one of the most recent ones being in the *Legal Consequences of the Construction of a Wall in the Occupied Palestinian Territory* Advisory Opinion (see pp.61 and 161).

Treaties

Key Principles: Customary international law and treaty law have equal authority. However if a treaty and custom exist simultaneously in respect of the issue in dispute then the treaty provision takes precedence.

The Wimbledon case (France, Italy, Japan and the UK v Germany) 1923

Facts: The case concerned the Kiel Canal, which cuts through Germany and links the Baltic and North Seas. According to Art.380 of the Treaty of Versailles (1919):

> "The Kiel Canal and its approaches shall be maintained free and open to the vessels of commerce and of war of all nations at peace with Germany on terms of entire equality".

The question before the Court was whether this provision violated the sovereignty of Germany.

Held: See p.54 for further discussion. The PCIJ declared that although it was prohibited under customary international law to permit the passage of armaments through the territory of a neutral state to the territories of a belligerent state, effect should be given to Art.380 of the Treaty of Versailles. The Court held that pursuant to this provision the Kiel Canal was to be "free and open to vessels of commerce and of war of all nations at peace with Germany on terms of entire equality". 1923 PCIJ Reports Series LA No.1.

Commentary
In this case the PCIJ was faced with a conflict between a rule of customary international law and a treaty provision. The Court held that in such instances, when there is a customary rule and treaty provision both dealing with the issue at dispute, the treaty law must take precedence. Thus an expressly intended treaty provision will take precedence over an earlier conflicting rule of customary international law. However, should there arise a new rule of customary international law, it would take precedence over an older treaty provision. See also *Nicaragua* case (below).

Key Principle: **Acknowledgement of the compatibility test with respect to reservations to a convention.**

Reservations to the Genocide Convention case Advisory Opinion 1951

Facts: The General Assembly requested an Advisory Opinion from the ICJ on three particular questions:

1) Whether a reserving state to the Genocide Convention could be regarded as a party to the Convention if some, although not all parties to the Convention objected to the reservation;

2) Given an affirmative answer, what relationship subsisted between the reserving and objecting states as well as the relationship between the reserving state and non-objecting states;

3) What would be the legal effect of an objection from a signatory state (i.e. a state, which had not yet ratified) or by a state entitled to sign or accede but which had not done so?

Held: The Court's opinion was that a state which had made a reservation on which there had been an objection made by some but not all parties to the Convention, could be regarded as being a party to the Convention provided the reservation was compatible with the object and purpose of the treaty. In the absence of such compatibility the reserving state could not be regarded as a party to the Convention.

As to the effect of a reservation on the relationship between the reserving state and those objecting and those not, the Court stated:

> "(a) if a party to the Convention objects to a reservation which it considers to be incompatible with the object and purpose of the Convention, it can in fact consider that the reserving State is not a party to the Convention;
> (b) that if, on the other hand, a party accepts the reservation as being compatible with the object and purpose of the Convention, it can in fact consider that the reserving State is a party to the Convention."

Finally the ICJ observed that an objection to a reservation made by a signatory state which has not yet ratified the

Convention would only have legal effect upon ratification. Until that moment it would only be a notice to the eventual attitude of the signatory state. An objection to a reservation made by a state which is entitled to sign or accede but which has not yet done so, the Court deemed to be without legal effect. 1951 ICJ Reports 15.

Commentary
This Advisory Opinion represented a different approach to reservations from what had previously been the position under international law. Prior to this Advisory Opinion reservations were required to be accepted by all Contracting Parties. This Advisory Opinion introduced a more flexible approach allowing the existence of different legal relationships between different parties to the same Convention.

In answering the first question, the Court formulated the "compatibility test", which represented a move away from the objective to the subjective interpretation of the object and purpose of a treaty. The object and purpose refers to both the substantive provisions and the nature and spirit of a treaty.

The approach of the Court in this Advisory Opinion is mirrored in Art.19 of the 1969 Vienna Convention on the Law of Treaties.

Key Principles: **Doctrine of *rebus sic stantibus*. Change of circumstances must be fundamental before a treaty is terminated on that ground.**

Fisheries Jurisdiction case (United Kingdom v Iceland) 1973

Facts: The case arose in the context of the "Cod War" over Iceland's unilateral extension of its exclusive fisheries zone to 12 miles. Iceland sought to have terminated a 1961 Exchange of Notes with the United Kingdom pursuant to which either party could refer a dispute relating to Iceland's extension of its fishing zone to the ICJ. It was on the basis of this Exchange of Notes that the United Kingdom had referred the case to the ICJ.

Held: The Court ruled that Art.62 of the Vienna Convention on the Law of Treaties, relating to termination of a treaty because of a fundamental change of circumstances, represented a codification of existing customary international law. The Court emphasised that an essential requirement of Art.62 was that the change must be fundamental or vital and must be such so as to "imperil" the existence of one of the parties. The Court highlighted that the change of circumstances alleged should have resulted in a radical transformation of the extent of the obligations still to be performed. The change must be such as to increase the burden of the obligation to be undertaken so as to make it essentially different from the original obligation. In this particular case it was held the jurisdictional obligation remained exactly as it had been when the agreement had been entered into in 1961. 1973 ICJ Reports 3.

Commentary
The doctrine of "change of circumstance" is one which can only be successfully invoked when the change brings about circumstances which were not contemplated by the relevant Contracting Parties at the time of the treaties conclusion. The decision in this case was referred to by the Court in *Gabcikovo-Nagymaros Project* case (see below).

Key Principles: **A "state of necessity" is not a ground for termination of a treaty; impossibility of performance cannot be invoked by the party for termination of a treaty; fundamental change of circumstance must be unforeseen.**

Gabcikovo-Nagymaros Project case (Hungary v Slovakia) 1997

Facts: Hungary and Czechoslovakia concluded a treaty in 1977 to assist in the construction of dams on the River Danube (Slovakia became a party to the 1977 Treaty as successor state to Czechoslovakia). In 1989 Hungary unilaterally suspended and subsequently abandoned the project in response to public concerns about the environmental consequences. Czechoslovakia then took unilateral measures which resulted in the diversion of the River Danube.

In 1993 the case was referred to the ICJ by special agreement and the Court was asked to determine the legality of Hungary's initial suspension and subsequent abandonment of the work, the legality of Czechoslovakia's actions in diverting the river, and Hungary's termination of the treaty, which it had intimated in May 1992. In practice the outcome of Czechoslovakia's diversion was that Czechoslovakia appropriated for its use, and benefit, some 80–90 per cent of the water of the river Danube before returning the waters to the main bed of the river. It did this despite the fact the river Danube is not only a shared international water course but also an international boundary river.

Hungary sought to argue the principle of the "impossibility of performance" by applying and contending the essential object of the 1977 Treaty, namely an economic joint investment regime had permanently disappeared, making the 1977 Treaty impossible to perform. Hungary also maintained a number of factors such as profound changes of a political nature, the diminishing economic viability of the project and the development of environmental knowledge acted accumulatively to fundamentally change circumstances.

Held: See p.195 for further discussion.

The Court ruled that the 1969 Vienna Convention of the Law of Treaties was not directly applicable to the 1977 Treaty as both countries had only ratified the Vienna Convention after the 1977 Treaty was concluded. Thus the only provisions of the Vienna Convention applicable to the 1977 Treaty were those which represented customary international law, namely, Arts 60–62 which deal with the termination and suspension of a treaty. The Court acknowledged that the 1977 Treaty was silent on the matter of termination and thus it could only be terminated on the limited grounds provided for in the 1969 Vienna Convention.

It was held that impossibility of performance as reflected in Art.61 of the 1969 Vienna Convention requires the "permanent disappearance or destruction of an object indispensable for the execution" of the Treaty. The Court highlighted that if the joint exploitation of the investment was no longer possible this was because Hungary had failed to carry out the work it was responsible for under the 1977 Treaty. The Court made reference to Art.61(2) of the 1969 Vienna Convention, precluding impossibility of performance being invoked by a party which has brought about that impossibility by its own breach of a treaty obligation and thus rejected Hungary's assertion.

In respect of a fundamental change of circumstance, the Court held that the prevalent political conditions were not so closely linked to the object and purpose of the 1977 Treaty that they went to the core of the consent of the parties and, in changing, so radically altered the extent of the obligations still to be performed.

The Court ruled that the changed circumstances put forward by Hungary were not of such a nature as to either individually or collectively radically transform the extent of the obligations still to be performed. The Court emphasised that the negative and conditional wording of Art.62 of the 1969 Vienna Convention was a clear indication that the stability of treaty relations demands the plea of fundamental change of circumstances be applied only in exceptional cases. In this case the ICJ held that the notification by Hungary of its termination of the 1977 Treaty in May 1992 was premature as Czechoslovakia had not at that time breached the 1977 Treaty. 1997 ICJ Reports 7.

Commentary
This case illustrates that in situations of treaty termination both impossibility of performance and radical change of circumstances will be applied only in very exceptional cases. The ICJ in this instance also acknowledged that Arts 60–62 of the 1969 Vienna Convention on the Law of Treaties represented customary international law.

Key Principle: **Subsequent practice important for the interpretation of international treaties.**

Competence of the General Assembly for the Admission of a State to the United Nations case Advisory Opinion 1950

Facts: The General Assembly in the Resolution of November 22, 1949 requested an Advisory Opinion, on the following question:

> "Can the admission of a State to membership in the United Nations, pursuant to Article 4, paragraph 2, of the Charter, be effected by a decision of the General Assembly, when the Security Council has made no recommendation for admission by reason of the candidate failing to obtain the requisite majority or of the negative vote of a permanent Member upon a resolution so to recommend?"

Held: See pp.81 and 209 for further discussion.
The ICJ held that according to the practice of the bodies entrusted with admission matters under Art.4 of the UN Charter, the General Assembly must receive a recommendation for membership from the Security Council. The Court noted that this

practice had even been reflected in the Rules of Procedure of the General Assembly. Consequently the ICJ came to the conclusion that the General Assembly must receive a recommendation from the Security Council on admission of a new member and the absence of such a recommendation could not be treated in the same way as that of a negative recommendation. 1950 ICJ Reports 4.

Commentary

In this Advisory Opinion the ICJ dealt with the interpretation of the UN Charter and while the Court took note of the text of the UN Charter, it paid special attention to the subsequent practice adopted by the organs. Thus, the interpretation of constituent documents of international organisations is treated differently from the interpretation of regular multilateral treaties.

Key Principle: **Endorsed subsequent practice as important for the interpretation of international treaties.**

Legal Consequences for States of the Continued Presence of South Africa in Namibia (South-West Africa) Notwithstanding Security Council Resolution 276 Advisory Opinion 1971

Facts: The Security Council of the United Nations requested the ICJ for an Advisory Opinion on the following question:

> "What are the legal consequences for States of the continued presence of South Africa in Namibia notwithstanding Security Council Resolution 276 (1970)?"

South Africa contended that the ICJ was not competent to deliver an opinion on this matter as, inter alia, two of the permanent members of the Security Council had abstained when voting for the resolution in question.

Held: See pp.57, 82 and 222 for further discussion.

The ICJ stated that the voluntary abstention by a permanent member of the Security Council did not constitute a bar for the adoption of a resolution since such a practice had been constantly and uniformly applied by the Security Council and had not been objected to by either the members of the Security Council or other UN members. Thus, the ICJ concluded that this constituted an accepted practice which was most important when interpreting the provisions of the UN Charter on the matter. 1971 ICJ Reports 16.

Commentary
The ICJ in this case underlined the difference between the rules of interpretation applicable to the regular multilateral treaties and those which constitute the founding documents of international organisations. It was held that for the latter type of agreements, the subsequent practice adopted by the organisation and its organs are of particular importance when interpreting its provisions. Thus, in the case of the interpretation of the constituent document of the organisation, the rule embodied in Art.31(3)(b) (importance of subsequent practice) in the Vienna Convention on the Law of the treaties is of particular importance.

Key Principles: **An oral undertaking can have legal effect; ordinary meaning of word applies in interpretation.**

Legal Status of Eastern Greenland case (Denmark v Norway) 1933

Facts: The Norwegian government, by way of an oral statement made by the Norwegian Minister of Foreign Affairs, Mr Ihlen, proclaimed that Norway "would not make any difficulties in the settlement of the question of the extension of Danish sovereignty over Greenland". The PCIJ was asked whether the Ihlen Declaration, if not amounting to a definitive recognition by Norway of Danish sovereignty, at least put Norway under an obligation to refrain from occupying any area of Greenland.

Norway submitted that the word "Greenland" in the legislative and administrative acts of the 18th century as invoked by Denmark was not used in the geographical sense, but rather referred to the colonised areas on the west coast.

Held: See p.94 for further discussion.
The Court held that because of the official position of the Minister of Foreign Affairs, the response given fell within his competencies and was therefore binding upon Norway. Norway

was under an obligation to refrain from contesting sovereignty over Greenland as a whole and *fortiori* to refrain from occupying a part of Greenland. The PCIJ maintained that the geographical meaning of the word Greenland should be regarded as the ordinary meaning of the word and if a party wishes to attribute either some unusual or exceptional meaning, then the burden of proof lies with the party making such an assertion. 1933 PCIJ Series A/B 53.

Commentary

This case shows that oral statements may also have legal effect, although the precise extent of such effects will depend upon the authority of the person making the statement, i.e. are they acting on the state's behalf and in what circumstances is such a statement being made.

This case is also important for the interpretation of treaties, as it illustrates that the ordinary meaning of a term must be applied. Therefore if a state is claiming otherwise, the burden of proof falls on the state to show the special or particular meaning is the one to be applied.

Key Principles: **Declarations made by way of unilateral acts concerning legal or factual situations may create legal obligations; such declarations may be, and often are, very specific; the form of the unilateral declaration makes no essential difference.**

Nuclear Test cases (Australia v France); (New Zealand v France) 1974

Facts: France carried out a number of nuclear tests in the South Pacific and indicated that no further tests would be conducted after 1973. The case was initiated by Australia and New Zealand against France seeking a declaration that the continuation of testing within the South Pacific was inconsistent with international law.

Held: The ICJ refrained from considering France's announcement of terminating nuclear testing as constituting a legal undertaking on the part of France. The Court also held that statements made by the President of the French Republic constituted an obligation on France. This was because of the official position held by the President. It was further stated that just as the very rule of *pacta sunt servanda* in the law of treaties is based on good faith so also is the binding character of an international obligation assumed by unilateral declaration. As to the form of such a declaration there is no special or strict requirement imposed by international law and "whether a statement is made orally or in writing makes no essential difference". 1974 ICJ Reports 253, 457.

Commentary

This judgment follows the earlier *Legal Status of Eastern Greenland* case (see above). The ICJ here deduced intention to discontinue any further nuclear testing as a legal obligation from the statement of the French President. The specific position of the French President played a central role in the Court's deliberations.

For the importance of intention in establishing the binding effect of an oral statement see *Burkina Faso v Mali* 1986 ICJ Reports 554, and *Armed Activities on the Territory of the Congo (Democratic Republic of Congo v Rwanda)* 2006, General List 126, where the ICJ found it had no jurisdiction to hear the merits.

Case Concerning the Application of the Convention on the Prevention and Punishment of the Crime of Genocide (Bosnia and Herzegovina v Yugoslavia) (Preliminary Objections) 1996

Facts: This particular case was one of a number relating to the application of the Genocide Convention between the two parties. Initially the Republic of Bosnia and Herzegovina lodged proceedings against the Federal Republic of Yugoslavia (FRY) regarding alleged breaches to the 1948 Geneva Convention on the Prevention and Punishment of Crimes of Genocide. Following the indication by the Court of certain provisional measures (see 1993 ICJ Reports 3 and 1993 ICJ Reports 325) FRY raised preliminary objections to the Court's jurisdiction.

Held: See p.220 for further discussion.

The Court determined that it had jurisdiction. 1996 ICJ Reports 595.

Commentary

This case is of interest not only because the Court found it had jurisdiction but also because of the separate opinions of Judges

Weeramanatry and Shaahbuddeen. The former maintained that there existed a principle of contemporary international law that there is automatic state succession to such conventions as the Genocide Convention which is considered a vital human rights convention. This reflected the opinion of Judge Shaahbuddeen when he stated "to effectuate its object and purpose, [the Genocide Convention] would fall to be construed as implying the expression of a unilateral undertaking by each party to the Convention to treat successor states as continuing as from independence any status which the predecessor state has a party to the Convention".

Both opinions endorsed the view expressed by the Human Rights Committee in 1992, namely "that all peoples within the territory of the Former Yugoslavia are entitled to the guarantees of the Covenants" and the General Comment No.26 of the Human Rights Committee (1997) which stated:

> "once people are accorded the protection of the rights of the Covenant, such protection devolves with territory and continues to belong to them, notwithstanding change in Government ... or state succession".

This highlights that international human rights instruments may be regarded as the exception to the principle that a new state starts with a clean slate and is not bound by the treaty obligations of its predecessor. The argument in favour of automatic succession to the Genocide Convention is that the rights recognised by it impose no burden on the state and the obligations imposed exist independently of conventional obligations.

The rights conferred by the Genocide Convention are non-derogable.

As Judge Weeramanatry also highlighted in his opinion continuity to the Genocide Convention was of particular importance in contemporary international law given the break up of so many states in many different parts of the world.

Equity

Key Principle: Under Art.38 of the ICJ Statute if not independently of that article the ICJ has some freedom to consider
principles of equity as part of the international law of which it
applies.

The Diversion of Water from the Meuse case (Netherlands v Belgium) (1937)

Facts: The case arose following the assertion by the Netherlands that Belgium had infringed a treaty obligation by building
canals which altered the flow of water in the river Meuse. The
argument being submitted by Belgium was that the Netherlands
had lost the right to bring its claim because it acted in a similar
way earlier.

Held: It was held by ten votes to three that the submissions of
the Netherlands and Belgium were not justified. However, the
separate opinion of Judge Hudson is cited as endorsing the
principles of equity and those common in national legal systems
generally. As such they were then seen as being a part of international law by virtue of Art.38(1)(c) of the ICJ Statute, if not
independently of that article. (1937) PCIJ Reports Series A/B
No.70.

Commentary
Judge Hudson was acknowledging that equity forms part of
international law. However there has been considerable academic debate as to whether equity should be treated under the
umbrella of general principles as provided for in Art.38(1)(c), is a
source in its own right, or whether it refers more to the way the
law is applied.

Key Principles: Maritime delimitation must be sought and effected by means of agreement following negotiations conducted in good faith and with genuine intention of achieving a positive result. In the event of not reaching an agreement recourse should be made to third parties. Whichever procedure is employed in delimitation was to be effected by the application of equitable criteria and practical methods so as to ensure an equitable result.

The Gulf of Maine case (Canada v US) Delimitation of the Maritime Boundary on the Gulf of Maine Area 1984

Facts: In 1981 Canada and the US referred this dispute to the ICJ following their inability to reach agreement on a joint fisheries management regime in the Gulf of Maine. This was after both countries had claimed a 200 mile fishing zone in 1976 and 1977.

Held: See p.112 for further discussion.

The Court endorsed the finding in the *North Sea Continental Shelf* cases (see above) that a solution should be sought by reference to equitable principles. 1984 ICJ Reports 246.

Commentary
Equitable principles are sought in resolving issues between states and should shape and be reflected in the solution decided.

Key Principle: It is an established rule of law that error cannot be relied upon if the party advancing it contributed to the error by its own conduct or could have avoided the error or if the circumstances were such to put the party on notice of a possible error.

Temple of Preah Vihear case 1962

Facts: The dispute arose between Cambodia and Thailand regarding the ownership of the Temple of Preah Vihear. The Temple was on an area of land that Cambodia claimed as successor to France. In support of its claim Cambodia relied on a map made in 1907 showing the Temple to be situated in French territory. The map was prepared by the Joint Franco Siamese Commission and was sent to the Siamese authorities.

It had been contended by Thailand that in respect of the disputed area of the Temple an error had been committed, an error which the Siamese authorities had been unaware of at the time when they accepted the map.

Held: The ICJ held that the persons who accepted the map, their character and qualifications, were such as to make it difficult for Thailand to plead error in law. It was also noted that the map in question had drawn such pointed attention to the Temple region that no interested party, or anyone charged, with the duty of scrutinising it would have failed to see what the map was purporting in the relevant region. It was known to the Siamese authorities that the work had been undertaken by French topographical officers to whom the work had been entrusted by the Siamese authorities. The Siamese authorities who had accepted the map without independent consideration were as a consequence precluded from pleading any error to their consent. 1962 ICJ Reports 6.

Commentary
The case highlights estoppel or personal bar as a general principle within the terms of Art.38(1)(c).

Key Principle: **Reparation is a principle of international law.**

Chorzow Factory case (Indemnity) (Merits) (1928)

Facts: The case concerns a dispute between Germany and Poland. The Polish government had taken possession of a nitrate factory at Chorzow in Poland and it was alleged that this was incompatible with the Geneva Convention of 1922 between Germany and Poland concerning Upper Silesia. The German government was seeking an indemnity from Poland in lieu of the damage experienced by the companies.

Held: See p.159 for further discussion.
The Court held in favour of Germany and declared that Poland owed reparations to Germany. (1928) PCIJ Reports Series A No.17.

Commentary
The case endorses the principle that reparation is a general principle recognised in international law. It also endorses that a

state which causes injury to another state by an internationally wrongful act is under a duty to make "full reparation".

Key Principle: *Actio popularis* **is not recognised as a general principle.**

See: South West Africa case 2nd Phase 1966 ICJ Reports 6

Key Principle: **In the absence of applicable international law cognisance must be given to the relevant institutions of domestic law.**

Barcelona Traction case (Belgium v Spain) (2nd Phase) 1970

Facts: See p.10 for further discussion.

Held: See pp.10, 171 and 220 for further discussion.

The Court denied that in the circumstances of this case Belgium enjoyed *locus standi* to bring a claim. The ICJ observed that the case involved factors which were derived from domestic law and as a consequence the Court was required to give cognisance to the relevant institutions of domestic law. To do otherwise was held to "invite serious legal difficulties" and the ICJ would lose touch with reality, particularly as there are no corresponding institutions of international law to which the Court could make reference. The ICJ specifically stated that not only would it take cognisance of domestic law but it would also refer to it. The Court noted that it was to the rules generally accepted by municipal legal systems recognising a limited company whose capital is represented by shares and not to the domestic law of a particular state that international law refers. The Court maintained that in making such reference it could not modify, still less reform, such rules. 1970 ICJ Reports 3.

Commentary
This case illustrates that in situations when international law is silent on a matter, a deciding body will make reference to domestic law. This underscores the reason for the inclusion of general principles in Art.38 of the ICJ Statute, namely to avoid such situations of *non liquet*.

2. RELATIONSHIP OF INTERNATIONAL LAW TO DOMESTIC LAW

Key Principle: Existence or absence of domestic legislative provisions is no defence for non-compliance with international obligations.

Alabama Arbitration Award

Facts: Vessels, of which the Alabama was the most notorious, were built in Liverpool for a private contractor but to specifications which made it quite evident the vessels were to be used in the Confederate cause in the American Civil War. The issue before the Claims Commission was whether Great Britain had violated its obligations as a neutral state.

The case arose out of a claim made by the US after damage had been caused by a number of vessels including the Alabama.

Held: That Great Britain could not rely on the absence of domestic legislation prohibiting interference with private contracts as a justification for non compliance with international obligations. Moore 1 Int. Arb. 495

Commentary

This case is authority for the position which international tribunals will adopt in the event of a conflict or incompatibility of domestic law and international law. A similar position was adopted in the *Freezones of Upper Savoy and Gex* (1932) PCIJ Reports Series A/B No.46. This claim is regarded as marking the start of the modern history of arbitration.

Key Principle: Domestic law provisions cannot be invoked as a valid justification for violating obligations arising under international law.

Applicability of the Obligation to Arbitrate under Section 21 of the United Nations Headquarters Agreement of June 26, 1947 Advisory Opinion 1988

Facts: The US Congress in 1987 adopted the Anti-Terrorism Act which forbade the Palestine PLO from, inter alia, establishing or maintaining an office of the UN on US territory. Since the PLO had been granted an observer status with the UN in 1974, the maintenance of its office was deemed by the UN Secretary-General to fall under the Headquarters Agreement concluded with the US in 1947. According to this agreement, parties are obliged to enter into arbitration for the settlement of their disputes.

The General Assembly requested an Advisory Opinion as to whether this would be the obligation of the US in the given situation.

Held: See p.84 for further discussion.

The ICJ answered the question in the affirmative by applying the long-standing principle of international law, which provides that international law prevails over domestic law. Thus the ICJ rejected the argument of the US that the measures against the PLO Observer Mission were taken irrespective of any obligations the US may have pursuant to the Headquarters Agreement. 1988 ICJ Reports 12.

Commentary
In this Advisory Opinion the ICJ reaffirmed the principle that provisions of domestic law cannot be invoked as a justification for a breach of an obligation arising from international law, in this case, an agreement with an international organisation.

The United Kingdom's position

Key Principle: **Customary international law is part of British domestic law.**

Triquet v Bath (1764)

Facts: The domestic servant of the Bavarian representative to Great Britain claimed diplomatic immunity in a case in which he had been named as a defendant.

Held: The immunity of foreign ministers and their domestic servants depended upon international law (The Law of Nations). The Diplomatic Privileges Act 1708 was declaratory of customary international law and part of the law of England. (1764) 3 Burr. 1478 Court of Kings Bench.

Commentary
This case endorsed a monistic approach to customary international law and reaffirmed the decision in an earlier case *Buvot v Barbuit* (1737) cases t Talb. 281, in which it was stated "the Law of Nations, in its full extent was part of the law of England".

Key Principles: **Customary international law is automatically incorporated into British law provided there is no legislative provision or judicial decision to the contrary.**

West Rand Central Gold Mining Company v R [1905]

Facts: South Africa allegedly unlawfully seized gold belonging to a British company. An action was raised against the British Crown for the gold's recovery or for compensation.
  This action was raised following British annexation of the South African Republic in 1900. The Court did not accept a conquering state assumed liability in international law for the financial obligations of its predecessor and thus was not required to determine the position of an alleged rule within English law.

Held: However the Court, in its opinion, did hold that whatever had received the common consent of civilised nations must have received the assent of Britain. Therefore such a rule could be properly called international law and should be acknowledged and applied as such by domestic tribunals. Such a rule however would have to be proved by satisfactory evidence and be so widely and generally accepted that it would be unlikely for any state to repudiate the rule. [1905] 2 KB 391.

Commentary

The opinion of the Court, which was delivered by Lord Alverstone, emphasised assent and the acknowledgement that consent had been given if the rule was acknowledged as customary international law. Hence the customary international law in question would automatically be incorporated into British law without the need for an express legislative enabling provision.

Key Principles: **Domestic courts will uphold domestic legislation even where that legislation is incompatible with alleged customary international law; state in question will still incur international liability.**

Mortensen v Peters (1906)

Facts: Mortensen, a Danish national and Master of a Norwegian ship, was convicted in the Scottish Courts of violating a bylaw issued pursuant to domestic legislation (Herring Fishery (Scotland) Act 1889). The bylaw prohibited fishing by beam or otter trawling in the Moray Firth, an area of water beyond the three mile territorial sea limit (as it was at that time). Persons convicted of such an offence were subject to a fine or imprisonment.

Mortensen was convicted of otter trawling in the Moray Firth and was therefore within the ambit of the relevant bye-law, however outside the three mile limit.

Mortensen appealed his conviction in the High Court of Justiciary.

Held: The Court held that the relationship of municipal law and international law was one of construction and emphasised "of construction only". It was not for the Court to decide whether an act of the legislature was ultra vires by virtue of having contravened what was accepted as customary international law.

The Court, faced with an Act of Parliament which had been duly passed according to the appropriate procedures, was bound to give effect to the terms of the legislative provisions. The Court acknowledged there was a presumption against Parliament contravening international law, however it was only a presumption and legislation must be applied particularly where the language is clear and express words are conclusive as to its plain implication. (1906) 8 F. (J) 93 Court of Judiciary Scotland.

Commentary

This case highlights that clear language contained in legislative provisions will be applied by the courts, albeit the provision may be at odds with recognised customary international law. A number of other successful prosecutions followed in the wake of this case and a number of those convicted went to prison rather than pay the fine. However they were released following protests from their state of nationality; Norway and subsequently the UK passed legislation prohibiting the landing in the United Kingdom of fish caught in the manner used by Mortensen.

This case emphasised the political sensitivity of the issue on the international stage and how a state can incur liability through a lack of competence to give effect to international obligations.

Key Principle: **Only an established rule of customary international law will be automatically incorporated into British law.**

R v Keyn (1876)

Facts: A collision took place between the *Francona*, a German ship, and a British ship, the *Strathclyde*, in the English Channel within three miles of the English coast. A passenger on board the *Strathclyde* died as a result of the collision and the German captain of the *Francona* was prosecuted in the English Central Criminal Court on a charge of manslaughter and found guilty.

However the question arose as to whether the English court had jurisdiction. That issue was reserved for Crown cases Reserved.

Held: This case was heard twice as initially the Court was equally divided on the matter.

On the second hearing the English courts held they did not
have such jurisdiction, the reason being that there was no
domestic legislation establishing a three mile territorial limit as
part of domestic law. Judge Cockburn C.J. stated "it is only in the
instances in which foreigners on the seas have been specifically
liable to our law by statutory enactment that the law can be
applied to them". (1876) 2 ExD. 63 Court for Crown cases
Reserved.

Commentary

This case did not represent a stance inconsistent with the
incorporation of customary international law into domestic law.
What actually was in dispute was the scope and extent of any
rule of international law relating to jurisdiction in territorial
waters. The Territorial Waters Jurisdiction Act 1878 reversed the
decision and provided:

> "the rightful jurisdiction of Her Majesty ... , extends and always has
> extended over the open seas adjacent to the coast of the United
> Kingdom and of all other parts of Her Majesty's dominions to such a
> distance as is necessary for the defence and security of such domin-
> ions ... "

Key Principles: **There is no immunity in respect of commercial transactions for a government department. Doctrine of
incorporation (adoption) was correct approach; international
law knows no rule of *stare decisis*.**

Trendtex Trading Corporation Ltd v Central Bank of Nigeria [1977]

Facts: *Trendtex Trading* sold cement which was to be used by
the Nigerian Government for a number of building projects. A
large number of similar contracts were made and on becoming
inundated with arriving shipments of cement the Nigerian
Government had to take contingency measures which included
ordering the central bank not to honour the letter of credit
involving Trendtex. Trendtex then sued the bank for payment.

Held: The Court considered the doctrine of sovereign immunity as based in international law. The Court also considered the
doctrines of "absolute immunity" and that of "restrictive

immunity". In respect of the latter it was noted that over the previous 50 years there had been a complete transformation in the function of the sovereign state. Nearly every country was engaged in some form of commercial activity, e.g. chartering of ships, buying commodities and issuing letters of credit. As a consequence of such activities a transformation had been brought about in the rules of international law relating to sovereign immunity. Many countries had departed from the rule of absolute immunity to such an extent that it could no longer be considered a rule of international law and it had been replaced by the doctrine of restrictive immunity. The Court highlighted examples from European countries and the 1952 "Tate" letter of the US. On the basis of such instances the restrictive approach was favoured by the Court of Appeal.

On the position of English law Lord Denning maintained that international law knew no rule of *stare decisis* and in support was satisfied that a rule of international law on a subject had changed from what it had been some 50–60 years previously, the Court could give effect to that change and apply the change in English law without waiting for the House of Lords to do so by way of legislation. [1977] 1 Q.B. 529 (CA).

Commentary

This decision apparently permitted an exception from an application of the principle of *stare decisis* and was founded on customary international law not being subject to this principle.

The question which confronted the Court of Appeal was whether the rules of precedent applied to rules of English law incorporating customary international law and were such that any change in international law, in the absence of legislation, would only be acknowledged by English Courts within the scope of the doctrine of *stare decisis*. It should be remembered the issue of sovereign immunity was one which was not covered by legislation but by judicial decision.

Note: this decision would appear to have precipitated the promulgation of the 1978 State Immunity Act which saw the UK adopting a restrictive immunity approach. The decision in Trendtex received judicial support in *Maclaine Watson v Department of Trade and Industry* [1989] 3 All ER 523 (see below).

Key Principle: **A treaty may only be incorporated into domestic law if there has been an express enabling act of Parliament.**

Parlement Belge (1878–79)

Facts: The vessel, the *Parlement Belge*, was the property of the King of Belgium. The vessel collided with *The Daring*, a steam tug, off the coast of Dover. After the collision the owners of *The Daring* served a writ on the *Parlement Belge* against the owners of that vessel and her freight. It was submitted the *Parlement Belge* was immune to the process of the English Courts on the grounds that she was the property of the King of Belgium and that the Coastal Convention of 1876, concluded between the British and Belgian monarchs, had placed the vessel in the category of a public ship of war.

Held: The Court denied that the provisions of the 1876 Convention could be incorporated into British domestic law without an enabling legislative provision. Sir Robert Philimore stated this would be:

> "a use of the treaty making prerogative of the Crown which I believe to be without precedent and in principle contrary to the laws of the Constitution".

(1878–79) 4 Pd 129 Probate Divorce and Admirality Division.

Commentary

This case remains good law for the principle that a treaty cannot produce adverse consequences for private law rights unless it has been made part of the UK's law by Parliament.

However on the point of immunity the Court of Appeal reversed the ruling of Sir Robert Philimore and upheld the immunity being sought as part of customary international law and thus part of British common law.

Key Principle: **Rejection of the automatic incorporation of alleged customary international law; international law only becomes part of British domestic law once accepted and adopted as such.**

Thakrar v Secretary of State 1974

Facts: The case arose as to the extent of the obligation incumbent on states under customary international law to accept its own nationals. The case came about at the time of the leaving from Uganda of numerous East Asians who claimed a right to enter the UK. However this right was curtailed by the Immigration Act 1971.

Held: In this decision Lord Denning maintained that the rules of international law only became part of English law insofar as they were accepted and adopted. 1974 Q.B. 684.

Commentary
It was being alleged there had been a customary rule of international law which required states to receive their own nationals.

The Immigration Act of 1971 had restricted the rights of a number of persons who previously enjoyed unfettered admission to the UK and therefore took precedence over any alleged rule of customary international law.

Key Principle: **A treaty is not part of domestic law unless specifically incorporated by an enabling legislative act.**

Maclaine Watson v Department of Trade and Industry [1990]

Facts: A number of claims were initiated against the International Tin Council (ITC) by its creditors. The ITC had been established by the Sixth International Tin Agreement, a treaty, and the ITC functioned in the UK on the basis of the Headquarters Agreement. Neither of the treaties had been incorporated into the domestic law of the UK. The creditors initiating the action maintained that the treaty provided them with a right of action against the state parties directly as opposed to the ITC.

Held: The Court unequivocally denied the applicant's claim and found:

"it is axiomatic that municipal courts have not and cannot have the competence to adjudicate upon or to enforce the rights arising out of the transactions entered into by sovereign states between themselves on the plane of international law".

It was further held that although as a matter of constitutional law, the Royal Prerogative embraced the making of treaties, it did not extend to amending the law or conferring rights upon individuals or depriving individuals of rights which they enjoy in domestic law without the intervention of Parliament.

The Court also acknowledged that there may be occasions when a court may be required to adjudicate upon the meaning or scope of the terms contained within an international treaty where domestic legislation, although not directly incorporating the treaty, requires reference to the terms of the treaty for the purpose of construing legislation. [1990] 2 A.C. 418 (H.L.).

Commentary

Treaties in the UK are not self-executing and treaty provisions are not part of domestic law unless they have been incorporated into law by legislation. If however a treaty has been incorporated into domestic law by way of an act of the legislature then of course, as acknowledged by the Court, its terms become subject to interpretative jurisdiction of the UK in the same way as any other piece of legislation. Likewise, if parties enter into a contract in which they choose to incorporate the terms of a treaty, then a court may be required to interpret the treaty for the purpose of determining the extent of the rights and obligations of the parties under the contract.

Treaty making power is an exercise of the Royal Prerogative in the UK. Legislation is the responsibility of Parliament and treaties must be incorporated by an enabling domestic legislative provision if they are to be relied upon in the courts of the UK.

Key Principle: **Unincorporated treaties into domestic law may create legitimate expectations on the part of individuals.**

Minister for Immigration and Ethnic Affairs re Teoh (1995)

Facts: This case before the Australian High Court involved Mr Teoh, a Malaysian citizen, who had gone to Australia in May 1988 and was granted a temporary entry permit. In July 1988 he married the *de facto* spouse of his deceased brother, namely Mrs

Jean Lim, an Australian citizen. Mrs Teoh had four children, one from her first marriage and three from the *de facto* relationship. Subsequently she and Mr Teoh had three children. Mr Teoh applied for, and was granted, a further extension of his temporary entry permit in October 1988, allowing him to remain in Australia until February 1989. Before the expiry of the permit he applied for a grant of resident status. However in November 1990 he was convicted on six counts of being knowingly involved in the importation of heroin and on three counts of being in possession of heroin. He was sentenced to six years imprisonment with a non-parole period of two years and three months. During his time in prison he was notified that, pursuant to the Migration Act of 1958, his application for residence status had been refused on the grounds that he did not meet the good character requirement. He applied for a review of the decision in February 1991 and although a strong argument was made on the basis of compassionate grounds, namely he was the only person capable of keeping the family together, the compassionate grounds were not considered sufficient for discretion to be exercised in his favour. Following acceptance of this recommendation an order was made in February 1992 for Mr Teoh to be deported. He sought a review of both the acceptance of the recommendation and the decision to deport.

This case eventually reached the Australian High Court where the main issue was whether a legitimate expectation existed and if so, what were its consequences.

Held: The Court found that;

> " ... ratification by Australia of an international convention is not to be dismissed as a merely platitudinous or ineffectual act, particularly when the instrument evidences internationally accepted standards to be applied by courts and administrative authorities in dealing with basic human rights affecting the family and children. Rather, ratification of a convention is a positive statement by the executive government of this country to the world and to the Australian people that the executive government and its agencies will act in accordance with the Convention. That positive statement is an adequate foundation for a legitimate expectation, absent any statutory or executive indications to the contrary, that administrative decision-makers will act in conformity with the Convention and treat the best interests of the children as 'a primary consideration'." (Mason C.J. and Dean C.J., Joint judgment).

However, notwithstanding the presence of a legitimate expectation, the Australian Court acknowledged that the decision maker was not compelled to act in a way that complied with such an expectation. To do so would be to incorporate the provisions of the unincorporated convention into domestic law. All that was required of the decision maker by way of procedural fairness, if he or she is proposing to make a decision inconsistent with the legitimate expectation, was to provide the affected person with the opportunity to present a case for not adopting the proposed course. (1995) C.L.R. 273.

Commentary

What the decision in this case suggests is that an individual may derive a legitimate expectation from the ratification of an international treaty. However that legitimate expectation does not bestow rights, benefits or obligations upon the individual.

See also acceptance of the principle in *R v Secretary of State for the Home Department ex parte Ahmed and Patel* [1999] Imm. A.R. 22. See in particular Lord Woolf M.R. at 36 CA.

Key Principle: **Cognisance given by domestic court to rules of international law.**

A & Others v Secretary of State for the Home Department [2005]

Facts: The issue before the House of Lords was whether evidence which had possibly been obtained by torture in a foreign state could be used in respect of a particular individual's alleged terrorist activity.

The case came before the House of Lords from the Special Immigration Appeals Commission.

Held: See p.224 for further discussion.

The House of Lords unanimously agreed that no Court or Tribunal in the UK could give cognisance to evidence which had allegedly been obtained by torture. The Court expressed the view that such evidence would be contrary to common law and was of course a crime under international law being a rule of *jus cogens*. [2005] UK HL 71.

Commentary

This case endorses that domestic courts recognise torture as *jus cogens* and as part of the common law.

UK Executive Certificate

Key Principle: **Executive certificate is conclusive.**

The Fagernes [1927]

Facts: The Court of Appeal sought the view of the Attorney General on whether a particular point in the Bristol Channel was regarded as British territory.

Held: The Court held that any definitive statement from a proper representative of the Crown should be treated as conclusive. See also *Duff Development Co v Government of Kelantan* [1924] A.C. 797 (H.L.). [1927] p.311.

Commentary
In the UK an Executive Certificate has been treated as conclusive by the Courts when it has been issued determining a factual situation. For example, as in the instant case whether recognition has been afforded. However an Executive Certificate is not regarded as conclusive in interpreting legislation or when it is with regard to the construction of documents, see for example *Re AL-FIN Corporations Patent* [1970] Ch.160 Chancery Division.

The US position

Key Principle: **International law is part of US law and where there is no treaty, no controlling executive act or judicial decision resort must be had to the customs and usages of civilised nations.**

Paquete Habana (1900)

Facts: The case involved the seizure of a foreign ship during the Spanish/US War. Two vessels were involved (*The Paquete Habana* and *The Lola*) and both were termed fishing "smacks" running in and out of Havana, regularly engaging in fishing off the coast of Cuba. Both vessels sailed under the Spanish flag and were owned by a Spanish subject of Cuban birth living in the city of Havana. The vessels' masters and crew had no "interest" in the vessels and were entitled to shares amounting, in all, to two thirds of the vessels catch, the other third going to the owner. The vessels cargo consisted of fresh fish landed as they were caught and kept and sold alive. Until stopped by the blockading squadron the vessels had no knowledge of the existence of the war, no knowledge of any blockade, carried no arms or ammunition on board, did not attempt to run the blockade after being made aware of its existence nor did any of the vessels resist capture. The vessels were brought by their captors into Key West.

An action for the condemnation of each vessel and their cargo as a prize of war was filed in 1898. The claim was interposed by the masters of both vessels on behalf of themselves, the crew and the vessels' owners. However on May 30, 1898 the final decree of condemnation and sale was entered. Each vessel was there upon sold in auction: the *Paquete Habana* for the sum of $490 and the *Lola* for the sum of $800. The question put to the US Supreme Court was whether fishing smacks were subject to capture by the armed vessels of the US during the war with Spain. The Court had to consider whether under international law coastal fishing vessels pursuing their vocation of catching and bringing in fresh fish had been recognised as exempt, with their crews, from capture as prizes of war.

Held: The Court held that on the basis of precedence and the general consent of the nations of the world, independently of any express treaty or other public act, it was an established rule of international law that coastal fishing vessels were exempt from capture as prizes of war. The Court stated this was a rule of international law which prize courts, administering the law of nations, were bound to take judicial notice of and give effect to in cases when there was no treaty or other US legislative provision in relation to the matter. (1900) 175 QS 677.

Commentary
The foregoing case illustrates that the US adopts a similar monistic approach to customary international law as does the UK. Customary international law will be automatically incorporated into US law provided there is no contradictory legislation or higher judicial decision.

This should be contrasted to the approach of the UK and the US to international treaties. These require a legislative act to become part of domestic law. For the particular position of self-executing treaties see below.

Key Principles: **Customary international law and norms of *jus cogens* are part of US law; torture is contrary to the law of the nations and a torturer like a pirate and slave trader is the enemy of all mankind.**

Filartiga v Pena-Irala (2d Cir. 1980)

Facts: This case was brought under the 1789 US Judiciary Act, also known as the Aliens Claims Tort Act (ACTA).

Civil proceedings for damages were brought for the wrongful death of their son and brother in Paraguay, in 1976, allegedly by torture. The proceedings were initiated against a Paraguayan citizen and the former head of police of Asuncion, Mr Pena-Irala. Both the applicants and the respondent were present in the US at the time the proceedings were initiated.

Under the ACTA, US courts have jurisdiction in any civil action brought by an alien for a tort committed in the violation of the law of nations or a treaty of the US. The jurisdictional issue went to the crux of the case because the existence of jurisdiction depended upon whether the conduct alleged violated the law of nations.

Held: See pp.137 and 224 for further discussion.

The US Court stated that torture had attracted a universal condemnation in numerous international instruments and it has been denounced as an instrument of official policy by virtually all of the nations of the world. Therefore the Court concluded that at least in principle if not in practice, an act of torture committed by a state official against an individual, indeed violated the established norms of the international law of human rights and hence the law of nations. (2d Circ. 1980) 630 F. 2d 876.

Commentary

This decision gave judicial endorsement to torture being contrary to customary international law. By doing so, the Court relied on customary international law and the *jus cogens* prohibition of torture as forming part of US law automatically. This supports the view that customary international law does not need incorporation into US legislation.

The case also marked the use of ACTA as a means of bringing claims for human rights violations committed abroad.

For UK position see *A & Ors v Secretary for the Home Department* [2005] UK HL 71.

US Self-Executing Treaties

Key Principle: **Self-executing treaties are regarded as part of US domestic law without further domestic enactment.**

Foster v Neilson (1829)

Facts: The case involved a treaty with Spain whereby Spain had ceded Florida to the US.

Held: The provision in the treaty preserving grants of land made by Spain within the ceded territory were not self-executing. The US Court held that the language used was such as to indicate that the provisions could not take effect as domestic law until they had been implemented by the legislature. 27 US (2 Pet.) 253 (1829).

Commentary

This was the first occasion in which the distinction between self-executing and non self-executing treaties was made and relied upon by the US Courts. The essence of the distinction is that in the absence of implementing legislation only self-executing treaties are judicially enforceable. A treaty, a contract between two nations, is not a legislative act. It does not generally provide the means whereby the object is to be accomplished. The US Constitution declares the treaty to be the law of the land and as such the US Courts will regard the treaty as equivalent to an act of the legislature and on occasions when it operates of itself without the aid of any legislative provision.

This will not be the case if the treaty imports a contract, whereby the parties engage to perform a particular act. Likewise the treaty will not be regarded as self-executing if further action by the legislature is required to give effect to the provisions of the treaty.

Key Principle: **Self-executing provision must stand alone and be enforceable in the courts.**

Sei Fugii v California (1952)

Facts: The Supreme Court of California had to determine whether the human rights provisions in the UN Charter (Arts 55 and 56) were self-executing so as to render obligatory provisions of a Californian Alien Land Law that prohibited Japanese citizens from owning land in California.

Held: The US Court held that in order to determine whether a treaty is self-executing it is necessary to look at the intention of the signatory parties. This intention will be expressed in the language of the instrument and in the event it is uncertain recourse may be made to the circumstances surrounding the treaty's execution. For a treaty provision to be operative without the assistance of an implementing legislative provision and to have the force and effect of a statute it must be evident that the framers of the treaty intended to prescribe a rule that could stand alone and would be directly enforceable in the courts.

The US Court held that the UN Charter was indisputably a treaty and under US Federal Constitutional law treaties are part of the supreme law of the land, thus binding all judges in every state. A treaty, however, would not automatically supersede local laws which were inconsistent with it unless the provisions were self-executing. The Court stated it was clear that neither the preamble nor Art.1 of the UN Charter were self-executing. These provisions stated general purposes and objectives of the UN as an organisation and did not purport to impose legal obligations on the individual member states or to create rights for private persons. The Court acknowledged that member states were, pursuant to Arts 55 and 56, obliged to co-operate with the UN in order to promote respect for and observance of human rights. However the Court maintained that it was evident that future legislative action by the nations concerned would be required for the accomplishment of the declared objectives. There was nothing to indicate that upon ratification of the UN Charter these provisions were intended to become rules of law incumbent on member states and in this case the Court of the US. The Court held the language used in Arts 55 and 56 was not of a type customarily employed in those treaties which would have been held to be self-executing and thus creating rights and duties for individuals. (1952) 242 P. 2d 617 (1952).

Commentary
This case explains the approach of the US courts in determining
if a particular treaty can be considered as self-executing. Therefore a treaty will be recognised as self-executing only if it is clear,
unambiguous and not demanding further action from the
legislator.

Key Principle: **There may be problems in giving effect within
a federal state to the provisions of a treaty.**

**Attorney General for Canada v Attorney General for Ontario
[1937]**

Facts: The Canadian Parliament initiated legislation to give
effect to certain International Labour Organisation conventions.
The case went on appeal from the Supreme Court of Canada to
the Judicial Committee of the Privy Council and the issue presented was whether the legislation required fell within the competence of the Dominion Parliament or was in fact ultra vires. It
was argued the legislative competence in the subject matter of the
international conventions dealing with the employment matters
lay within the competence of the provincial legislatures.

Held: The Privy Council held that it was necessary to keep in
mind the distinction between the formation of a treaty and the
performance of its obligations. Pursuant to the British system it
was well established that the making of a treaty was an executive
act but the performance of the treaty obligation required legislative action. Again it was held the provisions of a treaty do not
have the force of domestic law. If the government of the day
signs up to a treaty and domestic law is required then the government has to take the risk of obtaining the assent of Parliament. Therefore accession to treaties and undertaking
obligations thereunder is the exclusive competence of the
executive. However, if such a treaty requires assent from Parliament, the latter is not obliged to so consent. Consequently, if
Parliament does not give its assent to the treaty, the executive is
bound vis-à-vis other Contracting Parties, but is nonetheless
unable to give effect to the obligations undertaken, leaving the
state in default at an international level. [1937] A.C. 326 Judicial
Committee of the Privy Council.

Commentary
This case demonstrates the problems which may be encountered in a federal state where there is a division of internal competences. As the Canadian Court pointed out, in many instances, before finally ratifying a treaty, the executive will seek an expression of approval from Parliament, but the Parliament is not obliged to give such consent.

The foregoing can be contrasted with the decision in *Missouri v Holland* 252 US 416 (1920) US Supreme Court (see below).

Key Principle: **There is no fetter on what may be the subject of a treaty.**

Missouri v Holland (1920)

Facts: In 1913 an Act of Congress was passed to protect migratory wild fowl. However this legislation was declared ultra vires the legislative competence of the Federal Government and one which lay with the individual states.

In 1916 the US and Canada signed a treaty, namely the Migratory Bird Treaty, which was given internal effect by the Migratory Bird Treaty Act 1918.

The case came about as a result of an attempt by the State of Missouri to prevent a game warden (Holland) in his efforts to enforce the 1918 Act and the regulations made pursuant to that legislation. The issue before the US Court was whether or not the statute was an unconstitutional interference in subject matter which was reserved to the individual states by way of the Tenth Amendment of the US Constitution. The District Court held that the Act of Congress was constitutional and the State of Missouri appealed.

Held: The US Court ruled that the power to make treaties was delegated expressly and by Art.6 of the US Constitution. Treaties made under the authority of the US, along with the Constitution and the laws of the US made under the Constitution, are the supreme law of the land.

The Court articulated the question before it as an enquiry into the ground upon which there could be a possible exception to the supremacy of treaties. It was submitted that a treaty could not be valid if it infringed the US Constitution. The Court upheld the validity of the 1918 Act and stated there was no limitation on which could be the subject matter of a treaty and regardless of what was the subject matter the enforcement of a treaty fell within the Federal Government's exclusive competence. 252 US 416 (1920) US Supreme Court.

Commentary
This case highlights how the problem of a distribution of powers and differentiation of competences can be circumvented.

There are a number of cases which illustrate the decision in the event of a conflict between a treaty and a subsequent statute.

Key Principle: **An act of Congress which conflicts with an earlier US treaty will prevail.**

Edye v Robertson (1884)

Held: Treaty law is the law of the land and just like an Act of US Congress there was nothing inherent in the treaty which made it irrepealable or unchangeable, in other words, it could be amended. The US Constitution did not give a treaty any superiority over an act of US Congress. Thus a treaty could be repealed or modified by an act of a later date. 112 US 580 (1884).

Key Principle: **A later treaty provision will not be regarded as having repealed by implication of an earlier statute unless the statute and the treaty provision are so incompatible that the statute could not be enforced without "antagonising" the treaty.**

Johnson v Browne 205 US 309 (1907)

Key Principle: **A provision of a treaty cannot be rendered nugatory in any part of the US by municipal ordnances or state laws.**

Asakura v City of Seattle 265 US 332 (1924)

Key Principle: A treaty is not repealed or modified by a subsequent federal statute unless that is the clear express intention of the Congress.

Cooke v the United States 288 US 102 (1933)

Key Principles: The validity of a Presidential executive agreement was upheld and superseded otherwise applicable state law; Presidential executive agreements are those agreements made by the President of the US without the advice and consent of the US Senate. As such they have the same force as a treaty and are binding upon the US in international law.

US v Belmont 301 US 324 (1937)
A similar position was adopted in *US v Pink* 315 US 203 (1942).

Key Principle: The US Constitutional scheme is such that US Congress may denounce treaties if it sees fit to do so and there is nothing other branches of government can do about it.

Diggs v Schultz (1972)

Held: The Byrd Amendment allowing imports contrary to the UN Security Council embargo on Rhodesian products was in blatant disregard of the US treaty obligations. However the legality of the Byrd Amendment was upheld. 470 F (2d) 461 (1972).

Key Principle: Domestic practice although in breach of customary international law was held not to be contrary to US law because it was an exercise of a controlling executive act by the Attorney General.

Garcia Mir v Meese 788 F 2d 1446 (1986)

US Act of State Doctrine

Key Principle: **By virtue of the act of state doctrine the US courts will not determine the lawfulness under international law of acts executed by another state within its own territory.**

Banco Nacional de Cubas v Sabatino (1964)

Facts: The Cuban government confiscated and then resold for its own account to the same purchaser a cargo of sugar lying in a Cuban port. An action was brought, in New York, by a Cuban state bank seeking to recover the purchase price. However the bank's title to the sugar and the monies held in the US bank were challenged by a corporation registered in Cuba. This corporation, although registered in Cuba, was principally owned by American residents. The US Court at first instance and on appeal refused to apply the act of state doctrine, the reason being that the Cuban acts were retaliatory, discriminatory and without adequate compensation. The decision was reversed by the US Supreme Court.

Held: The US Supreme Court held the courts of the US would not examine the validity of the taking of a property within its own territory by a foreign sovereign government which the US recognised, at the time of the suit, even if the complaint alleged that the taking violated customary international law. 376 US 398 (1964).

Commentary
The immediate impact of the position was that Cuban decree, although contrary to international law, was given effect. The aftermath of this decision was the passing of the Hickenlooper Amendment to the Foreign Assistance Act 1961. This allowed US Courts to review the acts of foreign governments which violated international law and which affected property owned by American citizens.

Note: The act of state doctrine is one of American domestic law and international law does not demand the application of an act of state doctrine.

3. PERSONALITY INCLUDING RECOGNITION OF STATES AND GOVERNMENTS

Key Principles: **Definition of international legal personality; state as a primary and original bearer of international legal personality.**

Reparation for Injuries Suffered in the Service of the United Nations case Advisory Opinion 1949

Facts: See p.72 for further discussion.

The Chief United Nations Truce Negotiator Count Bernadotte, a Swedish national, was killed on September 17, 1948 in Jerusalem. The assassins were allegedly a gang of terrorists.

Israel was not a member of the United Nations at the time of the incident.

The General Assembly asked for the ICJ's Advisory Opinion on three questions:

(1) if the United Nations had legal personality

(2) if United Nations could bring a claim with the view to obtaining reparations in respect of the damage caused to itself

(3) to the victim or persons entitled through the victim.

Held: The ICJ stated that the subjects of law of different legal systems may differ in their nature or in the extent of their rights. Thus the extent of their legal nature is dependent upon the needs of the community. In revisiting the development of international law, the ICJ concluded that:

> "Throughout its history, the development of international law has been influenced by the requirements of international life, and the progressive increase in the collective action of States has already given rise to the instances which are not States".

The ICJ went on to examine the legal personality of the UN. However the ICJ also defined international legal personality as the possession of international rights and duties and the capacity to maintain these rights by bringing international claims. The ICJ recognised states as the original bearers of international legal personality. 1949 ICJ Reports 174.

Commentary
The most important implication of this Advisory Opinion concern the legal personality of international organisations (see p.72 for further discussion). However, when examining the extent of the legal personality attributed to an international organisation, the ICJ made constant parallels with the legal personality of a state, thus giving a significant insight into the content of the international legal personality of a state. First of all, the ICJ defined international legal personality in the abstract as the ability to possess international rights and duties and the power to sustain these rights by bringing international claims. Original international legal personality belongs to the main actors of international law, namely states, as the primary purpose of international law is to regulate the relations between states. This is also reflected in the ICJ Statute, namely Art.34, which provides that only states may be parties to a continuous case before the ICJ.

In this Advisory Opinion the ICJ established that the UN had international legal personality through the fact that its member states, by the very fact of creating such an organisation, must have transferred some of their powers over to the organisation. In other words, the ICJ drew a distinction between the original international legal personality belonging to states and derivative international legal personality, which in this instance belonged to the UN.

Key Principle: **A state is deemed to have suffered the alleged wrong.**

Mavrommatis Palestine Concession case 1924

Facts: See p.198 for further discussion.

Held: The PCIJ declared that despite the fact that the dispute having initially arisen between an individual and a state, namely, Mr Mavrommatis and Great Britain, since the Greek government subsequently took up the case, the dispute was transformed into one between the two states. It was maintained that:

> "by taking up the case of one of its subjects and by resorting to diplomatic action or international judicial proceedings on his behalf, a State is in reality asserting its own rights—its right to ensure, in the person of its subject, respect for the rules of international law".

1924 PCIJ Reports Series A No.212.

Commentary
This case confirms states as the main possessors of international legal personality. As such, they are the main actors in the area of international law and, as endorsed by this case, may take up a case on behalf of their nationals, but when they do so they are in effect exercising a sovereign right.

Key Principle: **Nationality must be real and effective to give a right to a state who has conferred it.**

Nottebohm case (Second Phase) (Liechtenstein v Guatemala) 1955

Facts: See p.162 for further discussion.

Held: See pp.131 and 163 for further discussion.
The ICJ declared that nationality is a matter of domestic jurisdiction of each state. However, since it may give rights to the state which conferred the nationality, for example the right to afford diplomatic protection, the conferral of the nationality must conform to the requirements of international law if it is to be relied upon in international law. Thus nationality must be real and effective. 1955 ICJ Reports 4.

Commentary
This case illustrates the limits of the rights to diplomatic protection and should be contrasted with the *Mavrommatis* case (see above). The state does not have an automatic claim on behalf of all of its nationals on the international scene. It will only have

such a claim if the nationality it confers corresponds to the requirements established by international law. Thus nationality must be real and effective if it is to give rise to any rights to a state.

Key Principle: **The borders of a state territory need not be definitely established.**

North Sea Continental Shelf cases (Federal Republic of Germany v Denmark) and (Federal Republic of Germany v Netherlands) 1969

Facts: See p.1 for further discussion.

Held: See pp.2, 105, 110 and 199 for further discussion.
The ICJ declared that:

> "there is no rule that the land frontiers of a State must be fully delimited and defined, and often in various places and for long periods they are not".

L 1969 ICJ Reports 3.

Commentary
The conditions of statehood are usually set as permanent population, defined territory, government and the ability enter into relations with other states. However, as evidenced by the ICJ judgment in this case, the requirement of defined territory should not be read in a restrictive manner. Just because the boundaries of a state are not definitely established does not automatically mean that an entity will not be recognised as a state. This resonates with the approach of the ICJ towards the requirement of government—see the *Western Sahara* Advisory Opinion.

Key Principle: **Meaning and extent of "independence" of a state.**

Austro-German Customs Union case Advisory Opinion 1931

Facts: Austria and Germany wanted to create a free trade customs union between themselves and requested an Advisory Opinion of the PCIJ as to whether such an arrangement between the two states would be contrary to the 1919 Peace Treaties and the subsequent protocol of 1922. According to these, Austria had undertaken not to take any action which could compromise its independence.

Held: In its discussion on the independence of states, the PCIJ stated that in the case before it, the independence of Austria should be understood as the continued existence of Austria within its existing borders as a separate state with the sole decision making power in all economic, political and financial matters. Thus such independence would be violated if there were to be an encroachment upon the economic, political or financial fields as these different aspects of independence in practice are one and indivisible.

The PCIJ went on to examine the concept of "alienation", which is referred to in Art.88 of the Treaty of Saint-Germain of 1919 and according to which Austria's independence was inalienable. It was stated that any voluntary act by Austria which would lead it to lose its independence or which would modify its existing independence in the way that its sovereignty would be subordinated to another power or group of powers, would constitute such "alienation". 1931 PCIJ Reports Series A/B No.41.

Commentary
This case is the cornerstone of the concept of independence and sovereignty of states in international law. Independence is a crucial requirement for statehood and, as evidenced by the approach of the PCIJ here, can be ascertained in the light of the circumstances of each individual case. The PCIJ provided guidelines for defining the concept of "independence" but was careful to underline that each case should be assessed on its merits.

Particularly noteworthy is the separate opinion of Judge Anzilotti, who stated that independence is the normal condition of a state in international law. According to him, restrictions upon the freedom of a state, irrespective of whether these arise from international law or contractual obligations, do not per se affect the independence of a state. As long as such restrictions do not place a state under the legal authority of another state, the former state remains independent regardless of how extensive and onerous these obligations may be.

Key Principle: **Right of entering into international engagements is an attribute of state sovereignty.**

The Wimbledon case (France, Italy, Japan and the UK v Germany) 1923

Facts: See p.12 for further discussion.

Held: The PCIJ stated that:

> "No doubt any convention creating an obligation of this kind places a restriction upon the exercise of the sovereign rights of the State, in the sense that it requires them to be exercised in a certain way. But the right of entering into international engagements is an attribute of State sovereignty".

1923 PCIJ Reports Series A No.1.

Commentary
The PCIJ in this case noted that the rights of states in international law can be restricted by, for example, an international treaty to which the state is a party. However the Court proclaimed that every state is free to enter into any international arrangements it wishes as the right to enter into international agreements is an attribute of state sovereignty.

Key Principle: **Restrictions upon the independence of states cannot be presumed.**

SS Lotus case (France v Turkey) 1927

Facts: See p.8 for further discussion.

Held: See pp.9 and 134 for further discussion.
The PCIJ emphasized that there cannot be any presumptions made about the restrictions of the independence of states. 1927 PCIJ Series A No.1081.

Commentary
The sovereign independence of a state is possibly the most distinctive and important characteristic of a state as the subject of international law. In international law, the term independence is a legal one and while in reality a state may be politically or economically dependent upon another state, this per se does not affect the legal status of its independence unless the state in question formally submits to another state. The PCIJ in the *Lotus* case made a very strong proclamation about the extent of the independence of a state—no presumptions about the restrictions upon such independence should be made.

Key Principles: **Restrictions upon the independence of states cannot be presumed; equality of states.**

Nicaragua case (Nicaragua v United States; Military and Paramilitary Activities in and against Nicaragua) 1986

Facts: See p.4 for further discussion.

Held: See pp.5, 110 and 182 for further discussion.
When examining the issue of armaments, the ICJ stated that:

> "in international law there are no rules, other than such rules as may be accepted by the state concerned, by treaty or otherwise, whereby the level of armaments of a sovereign state can be limited, and this principle is valid for all states without exception" (para.135).

1986 ICJ Reports 14.

Commentary

While this excerpt from the *Nicaragua* case may appear somewhat insignificant, in fact the ICJ once again confirmed the long
established principle that restrictions upon the independence of
states may not be presumed. In this particular case the ICJ
declared that every state has the right to such level of armament
as it chooses. It is also the choice of every sovereign state to limit
this right by, for example, acceding to a specific treaty which
would limit its right to armament. Otherwise no restrictions
upon the sovereignty of a state can be presumed. Thus the ICJ
also made a proclamation on the equality of all states.

Key Principle: **Restrictions upon the independence of states
cannot be presumed.**

Legality of the Threat or Use of Nuclear Weapons case
Advisory Opinion 1996

Facts: See p.7 for further discussion.

Held: See pp.7, 193 and 211 for further discussion.

In its examination on the legality of the use of nuclear weapons, the ICJ stated that, as is evidenced by state practice, the use
of certain weapons is considered illegal not because there would
be an authorisation to use certain weapons but because there are
specific prohibitions on the use of certain types of weapons. 1996
ICJ Reports 226.

Commentary

While this proclamation of the ICJ might appear insignificant, the
Court actually endorsed the principle that no restrictions upon
the independence of a state can be presumed. Thus the freedom
of every independent state is unlimited unless there is a rule of
international law which constraints its freedom. Therefore the
only limitations upon the sovereign independence of a state are
those which are imposed by rules of international law.

Key Principle: **Limits of powers of states vis-à-vis other states; principle of non-intervention.**

Corfu Channel case (Merits). United Kingdom v Albania 1949

Facts: See p.152 for further discussion.

Held: See pp.108, 152 and 188 for further discussion.
   The ICJ declared that the respect for territorial sovereignty between independent states is an essential foundation of international relations. 1949 ICJ Reports 4.

Commentary
The principle of sovereignty of a state is closely related to other core principles of international law and one of the most important ones is the principle of non-intervention. This is based on the idea that every state is equal in the exercise of its sovereignty and therefore no state can dictate to another state how this sovereignty should be exercised.

Key Principle: **Principle of self-determination is part of customary international law.**

Legal Consequences for States of the Continued Presence of South Africa in Namibia (South-West Africa) Notwithstanding Security Council Resolution 276 Advisory Opinion 1971

Facts: See pp.18 and 82 for further discussion.

Held: See pp.18, 82 and 222 for further discussion.
   The ICJ declared that:

> "the subsequent development of international law in regard to non-self-governing territories enshrined in the Charter of the United Nations, made the principle of self-determination applicable to all of them" (para.52).

Thus the ICJ upheld the applicability of the principle to self-determination to the peoples of Namibia. 1971 ICJ Reports 16.

Commentary
The principle of self-determination is the cornerstone of the UN decolonisation process which started in the 1960s. However, the
judicial discussion of the principle of self-determination is not very
extensive. The essence of the principle is dealt with by the ICJ in its
two Advisory Opinions—the *Namibia* case and the *Western Sahara*
case (see below). In essence the latter reaffirms the principles
established in the former. In *Namibia* the ICJ made it clear that the
principle of self-determination is not just a political concept, but
rather a legal one and in the context of colonial territories and
trusteeships, it is applicable and involved the right of the concerned
peoples to decide freely on their future. Self-determination thus is a
way of conferring international legal personality upon peoples.

   Perhaps the greatest controversy surrounding the right to self-
determination today concerns the claims advanced by some
minority groups: the right to self-determination is claimed by
national minority groups in an attempt to create their own states.
This however goes beyond the right to self-determination as
elaborated upon by the ICJ in *Namibia* and *Western Sahara* cases.
Both of these Advisory Opinions must be read in the context of
their specific facts: both dealt with colonised territories and the
right of the peoples of these colonised territories to decide their
own future, even if this would involve the creation of new states.

   It should also be noted that the right to self-determination has
many dimensions to it and the ICJ in the *Namibia* and *Western
Sahara* cases dealt with only one aspect, namely, the creation of a
new entity. Other aspects of self-determination include cultural,
linguistic and even political autonomy. These options have been
widely and correctly utilised by some minority groups.

Key Principles: **Display of state authority; no prescribed state
structure; principle of self-determination as a rule of customary
international law; possible outcomes of self-determination;
exercise of self-determination.**

Western Sahara case Advisory Opinion 1975

Facts: See p.98 for further discussion.

Held: See pp.98 and 221 for further discussion. The ICJ stated
that a claim to sovereignty must be based upon a continued

display of authority, which in turn involves two elements: intention, the will to act as a sovereign as well as some actual exercise or display of this authority. The ICJ accepted that in certain circumstances, for example, when the claims are directed towards sparsely populated areas or countries with unsettled borders, the actual exercise of authority might be very little, but could still be sufficient in sustaining a claim to sovereignty in the absence of competing rights.

The Court went on to observe that there was no rule of international law which required the structure of a state to adhere to any particular pattern. However, it stated that:

> "where sovereignty over territory is claimed, the particular structure of a State may be a relevant element in appreciating the reality or otherwise of a display of State activity adduced as evidence of the sovereignty" (para.94).

The ICJ upheld the principle of self-determination of all peoples and noted its particular importance in bringing an end to the colonial situations. The Court recalled its earlier Advisory Opinion in the *Namibia* case (see above) where it concluded that the interpretation of the content of the principle of self-determination in the colonial context "leaves little doubt that the ultimate objective of the sacred trust was the self-determination and independence of the peoples concerned".

The ICJ went on to state that there are three possible outcomes for non-self-governing territories:

(i) emergence as a sovereign and independent state;

(ii) free association with an independent state; and

(iii) integration with an independent state.

The main factor determining the choice between these three options, however, in the view of the ICJ, was the freely expressed will of the peoples concerned. The Court also noted that just because previously on some occasions the UN General Assembly had not consulted the peoples concerned, did not mean that such consultations should not take place. Rather in the view of the Court this had happened because:

> "Those instances were based either on the consideration that a certain population did not constitute a 'peoples' entitled to self-determination

or on the conviction that a consultation was totally unnecessary, in the view of special circumstances''.

The ICJ, in defining self-determination as the need to pay regard to the freely expressed will of peoples ruled that a full exercise of the principle of self-determination in the colonial context required consultation with the peoples concerned and that such peoples must have been given the opportunity to freely express their will.

The ICJ also recognised that the principle of self-determination is a part of customary international law. 1975 ICJ Reports 12.

Commentary

The ICJ in this Advisory Opinion made some very significant statements about statehood, thus giving important insights into the requirements necessary for an entity to be recognised as a state, the main subject of international law. The ICJ made it clear that as evidenced by the great variety of the diversity of state forms around the world, there is no prescribed rule as to what pattern of state structure an entity should follow. The main decisive element in the view of the Court was the display of authority. Two essential elements were pointed out: intention and the will to act as a sovereign, and some actual exercise or display of such authority.

The ICJ examined the claims about religious, political and cultural ties, but noted that these per se were not enough when a claim of sovereignty over a certain territory is advanced. Rather, the Court went on to examine the ways whereby Morocco had exercised and displayed its authority over the territory. There were no strict prescriptions on how this display of authority must take place and no requirements for particular political structures, for example, were set. It is thus clear that the assessment of each entity will depend on the specific circumstances. Therefore, just as in the case of state territory, discussed in the *North Sea Continental Shelf* cases (see above), the ICJ showed flexibility in applying the criteria for statehood, bearing in mind the reality of each situation.

The essence of the principle is dealt with by the ICJ in the Advisory Opinion—the *Namibia* case (see above).

Key Principles: **The right to self-determination is obligation *erga omnes*; content of the right to self-determination.**

Case Concerning East Timor (Portugal v Australia) 1995

Facts: See p.199 for further discussion.

Held: See pp.199 and 223 for further discussion.

The ICJ accepted the claim advanced by Portugal that the right to self-determination as evolved from the United Nations Charter and the practice of the United Nations was of *erga omnes* character, constituting one of the essential principles of contemporary international law. The ICJ also made it clear that the right to self-determination includes sovereignty over the natural resources of the country and may provide criteria for the resolution of disputes. 1995 ICJ Reports 90.

Commentary

The ICJ in accepting Portugal's claim that the right to self-determination was of *erga omnes* character endorsed Portugal's right to make such an individual request to Australia to respect this right. The Court's decision makes it clear that the right to self-determination is part of customary international law. Moreover, the circumstances of this case allowed the ICJ to make a further proclamation on the content of the right to self-determination: such aspects as sovereignty over natural resources and the applicable criteria for the resolution of disputes are also affected.

Key Principles: **Self-determination is an *erga omnes* obligation; the elements of the right to self-determination; breach of *erga omnes* obligation and the consequences thereof.**

Legal Consequences of the Construction of a Wall in the Occupied Palestinian Territory Advisory Opinion 2004

Facts: The General Assembly in its Resolution ES-10/14, adopted on December 8, 2003, posed the following question to the ICJ:

> "What are the legal consequences arising from the construction of the wall being built by Israel, the occupying Power, in the Occupied

Palestinian territory, including in and around East Jerusalem, as described in the report of the Secretary-General, considering the rules and principles of international law, including the Fourth Geneva Convention of 1949, and relevant Security Council and General Assembly resolutions?"

Held: See pp.161, 187, 212 and 219 for further discussion.

The ICJ initially ascertained Israel's status as an occupying power in relation to the Palestinian territories. In its affirmative response, the ICJ also noted that the Palestinian territories in question are occupied territories. The Palestinian people, in the opinion of the Court, constitute "peoples" as required for the application of the right to self-determination and the ICJ went on to observe this has been recognised by Israel itself in various communications it has made. Thus, since Israel was recognised as the occupying power of the Palestinian territory and the Palestinian population was recognised as constituting peoples, the ICJ concluded that they are entitled to the right of self-determination.

The Court went on to examine the construction of the wall by Israel and concluded that this constituted a breach of Israel's obligation to respect the right of the Palestinian peoples to self-determination. The ICJ stated: "That construction, along with the measures taken previously, thus severely impedes the exercise by the Palestinian peoples of its right to self-determination, and is therefore a breach of Israel's obligations to respect that right" (para.122).

The ICJ reaffirmed its position in the *East Timor* case (see above) and once again stated that the right to self-determination con-stitutes an obligation *erga omnes*. The ICJ not only declared that the breach of this obligation by Israel engaged its state responsibility under international law, but also held that because of the *erga omnes* character of the right breached, other states also have certain obligations such as not recognising the illegal situation resulting from the construction of the wall, not rendering any assistance to Israel in maintaining the situation and seeing that any impedi-ment, resulting from the construction of the wall, to the exercise of the right to self-determination by the Palestinian peoples is brought to an end. The ICJ also went on to express its view that the UN General Assembly and the Security Council should take further steps to resolve the situation. 2004 ICJ Reports 134.

Commentary

This Advisory Opinion is a further confirmation of the ICJ's earlier declaration that the right to self-determination has *erga omnes* character. The Court in this case provided a detailed examination of all the elements of the right to self-determination: it examined whether Israel was an occupying power, whether the territory in question was occupied and whether the population of the territory in question constitute "peoples" in the meaning of the right to self-determination. Answering each of these three issues in the affirmative, the ICJ not only declared that the Palestinian peoples are entitled to the right to self-determination, but also concluded that the construction of the wall by Israel was an impediment to the exercise of this right and thus constituted a breach of international law by Israel. The ICJ proceeded to draw the necessary consequences of such a conclusion. Namely, the state responsibility of Israel was engaged and it was required to bring an end to the violation, to make reparation for the damages and in the event when restitution would not be possible—to compensate the victims. The Court also drew the necessary conclusions in respect of other states since it was an *erga omnes* obligation, which had been violated, a right in the protection of which all states have an interest because such a right constitutes an intransgressible principle of international customary international law.

This Advisory Opinion certainly constitutes one of the most complete and thorough judicial proclamations of the Court: the ICJ not only engaged in a detailed examination of the circumstances of the case, but also elaborated in detail on the legal concepts, showed their application to the facts and drew the necessary conclusions from such application.

Key Principle: **Relationship between the principle of *uti possidetis* and self-determination.**

Burkina Faso v Mali 1986

Facts: See p.99 for further discussion.

Held: The ICJ declared that *uti possidetis* is:

"not a special rule which pertains solely to one specific system of international law. It is a general principle, which is logically connected with the phenomenon of the obtaining of independence, wherever it occurs. Its obvious purpose is to prevent the independence and stability of new States being endangered by fratricidal struggles".

1986 ICJ Reports 554.

Commentary
The ICJ in this case elaborated on the relationship between the long standing principle of *uti possidetis* and self-determination: in case of the emergence of a new state as a result of the exercise of the right to self-determination, respect for the principle of *uti possidetis* must be maintained.

Key Principles: Uti possidetis and condominium.

Case Concerning the Land, Island and Maritime Frontier Dispute El Salvador v Honduras, Nicaragua intervening 1992

Facts: See p.100 for further discussion.

Held: The ICJ accepted the earlier conclusion by the Central American Court of Justice of 1917 that there existed condominium arrangement between the three states and characterised it as "a structured system for the joint exercise of sovereign government powers over a territory". 1992 ICJ Reports 355.

Commentary
The ICJ in this case not only endorsed the applicability of *uti possidetis* principle, but accepted that in case of *condominium*, all states which are involved in the arrangement, exercise their sovereign powers. Thus, such types of arrangements as *condominiums* do not affect the sovereign independence of states.

Key Principles: **Scope of the right to self-determination; right to self-determination and minority groups; territorial integrity of states.**

Re Reference by Governor in Council Concerning Certain Questions Relating to Secession of Quebec from Canada (1998)

Facts: In the light of the secessionist advances of the Province of Quebec in Canada, three questions were posed to the Canadian Supreme Court for its Advisory Opinion. First, whether there existed in Canadian constitutional law a right to secede. Secondly, whether there existed a right to self-determination in international law which would give the right to unilateral secession to Quebec. Thirdly, whether international or constitutional law of Canada would prevail in the event of conflict between these two sets of laws.

Held: See p.101 for further discussion.

The Canadian Supreme Court declared that such unilateral secession is not permissible neither under Canadian constitutional nor under international law. The Canadian Supreme Court declared that the right to self-determination had acquired a status of a rule of customary international law, but this right does not automatically imply the right of a province to secede. It was recognised that as long as the government of the country represents the whole of the population of the territory and this representation is equal and without discrimination, there is no right to secession. Thus the Supreme Court examined two important principles of international law: the sovereign integrity of states and the principle of self-determination. The Court concluded that international law expects that the right to self-determination will be exercised within the existing borders of the states in consistency with the maintenance of the territorial integrity of states. While the Canadian Supreme Court did refer to exceptional circumstances which may lead to the right of secession from an existing state to arise, these exceptional circumstances, in the view of the Court, were colonial contexts or situations where ''a definable group is denied meaningful access to government to pursue their political, economic, social and cultural development'' (para.442). The Supreme Court concluded that neither of these exceptional circumstances were applicable to the province of Quebec. (1998) Supreme Court of Canada 161 D.L.R. (4th) 385.

Commentary
This is certainly the most well-known case internationally which
has dealt with the acclaimed exercise of the right to self-determination in the form of secession from an existing state. In this
case a claim advanced by a national minority group that a right
self-determination entails a right to secede was rejected. The
Canadian Supreme Court found that both its national constitutional law and international law were in agreement on the
matter. Thus the boundaries of the right to self-determination
outside a colonial context were set: national minorities do have a
right to self-determination, but this right does not include a right
to secession. It should be noted however that the Court stated
that in a case where there was clear support to secession
expressed in a future referendum, there would be a constitutional duty upon the government to negotiate.

Key Principles: **The international legal personality of the
Sovereign Order of Malta; states are prime subjects of international law.**

Nanni v Pace and Sovereign Order of Malta (1935–37)

Facts: The Italian Court of Cassation was asked to deliver its
opinion on the legal status of the Order of Malta.

Held: The Court recognised that states are the prime subjects of
international law, but declared that it is impossible to deny to
other international entities limited capacity to act under international law:

> "within the ambit and the actual exercise of their own functions with
> the resulting international juridical personality and capacity which is
> its necessary and natural corollary".

The Court went on to state that theory on subjects of international law recognises various collective units:

> "whose composition is independent of the nationality of their con-
> stituent members and whose scope transcends by virtue of their
> universal character the territorial confines of any single state".

Thus the international legal personality of the Sovereign Order of Malta was upheld. (1935–37) 8 A.D. Italian Court of Cassation.

Commentary
While states remain main subjects of international law, there are other entities that possess international legal personality. In this case, the Sovereign Order of Malta was recognised as a subject of international law even though it lost its sovereignty over its territories in 1798. Following this the Order established its headquarters in Rome in 1834 as a humanitarian organisation. Today many states have diplomatic relations with the Order. This is an example of a special case when international legal personality is accorded to non-state entities.

Key Principles: **The effect of recognition under UK domestic law.**

Luther v Sagor [1921]

Facts: In 1919 a Soviet government decree nationalised a factory in the USSR. In 1920 the defendant company bought wood from the new Soviet government and the Russian company which was the previous owner of the factory claimed title to the wood on the grounds it had come from a factory that it had owned before nationalisation. The argument continued that the nationalisation legislation should not be recognised by an English court as the UK had, in 1919, not recognised the Soviet Government.

Initially the Court of First Instance accepted this argument and found in favour of the plaintiff. However the defendants appealed and in 1921 the UK government recognised the Soviet government. The retroactive effect of recognition meant that recognition was backdated to December 1917, the date when the Soviet authorities took over control from the Provisional Government.

Held: The Court of Appeal held that the UK government had recognised as *de facto* the government of Russia and "this government had begun its existence at a date anterior to any date material to the dispute between the parties to this appeal". The Court, accordingly, held that recognition was retroactive in effect and that was retroactive to the time that the recognised government established itself. Accordingly, on the basis of retroactivity it followed that the recognised government had *locus standi* in the UK courts. A recognised government also enjoys immunity from suit in the UK courts and its legislative and administrative acts will be given effect in the UK. [1921] 3 KB 532, CA.

Commentary

The significance of this decision was more relevant when the UK made a distinction between *de facto* and *de jure* recognition. The consequences of *de facto* and *de jure* recognition were the same except there were a further two legal consequences which flowed exclusively from *de jure* recognition. Namely, *de jure* recognition implied full diplomatic relations and a recognised competence to recover a public debt or state asset. However this distinction is now largely academic as the UK has, since 1980, ceased to make announcements affording explicit recognition.

Key Principle: **Mitigating the consequences of non-recognition.**

Carl Zeiss Stiftung v Rayner and Keeler Ltd (No.2) [1969]

Facts: This case involved a German charitable foundation CZS which made optical instruments. The foundation under its constitution was administered by a Special Board, which after the First World War, was the Minister of Education of Thuringia. Thuringia after 1945 was part of the Russian zone of occupied Germany. However in 1949 the USSR handed its zone over to the German Democratic Republic (GDR). Thuringia ceased to exist in 1952 following a reorganisation of local government by the GDR and the Special Board of CZS was constituted as the Council of Gera.

The issue over recognition was raised when CZS, acting through its new board, brought a claim in the English Courts.

In the domestic proceedings it was initially argued that the claim should be dismissed because it had been brought without the proper authority of the Appellants. The requested order was denied, but subsequently allowed by the Court of Appeal. The argument presented to the Court of Appeal was that as the

United Kingdom had not recognised the GDR the new Special Board, a creation of the GDR, could not be recognised by an English court.

Held: The House of Lords reversed the Court of Appeal's decision. Lord Reid emphasised that the consequences of applying non-recognition rigidly would be that:

> "the incorporation of every company in East Germany under any new law made by the Democratic Republic or by the official act of any official appointed by its government would have to be regarded as a nullity. So that any such company could neither sue or be sued in this country. And any civil marriage under any such new law, or owing its validity to the act of any such official, would also have to be treated as a nullity, so that we should have to regard the children as illegitimate. And the same would apply to divorces and all manner of judicial decisions, whether in family or commercial questions. And would affect not only the status of persons formerly domiciled in East Germany but property in this country the devolution of which depended upon East German law." (at para.907)

The House of Lords in essence maintained that as Britain recognised the Soviet government as the *de jure* authority in East Germany, the acts of the unrecognised East German regime could nevertheless be recognised as those of a subordinate body acting pursuant to the authority of the Soviet Union. In other words, as far as the House of Lords was concerned, the GDR was irrelevant and was merely an administrative organ of the *de jure* Soviet regime.

The Court's approach was endorsed in the *Gur Corporation v Trust Bank of Africa Ltd* [1987] Queens Bench 599, Court of Appeal.

The facts of this case involved the Republic of Siskei (an entity created pursuant to South Africa's homelands policy). A Panamanian company made a contract with Siskei to build two schools and a hospital. A guarantee was obtained from the Trust Bank of Africa in favour of the Siskei Department of Public Works so as to cover the costs of any defective building works.

In the proceedings raised in the English Courts the Bank sought to recover a sum paid to the defendant as security for the guarantee. The defendant joined the Republic of Siskei as a third party and the Republic of Siskei brought a counter claim for the money paid as security. The issue was raised as to whether or not the Republic of Siskei had *locus standi* before an English court. At the Court of First Instance it was held it did not have *locus standi.*

The Court of Appeal reversed the decision of the Judge at First Instance. The Court of Appeal applied the principle used in Carl Zeiss, namely the Siskei government was acting as a subordinate body of the South African government and thereby enjoyed *locus standi* before English courts. [1967] 1 A.C. 853 UKHL.

Commentary
The foregoing cases demonstrate the somewhat harsh consequences of a rigid approach to non-recognition and the way in which UK Courts may seek to mitigate such adverse consequences.

Key Principle: **Judicial guidance on the criteria to be employed in determining whether a government should be recognised.**

Somalia (A Republic) v Woodhouse Drake and Carey (Suisse S.A.) [1993]

Facts: The proceedings raised in the English court were as to whether £2 million, which had been paid into the Court, could be paid to the solicitors who were acting for the interim government of the Prime Minister appointed by the interim President of Somalia. The £2 million was the proceeds from the sale of a cargo of rice which had been bought in the Republic of Somalia in 1991 but by the time the cargo vessel bringing it to Somalia arrived offshore, the captain decided it was to dangerous to land.

The question before the Court of Appeal was whether Somalia had *locus standi* before an English court.

Held: The Court held that the interim government did not qualify, when regard was made to a number of identified important factors. The factors identified by the Court were:

a)   whether the government of a state is the constitutional government of the state;

b)   the degree, nature and stability of administrative control, if any, that it of itself exercises over the territory of the state;

c)   whether the British government has any dealings with that government and if so the nature of these dealings; and

d)   in marginal cases the extent of international recognition, which has been accorded to the government of the state.

[1993] Q.B. 54.

Commentary
The criteria identified by the Court in this case have been used subsequently, e.g. *Sierra Leone Telecommunications Co Ltd v Barclays Bank Plc* [1998] 2 All E.R. 820, in denying that the military junta in Sierra Leone was a constitutional government of Sierra Leone.

4. INTERNATIONAL ORGANISATIONS

Key Principles: Definition of international personality; international legal personality of the United Nations; United Nations not a "super state"; international legal personality of international organisations.

Reparation for Injuries Suffered in the Service of the United Nations case Advisory Opinion 1949

Facts: The Chief United Nations Truce Negotiator, Count Bernadotte, a Swedish national, was killed on September 17, 1948 in the "new" city of Jerusalem. The alleged killers were a gang of terrorists. Israel was not a member of the United Nations (UN) at the time of the incident. The General Assembly asked for the ICJ's Advisory Opinion on three questions:

(1) if the United Nations has legal personality;

(2) if the United Nations can bring a claim with the view of obtaining reparations in respect of the damage caused to itself; and

(3) as to the victim or persons entitled through the victim.

Held: See p.49 for further discussion.

The ICJ initially stated that the establishment of the UN was the culmination of the requirements of international life and the progressive increase in the collective action of states. The Court maintained that the purposes and principles of the organisation were specified in the Charter of the UN and the achievement of these meant that the attribution of international legal personality was essential for the organisation. The UN had not been created as a mere centre for harmonising certain actions among states to achieve some common ends. On the contrary, the organisation had been equipped with various organs which in turn had been entrusted with specific tasks. Moreover, the members of the UN are also obliged to give the organisation and its organs every assistance in any action the organisation undertakes, as stated in Art.2(5) of the UN Charter. Thus:

"In the opinion of the Court, the Organisation was intended to exercise and enjoy, and is in fact exercising and enjoying, functions and rights which can only be explained on the basis of the possession of a large measure of international personality and the capacity to operate upon an international plane. It is at present the supreme type of international organisation, and it could not carry out the intentions of its founders if it was devoid of international personality. It must be acknowledged that its Members, by entrusting certain functions to it, with the attendant duties and responsibilities, have clothed it with the competence required to enable those functions to be effectively discharged."

The ICJ then drew a comparison between the legal personality of a state and that of an organisation, stating that the fact that the UN had legal personality did not turn it into a state or "a super-state". The attribution of legal personality was said to mean that the organisation was a subject of international law as it possessed international rights and duties and had the capacity to maintain its rights by bringing international claims. The ICJ maintained that while a state possessed the totality of international rights and duties recognised by international law:

"the rights and duties of an entity such as the Organisation must depend upon its purposes and functions as specified or implied in its constituent documents and developed in practice. The functions of the Organisation are of such a character that they could not be effectively discharged if they involved the concurrent action, on the international plane, of fifty-eight [Note: this was the number of the UN member states at the time] or more Foreign Offices, and the Court concludes that the Members have endowed the Organisation with capacity to bring international claims when necessitated by the discharge of its functions".

Thus the ICJ concluded that the UN as an organisation had the capacity to bring an international claim. If such capacity was denied the UN would not have been able to obtain reparations for the damage sustained to one of its agents.

The ICJ then examined the question as to whether the UN could bring such a claim on behalf of a national of one of its member states. This question was answered in the affirmative and the Court acknowledged that the agent of the organisation must have the confidence that he is protected when carrying out his duties on behalf of the UN. Otherwise his/her protection would be dependant upon various factors of international affairs, for example the fact of whether he/she is a national of a powerful state or not. Moreover, the ICJ also noted that the agent should be perceived as neutral and thus, if he/she had to rely on the state of nationality, the UN's independence might have been jeopardised. Thus the ICJ concluded that:

> "In claiming reparation on the injury suffered by its agent, the Organization does not represent the agent, but is asserting its own right, the right to secure respect for undertakings entered into towards the Organization".

The final issue the ICJ addressed was that of whether the UN has the right to claim reparations from a country which is not a member of the UN. The ICJ maintained that:

> "fifty states, representing the vast majority of the members of the international community, had the power, in conformity with international law, to bring into being an entity possessing objective international personality and not merely personality recognised by them alone, together with capacity to bring international claims".

Thus the ICJ concluded that the UN could bring a claim against a state which was not a member of the UN. 1949 ICJ Reports 174.

Commentary
This Advisory Opinion is the leading statement on the issue of the legal personality of international organisations. The ICJ laid down some important requirements of how the existence of international legal personality of an organisation could be established. First of all the documents establishing the organisation must be examined and the intentions of its creators determined. In the case of the UN the ICJ noted that the UN Charter, while not specifically stating that the UN as an organisation has legal personality, vests the UN with important duties and responsibilities, creates various organs for the discharge of these duties and requests full co-operation from the member states. Thus the ICJ was of the opinion that the members of the UN, by creating such an organisation, meant it to have international legal personality, otherwise it would not have been able to carry out its envisaged functions as members had planned.

The ICJ confirmed the so-called doctrine of implied powers whereby the organisation must be deemed to have those powers which, though not expressly provided for in the UN Charter or in another constituent document, are conferred upon it by necessary implication as being essential to the performance of its duties.

The ICJ also made clear that the UN did not possess the totality of legal personality possessed by states. The legal personality of any organisation is limited by the remit of its functions and purposes. It is important to remember that the scope of the legal personality possessed by different international organisations may differ. This is in sharp contrast to the position of states. All states enjoy the same legal personality; such legal personality is an inherent attribute of statehood. Thus an international organisation may be a subject of international law and is capable of possessing international rights and duties.

Finally, the ICJ noted that of the number of member states of the UN indicated, there had been almost universal acceptance of the UN as an organisation.

Hence the Court's conclusion that the UN enjoyed objective personality which could be enforced against all members of the international community.

Given the unique position of the UN, it was important that it was attributed with international personality so early in its history.

However for the rights and duties to be effective, international procedural capacity, namely the competence to bring claims and to seek redress, is also required. Hence recognition that the UN was capable of bringing international claims in cases in which its rights have been trespassed was important. Also important was the recognition that the UN possessed such a right, both on behalf of itself and its agents. The latter was particularly important so as to provide the agent with protection when fulfilling his duties in the service of the UN. The ICJ observed that "there was no necessary order of priority" between the diplomatic protection right of an agent's national state and the functional protection rights of the UN.

Key Principles: Limitations of the legal personality of an organisation: the principle of speciality; constituent documents are not regular treaties.

Legality of the Use by a state of Nuclear Weapons in Armed Conflict case (the WHO Nuclear Weapons case) Advisory Opinion 1996

Facts: The General Assembly of the World Health Organisation (WHO) asked the ICJ for its Advisory Opinion on the following question:

> "In the view of the health and environmental effects, would the use of nuclear weapons by a state in war or other armed conflict be a breach of its obligations under international law including the WHO Constitution?"

Held: The ICJ refused to give the Advisory Opinion on the question posed stating that in accordance with Art.96 (2) of the UN Charter, an Advisory Opinion may be requested by an authorised, specialised agency regarding issues that fall within the scope of its activities. Since the question was dealing with the legality of the use of nuclear weapons, it did not correspond to the competence of the WHO as defined in its Constitution, thus falling outside the scope of Art.96(2) of the UN Charter.

The ICJ did make an important statement regarding the constituent instruments of organisations, saying that the intention of these is to create new subjects of international law, which are endowed with a certain autonomy. 1996 ICJ Reports 66.

Commentary

The WHO Constitution empowers the organisation to deal with the effects on health of the use of nuclear weapons and to act preventively to protect people from these effects. The ICJ established that the question posed by the WHO fell outside the scope of these activities, but rather fell in the area of use of force. Thus the ICJ emphasised that in marked contrast from states, which possess total legal personality, organisations are governed by the principle of speciality: states who create organisations do so for specific reasons, vesting these organisations with certain powers. These powers are limited and the limits are set by the states who have created these organisations for the promotion of their common interest. In other words, an organisation is limited in its legal personality and actions by its constituent document and subsequent practice and is not entirely autonomous. The ICJ found the WHO, in requesting an Advisory Opinion on the legality of the use of nuclear weapons to be going beyond the scope of its activities and hence the Advisory Opinion was refused.

Thus, in the case of organisations, the constituent documents are not treated as mere agreements between the states which are creating the organisation.

Key Principle: **Not every arrangement between states constitutes an international organisation with separate legal personality.**

Case Concerning Certain Phosphate Lands in Nauru (Nauru v Australia) (Preliminary Objections) 1992

Facts: Nauru initiated proceedings before the ICJ over its dispute with Australia about the rehabilitation of certain phosphate lands in Nauru which Australia had worked out before Nauru independence. Australia, along with New Zealand and Great Britain, was the Administrating Authority of Nauru until 1965, when Nauru attained independence. Australia raised preliminary objections by claiming that the ICJ has no jurisdiction to hear the case and the ICJ upheld this position.

Held: Australia, New Zealand and Great Britain were agreed as the Administrating Authority of Nauru pursuant to the Trusteeship Agreement, approved by the United Nations in 1947. The ICJ held that this arrangement between states did not create a separate legal entity and thus the Administration Authority did not possess a separate legal personality from that of the three states. 1992 ICJ Reports 240.

Commentary
The ICJ took a special note of the fact that the operation of the Administrative Authority did not take place through special organs created by the body itself. Rather, for example, the Administrator was appointed by Australia and certain powers were entrusted to the Governor-General of Australia and the Australian Parliament. Therefore, the ICJ does not automatically

consider any arrangement between states as a separate legal entity with international legal personality.

Key Principle: **Art.4 of the UN Charter prescribes the conditions for UN membership; these conditions are exhaustive.**

Conditions for Admission of a State to Membership of the United Nations, Advisory Opinion 1948

Facts: The UN General Assembly requested the ICJ for an Advisory Opinion as to whether a Member of the United Nations could, pursuant to Art.4 of the UN Charter:

> "pronounce itself by its vote, either in the Security Council or in the General Assembly, on the admission of a State to membership... juridically entitled to make its consent ... dependent on conditions not expressly provided by paragraph I of the said Article? In particular, can such a Member, while it recognizes the conditions set forth in that provision to be fulfilled by the State concerned, subject its affirmative vote to the additional condition that other States be admitted to membership in the United Nations together with that State?"

Held: The Court initially made some comments on the question as posed. The Court acknowledged that the General Assembly could not have intended to ask the Court's opinion as to the reasons which, in the mind of a Member, may prompt its vote, as that refers to a "mental process". The Court observed that it was not called upon to define the meaning and scope of Art.4 of the UN Charter, but rather on the exhaustive nature of the conditions contained therein. If an affirmative view was expressed, that would mean a Member State would not legally be able to make admission dependent upon a condition not expressly provided for in Art.4.

The Court characterised the question as one of interpretation and a "purely legal one".

The ICJ dismissed the contention that the General Assembly's request should be regarded as political, falling outside the ICJ's jurisdiction. The Court expressed the view that a political character could not be attributed to a request, which framed in abstract terms, required it (the Court) to undertake an essentially judicial task, viz the interpretation of a treaty provision. Furthermore the Court denied that it should not deal with a question couched in abstract terms. In the Court's opinion this was a "mere affirmation devoid of any justification" (p.61). On the basis of Art.96 of the UN Charter and its own Statute Art.65 the ICJ maintained it could "give an advisory opinion on any legal question, abstract or otherwise." (p.61)

The Court further denied the assertion that it could not render an opinion as to do so would have involved an interpretation of the UN Charter. The Court observed that there was no prohibition in the UN Charter forbidding it as "the principal judicial organ of the United Nations" from exercising an interpretative function, such a function being a normal exercise of judicial powers. The ICJ analysed Art.4 para.1 and enumerated the five conditions, which must be satisfied by a prospective member of the UN, namely a candidate for membership must show that it is a State, is peace loving, accepts the obligations of the UN Charter, and is able and willing to carry out these obligations.

The Court expressed the view that the conditions as prescribed by Art.4 were exhaustive and not merely stated by way of information or of example. The conditions set out in Art.4 were not merely the necessary conditions, but constituted those recognised as suffice for membership. The Court, in giving its Opinion, highlighted that the English and French texts of Art.4 para.1 reflected the same meaning and that it was impossible to discern any conflict between the texts. The Court was unequivocal in its Opinion that the conditions for membership as set out in Art.4 were exhaustive and denied that any argument to the contrary could be drawn from para.2 of Art.4 as that paragraph relates only to the procedure for admission to the UN. The ICJ maintained that if the drafters of the UN Charter had intended to allow Member States the freedom to import conditions over and above those of the UN Charter, this would have been expressly adopted in the wording of the Article. However, the exhaustive character of Art.4 did not, in the Court's view, preclude recognition and appreciation of such factual circumstances which would allow verification as to the existence of the requisite conditions. Nevertheless, according to the Court Art.4 did not forbid the taking into account of any factor which in good faith it was possible and reasonable to connect with the conditions as prescribed. The ICJ maintained that the taking into account of such factors was "implied in the very wide and very elastic nature of the prescribed conditions; no relevant political factor— that is to say, none connected with the conditions of admission" were excluded (p.63). The Court noted the reference to the "recommendation" of the Security Council and the "decision" of the General Assembly was designed only to determine the respective functions of these two organs, and that the "political character of an organ" could not release it from the "observance of the treaty provisions established by the UN Charter and when they constitute limitations on its powers or criteria for its judgment". In the Court's view, there was "no conflict between the functions of the political organs on the one hand, and the exhaustive character of the prescribed conditions, on the other."(p.64). As to whether a Member could make its consent to the admission of an applicant dependent on the admission of the other applicants the Court stated that this would constituted "a new condition, since it is entirely unconnected with those prescribed in Art.4". The Court also noted that such a condition was of a different category from that of the Art.4 conditions, since it made admission dependent not upon the fulfillment of conditions but rather on "an extraneous consideration concerning States other that than the Applicant State" (p.65). 1948 ICJ Reports 57.

Commentary

This Opinion witnessed the Court establishing that it would not be deterred from dealing with issues on the grounds that the request was allegedly of a political nature. It established that membership of the UN was to be reflected in the fulfillment of criteria, criteria which were laid down in the UN Charter and thus established a legal rule which by prescribing conditions for admission also provided reasons for refusal. The Court made it quite clear that the conditions prescribed were exhaustive and that political considerations could not be superimposed. The political responsibilities assumed by the Security Council were not such to warrant a more extensive interpretation to Art.4 than was the intention of the framers of the UN Charter.

Key Principle: **Interpretation of the constituent documents of international organisations; importance of subsequent practice.**

Competence of the General Assembly for the Admission of a State to the United Nations case Advisory Opinion 1950

Facts: The General Assembly in its Resolution of November 22, 1949, requested the ICJ for an Advisory Opinion, on:

> "Can the admission of a State to membership in the United Nations, pursuant to Article 4, paragraph 2, of the Charter, be effected by a decision of the General Assembly, when the Security Council has made no recommendation for admission by reason of the candidate failing to obtain the requisite majority or of the negative vote of a permanent Member upon a resolution so to recommend?"

Held: See pp.17 and 209 for further discussion.

The ICJ noted that those bodies which Art.4 of the UN Charter had entrusted with admission matters, have consistently interpreted this Article as meaning that the General Assembly can only admit a member on the basis of a recommendation of the Security Council. The Court noted that this is also specifically reflected in the Rules of Procedure of the General Assembly. Consequently the ICJ came to the conclusion that the General Assembly must receive a recommendation from the Security Council when admitting a new member and the absence of such a recommendation cannot be treated in the same way as receiving a negative recommendation. 1950 ICJ Reports 4.

Commentary

In this Advisory Opinion the ICJ was asked to deal with the interpretation of the UN Charter and the Court took special note not only of the text of the UN Charter but also of the practices established. Therefore the interpretation of constituent documents of international organisations is different from the interpretation of regular multilateral treaties: rule embodied in Art.31(3)(b) (importance of subsequent practice) in the Vienna Convention on the Law of Treaties is of particular importance.

Key Principles: Interpretation of the constituting documents of international organisations; importance of subsequent practice.

Legal Consequences for States of the Continued Presence of South Africa in Namibia (South-West Africa) Notwithstanding Security Council Resolution 276 Advisory Opinion 1971

Facts: The Security Council of the UN asked the ICJ for an Advisory Opinion on the following question:

> "What are the legal consequences for States of the continued presence of South Africa in Namibia notwithstanding Security Council Resolution 276 (1970)?"

South Africa contended that the ICJ was not competent to deliver an opinion on this matter as, inter alia, two of the permanent members of the Security Council had abstained when voting for the resolution in question.

Held: See pp.18, 57 and 222 for further discussion.

In examining the issue of whether the voluntary abstention by a member of the Security Council should be considered as a bar to the adoption of a resolution, the ICJ stated that members of the Security Council, and in particular the permanent members, have "consistently and uniformly" interpreted that this practice did not constitute an obstacle to the adoption of a resolution. The ICJ emphasised that this practice had also been generally accepted by UN members and amounted to evidence as a general practice of the UN. 1971 ICJ Reports 16.

Commentary

As already noted, the interpretation of constituent documents of international organisations is approached differently from interpretation of regular multilateral treaties. The main distinguishing factor, according to the ICJ, in this instance is the practice that the organisation has adopted. Thus the ICJ noted the uniform and constant practice of the Security Council of not treating abstentions by its members as a bar to the adoption of a resolution. The ICJ specifically noted that this practice had also been accepted by other UN member states.

In cases of the interpretation of the constituent document of an organisation, the rule embodied in Art.31(3)(b) (importance of subsequent practice) in the Vienna Convention on the Law of Treaties is again seen to be of particular importance.

Key Principle: **Responsibility is the necessary consequence of international personality.**

The WHO Regional Offices case (Interpretation of the Agreement of 25 March 1951 between the WHO and Egypt) Advisory Opinion 1980

Facts: The WHO Assembly submitted a request for an Advisory Opinion about the legal principles and rules concerning consultation, negotiation and notice which should apply between the WHO and Egypt in the event the WHO regional office would be transferred from Alexandria in the Egyptian territory.

Held: See p.211 for further discussion.
    The ICJ initially reiterated its position in the *Reparations* case (see above) that international organisations are subjects of international law and as such:

"are bound by any obligations incumbent upon them under general rules of international law, under their constitutions or under international agreements to which they are parties to" (para.37).

The consequence of such legal personality is that just as a state can be held responsible for an injury to an organisation, so an organisation can be held responsible for an injury to a state. The ICJ accordingly established that the agreements between Egypt and WHO about having their regional office on Egyptian territory constituted a legal regime between the two entities and in accordance with these agreements, the WHO regional offices had been operational in Alexandria (Egypt) for over thirty years. The ICJ concluded that the obligation to cooperate in good faith would fall both upon Egypt and WHO if the negotiations about the transfer of the regional office should take place. 1980 ICJ Reports 73.

Commentary
This Advisory Opinion highlights that not only the constituent documents of organisations can impose legal obligations upon such organisations. In this opinion the Court acknowledged these were headquarters agreements that the ICJ saw as imposing obligations upon WHO. Moreover, the ICJ spelt out the necessary consequence of the attribution of international legal personality to an organisation, namely the international organisation can be held responsible for a breach of international law.

Key Principle: **Domestic law provisions cannot be invoked to override the obligations arising from an international agreement with an international organisation.**

Applicability of the Obligation to Arbitrate under s.21 of the United Nations Headquarters Agreement of June 26, 1947 Advisory Opinion 1988

Facts: In 1987 the United States Congress adopted the Anti-Terrorism Act which forbade the Palestine Liberation Organisation (PLO) from, inter alia, establishing or maintaining an office of the UN on the territory of the United States. Since the PLO had been granted an observer status with the UN in 1974, the maintenance of their office was deemed by the Secretary-General of the UN to fall under the Headquarters Agreement concluded with the United States in 1947. According to this agreement, parties are obliged to use arbitration for the settlement of their disputes. The General Assembly requested an Advisory Opinion from the ICJ asking if this should be the obligation incumbent on the United States in the given situation.

Held: See p.28 for further discussion.
The ICJ answered in the affirmative by applying the long-standing principle of international law, which provides that international law prevails over domestic law. Thus the ICJ rejected the argument of the United States that the measures against the PLO Observer Mission were taken irrespective of any obligations the United States might have pursuant to the Headquarters Agreement. 1988 ICJ Reports 12.

Commentary
While this opinion is of more relevance when considering the relations between the international and domestic law (see p.28), it is also important for the law concerning international organisations. In this instance a state was held to the obligations it had undertaken in its agreement with an international organisation, the UN, and the argument, that a domestic law could override the obligations arising from such an agreement, was rejected.

Key Principle: **Special privileges and immunities of the experts of the UN are such that are necessary for the exercise of their functions.**

Difference Relating to Immunity from Legal Process of a Special Rapporteur of the Commission on Human Rights Advisory Opinion 1999

Facts: Mr Cumaraswamy, a Malaysian jurist, serving as the UN Special Rapporteur on the UN Commission of Human Rights on the Independence of Judges and Lawyers was charged with defamation in Malaysia. The charges were brought against him after an article, based on an interview with him, was published. The legal counsel of the UN, acting on behalf of the Secretary-General of the UN, considered that the interview was given by Mr Cumaraswamy in his capacity as the UN Special Rapporteur which in turn would make him immune from the Malaysian proceedings, on the basis of the UN Convention on the Privileges and Immunities of the United Nations and its activities. These views of the Secretary-General were communicated to the Malaysian government, but the legal proceedings did not stop and the courts were not aware of such communications from the UN.

The Malaysian authorities in effect refused to accept the position of the UN and the Economic and Social Council of the UN applied to the ICJ for an Advisory Opinion on the matter.

Held: See pp.151 and 169 for further discussion.
The ICJ concluded that Special Rapporteurs are entrusted with a mission by the UN and this is the decisive element in determining that they are entitled to privileges and immunities as

provided for by Art.VI, s.22 of the UN Convention on the Privileges and Immunities of the United Nations and its activities.
The ICJ underlined that the Secretary-General of the UN plays a
pivotal role in determining whether a particular expert on a
mission is entitled to the immunity in the prevailing circumstances. The Court observed that the Secretary-General had on
numerous occasions made communications to the Malaysian
authorities stating that in this instance Mr Cumaraswamy should
be immune from the proceedings. Moreover, the ICJ also took
note that the article referred to Mr Cumaraswamy as the UN
Special Rapporteur on various occasions. Therefore the ICJ
concluded that Mr Cumaraswamy was entitled to immunity in
respect to the words spoken during the course of the interview in
question. The ICJ also declared that the Malaysian government
was obliged to communicate the view of the Secretary-General
regarding the immunity of Mr Cumaraswamy to the relevant
Malaysian authorities and that in this particular instance the
state responsibility of Malaysia was engaged: even though the
breach of its obligations resulted from the judicial proceedings, a
state is responsible for the actions of its agents, even if these
agents are free from the executive. 1999 ICJ Reports 62.

Commentary
The ICJ confirmed that agents of the UN are entitled to such
privileges and immunities as are necessary in the course of their
actions as experts of the UN. In this particular case, the provision
of immunity arose from the UN Convention on the Privileges
and Immunities of the United Nations and its activities. In the
case of other international organisations, the relevant agreements
concerning the privileges and immunities have to be consulted
as there are no general rules in this area.

   The ICJ also underlined the central role of the Secretary-General in determining the scope of such immunities and privileges,
noting that he/she must ensure that such immunities are not
abused. However the judgment of the Secretary-General that Mr
Cumaraswamy had immunity along with the fact that the article
referred to him as the UN Special Rapporteur, were factors
enough for the ICJ to conclude that immunity should apply in
this case.

Key Principle: **Succession of international organisations may take place without express provision.**

International Status of South-West Africa Advisory Opinion 1950

Facts: The territory of South-West Africa was placed under a mandate conferred upon the Union of South Africa by the League of Nations in 1920. The Union of South Africa continued to administer this territory also after the dissolution of the League of Nations and the formation of the UN, but constantly refused to submit reports to the UN and transmit petitions from the inhabitants of the territory.

The General Assembly requested the Advisory Opinion of the ICJ in its Resolution of December 6, 1949 about the international status of the South-West African territory and the obligations of the Union of South Africa.

Held: The ICJ held that the supervisory responsibilities, which were entrusted to the Union of South Africa by the League of Nations mandate, continued to exist also after the dissolution of the League of Nations. The ICJ analysed the resolutions of the League of Nations and concluded that:

> "the Assembly said that the League's functions with respect to mandated territories would come to an end; it did not say that the Mandates themselves came to an end. In confining itself to this statement, and in taking note, on the other hand, of the expressed intentions of the mandatory Powers to continue to administer the mandated territories in accordance with their respective Mandates, until other arrangements had been agreed upon between the United Nations and those powers, the Assembly manifested its understanding that the Mandates were to continue in existence until 'other arrangements' were established".

1950 ICJ Reports 128.

The ICJ went on to examine the statements of the representatives of the Union of South Africa and concluded that those expressed a similar view, namely, that the Union did not regard the dissolution of the League of Nations as diminishing or ceasing its Mandate and that it would carry on the administration until other arrangements had been made.

Therefore the ICJ concluded that the obligation to submit reports did not cease only because the League of Nations as a supervisory organ had ceased to exist since another, albeit not identical, supervisory body existed, namely, the UN General Assembly.

Commentary
In this Advisory Opinion the ICJ confirmed that succession of international organisations may also take place without express provisions to that effect. In this opinion, the UN General Assembly was recognised as legally qualified to exercise the supervisory powers that belonged to the Assembly of the League of Nations. Thus the UN was in essence recognised as a successor to the League of Nations.

Key Principles: **Obligations of successor states; representation in international organisations.**

Case Concerning Application of the Convention on the Prevention and Punishment of the Crime of Genocide (Bosnia and Herzegovina v Serbia and Montenegro) Preliminary Objections (Bosnia and Herzegovina v Yugoslavia) 1996

Facts: The case concerned the application of the 1948 Convention on the Prevention and Punishment of the Crime of Genocide (Genocide Convention) and whether the Respondent (Serbia) was in breach of its obligations under the Genocide Convention.

There were a number of stages prior to a judgment on the merits including an objection to the Court's jurisdiction raised by Yugoslavia. Yugoslavia objected to the contention that the Convention bound the two parties or that it had entered into force between them and also denied the dispute fell within the provisions of Art.IX of the Genocide Convention. At the time of the creation of FRY in 1992, Yugoslavia had formally declared its intention to be bound by international treaties to which the former Yugoslavia was a party. The Court observed that it had not been contested that Yugoslavia was a party to the Genocide Convention. Accordingly Yugoslavia was bound by the provisions of the Convention on the date of the filing of the Application of the preliminary objections.

Bosnia-Herzegovina had transmitted on December 29, 1992 a Notice of Succession to the Secretary-General of the UN, as depositary of the Genocide Convention. Yugoslavia had contested that notice on the grounds Bosnia-Herzegovina was not qualified to become a party to the Genocide Convention.

Held: See pp.21 and 220 for further discussion.

The Court noted Bosnia-Herzegovina had been admitted to UN in May 1992. On this basis the Court concluded Bosnia-Herzegovina could become a party to the Genocide Convention.

The Court did not address further the dispute between the parties concerning state succession in respect to treaties as it was evident that Bosnia-Herzegovina was a party to the Genocide Convention on the date that preliminary objections were lodged.

As to Yugoslavia's objection that the Convention could not have entered into force between the Parties, because the two states did not recognise one another the conditions necessary to found the consensual basis of the Court's jurisdiction were lacking. However the Court observed that pursuant to the Dayton-Paris Agreement, which entered into force December 14, 1995 the Parties "recognize each other as sovereign independent States within their international borders". (Art.X)

The Court then addressed the issue as to whether it had jurisdiction on the basis of Art.IX of the Genocide Convention and whether the dispute between the parties was one that fell within the scope of Art.IX.

The Court held that there was a legal dispute between the parties and as such fell within Art.IX of the Genocide Convention thus giving the Court jurisdiction. 1996 ICJ Reports 595.

Commentary

The foregoing case subsequently led to an application from Yugoslavia requesting a revision of the 1996 judgment (see Application for Revision of the Judgment of July 11, 1996 in the case concerning Application of the Convention on the Prevention and Punishment of the Crime of Genocide (*Bosnia and Herzegovina v Yugoslavia*), Preliminary Objections (*Yugoslavia v Bosnia and Herzegovina*, February 3, 2003) maintaining Yugoslavia's membership of the UN amounted to a new fact which was not known in 1996. Yugoslavia was admitted as a new member to the UN on November 1, 2000. Yugoslavia further maintained that at the time FRY had not been a party to either the ICJ Statute or the Genocide Convention. In September 1992, pursuant to General Assembly Resolution 47/1 the UN General Assembly had

considered that FRY did not automatically continue in, or succeed to, the membership in the UN of the former Socialist Federal Republic of Yugoslavia. However the Court in 2003
maintained that GA Resolution 47/1 did not affect FRY's right of
locus standi before the ICJ nor did it affect FRY's position in
relation to the Genocide Convention. The Court therefore rejected the application for revision.

5. TERRITORY

Key Principles: **Title to territory; what is required for and the characteristics of territorial sovereignty.**

Island of Palmas case, Netherlands v United States (1928)

Facts: Pursuant to the Treaty of Paris 1898, following the Spanish-American war, the Philippines were ceded by Spain to the United States. Palmas (or Miangas), a small island situated some 50 miles south east of the Philippines was visited in 1906 by an American official. On the island he found the Dutch flag was being flown and during his visit it was evident the Netherlands considered the island to be part of the Dutch East Indies.

The United States maintained that the island was part of the Philippine archipelago ceded by the Spanish, whereas the Netherlands maintained that sovereignty was based on the continuous and undisputed display of authority over the territory for a long period of time. The matter of sovereignty over the island was referred to arbitration.

Held: See p.137 for further discussion.

It was held the Netherlands' title of sovereignty had been acquired by continuous and peaceful display of state authority during a long period of time going back beyond the year 1700 and that that title held good.

In respect of the United States it was noted that Spain could not transfer more rights than she had herself possessed. It was noted that from the moment when the Spaniards had withdrawn from the Moluccas in 1666 up until the US protests in 1906, the exercise of territorial rights by the Netherlands had not been tested.

Max Huber, the sole arbitrator, highlighted that sovereignty in inter-state relations signified independence and territorial sovereignty provided an exclusive right to the state concerned to exercise the functions of a state to the exclusion of any other state. Territorial sovereignty is generally acknowledged either by natural frontiers as recognised by international law or, in the words of the arbitrator, by:

> "outward signs of delimitation that are undisputed, or else by legal engagement entered into between interested neighbours, such as

frontier conventions or by acts of recognition within fixed boundaries".

In the event of a dispute it is not sufficient to establish the title by which territorial sovereignty was validly acquired at a certain moment. It is necessary to show that the territorial sovereignty had continued to exist and did exist at the moment at which the decision of the dispute would be considered as critical. This involves an actual display of state activities of a type which can be exercised only by the territorial sovereign.

The right of the territorial sovereign, however also has a corollary, a duty, namely an obligation to afford protection within the territory to the rights of other states, in particular their right to integrity and inviolability in both peace and in war, as well as the right which may be claimed for other states' nationals.

The arbitrator highlighted the continuous and peaceful display of territorial sovereignty, peaceful that is in relation to other states, was as good as title. He maintained that effective occupation was required for the maintenance of the right. Arbitrator Huber recognised territorial sovereignty could be manifested in different ways according to time and place. He acknowledged that although sovereignty should be continued, it could not be exercised in fact at every moment on every point of a territory. It was recognised that the extent of sovereignty could differ according to whether the region is inhabited or uninhabited, whether it is readily accessible, or whether it was enclosed within territories.

Arbitrator Huber discussed the title arising from the principle of contiguity but maintained there was no rule of international law to the effect that islands situated outside territorial waters should belong to a state simply because its territory forms the *terra firma* (nearest continent or island of considerable size). There was insufficient practice to demonstrate a rule of international law and he maintained the alleged principle itself was so uncertain and contested that even successive governments of the same state had on different occasions maintained contradictory opinions.

The arbitrator stated the display of sovereignty should be open and public and on the point of discovery he held that discovery could only exist as an inchoate title, as a claim to establish sovereignty by effective occupation. An inchoate title could not prevail over a definitive title founded on a continuous and peaceful display of sovereignty. (1928) 2R. 1AA 829.

Commentary

The arbitrator's decision has stood the test of time and remains the leading authority on the acquisition of title to territory, the nature of territorial sovereignty and what is understood by a continued and peaceful display of state authority. It is also important with respect to critical dates, namely the date which is relevant for determining territorial sovereignty.

The case is also important for the point which Arbitrator Huber made in respect of intertemporal law, namely that title must be valid according to the law prevailing at the time at which it is claimed title had been established.

Key Principle: **The taking of possession for the purpose of establishing title to territory may vary according to the geographical and geological characteristics of the territory in question.**

Clipperton Island Arbitration, Mexico v France (1931)

Facts: Sovereignty over Clipperton Island was established by a French Navy Commissioner in 1858. Although no evidence of sovereignty was left on the island, the naval official sent a communication to the Government of Hawaii and the French Consulate in Honolulu and published in *The Polynesian*, an English Journal, claiming sovereignty over the island. No act of sovereignty was made on the island, the island had no population and no administrative or economic activities were undertaken. However, in 1897 three people were apparently seen on the island collecting guano and when spotted by a French vessel the individuals had raised the American flag. The US stated that it did not intend to claim sovereignty over the island.

Mexico claimed Clipperton Island on the grounds of a long period of ownership and sent an expedition to the island, ignoring the French claim to sovereignty.

Held: The arbitrator looked at the history of the island and maintained there was no evidence to prove the island had actually been discovered by Spain. This would have been necessary for Mexico to establish good title. The arbitrator maintained that when sovereignty had been claimed by France in 1858, the island was *terra nullius* and susceptible to occupation. The question was whether the French had established effective occupation.

The arbitrator held that the actual *(animus occupandi)* and not the nominal taking of possession was what was necessary. The taking of possession was held to consist of an act or series of acts, by which the occupying state reduces to its possession the territory in question. That normally occurs when the occupying state establishes the legal apparatus whereby its laws are respected. If a territory was completely uninhabited then from the time that the occupying state makes its appearance it becomes the absolute and undisputed possession of that state; from that moment the taking of possession must be considered as accomplished and the occupation complete.

It was noted that France had intimated her intention through the naval officer's publication and thereby had legitimately acquired sovereignty in Clipperton Island. Furthermore there was no reason to suppose that this sovereign right had been subsequently lost as France had never expressed any intention of abandoning the island. (1931) 2R. 1AA 1105.

Commentary
The decision highlights that what is important in establishing sovereignty over territory is intention, and intention must be made public and should not be protested against from other states. The decision further reinforces that the nature and scope of actual acts whereby territory is claimed will differ according to the nature of the territory in question.

Key Principle: **The actual exercise of sovereign rights may be quite minimal and little more than symbolic.**

Legal Status of Eastern Greenland Case, Denmark v Norway (1933)

Facts: The dispute which arose between Denmark and Norway came about as a result of Norway proclaiming sovereignty over Eastern Greenland, an uninhabited and uncolonised part of the island. Denmark claimed sovereignty over all of the island and raised proceedings against Norway in the PCIJ.

Held: The Court held that in many instances in international law very little may be demanded regarding an actual exercise of sovereign rights, provided that is, that other states could not make a superior claim. The Court held that this was particularly true in the case of claims to sovereignty over areas in sparsely populated or unsettled countries.

However, the Court maintained the superior claim was made out in this instance by Denmark. Denmark had succeeded in demonstrating a valid title to the sovereignty of all Greenland at the critical date. (1933) PCIJ Reports Series A/B 53.

Commentary
This case endorses the principles established in the *Clipperton Arbitration* case (see above).

Key Principle: **The state which can show the most recent evidence of state functions will establish good title.**

Minquiers and Ecrechos case, France v United Kingdom 1953

Facts: The case came before the ICJ under a special agreement between France and the UK to determine the sovereignty over a number of islets and rocks in the English Channel. Under that agreement the concept of *terra nullius* was excluded as a basis for resolving the claims, as was that of *condominium*.

[*Condominium* refers to an unusual situation when authority is exercised jointly over a particular territory by two or more external powers. Such an instance might be that of territory being taken from a defeated state and handed over to the victors jointly. Such a situation is not one which would arise in contemporary international law.]

The claim of both parties was that they had an ancient or original title to the Ecrechos and Minquiers islands and that title had always been maintained and had never been lost.

Held: See p.19 for further discussion.

The Court considered the evidence of sovereignty provided by each party. In considering the evidence produced by the UK, regarding its claim to sovereignty in the 19th century, attached particular probative value to those acts which related to an exercise of jurisdiction, local administration and legislative

activity. The ICJ, in looking at the relative strengths of the
opposing claims, concluded the Ecrechos, at the beginning of the
13th century, was considered and treated as an integral part of
the fief of the Channel Islands, which were held by the English
King and that the group continued under the dominion of the
King. At the beginning of the 14th century jurisdiction over the
islands was exercised by the English King.

In the 19th and 20th centuries the British authorities had
exercised state functions, functions which had not been exercised
by the French Government. On the basis of the evidence put to it
in both instances the Court concluded that the UK had sovereignty over the islands and rocks, as far as these were capable of
appropriation. 1953 ICJ Reports 47.

Commentary
What emerges as the most important principle from this judgment is that a state claiming sovereignty must be able to
demonstrate that it has performed state functions over the territory in question.

***

Key Principle: **Protest can negate a prescriptive claim.**

Chamizal Arbitration case, United States v Mexico 1911

Facts: Treaties of 1848 and 1853 established the Rio Grande
River as the boundary between Mexico and the US. Over a
period of time the course of the river changed. A joint boundary
commission was established to determine the sovereignty over
the tract of land which, as a consequence of the river's change in
course, was established on the American's side.

Held: The consistent and constant challenge by Mexico
through official sources over the physical possession of the area
by American citizens denied the US obtaining a prescriptive title
to the land in question. It was held that the possession by the US
citizens was not undisturbed, uninterrupted and unchallenged.
The initiating of a treaty establishing the competent tribunal to
decide the question precluded the US from acquiring a valid title
through prescription. 5 AJIL 1911 782.

Commentary
Prescription cannot give rise to a valid title to territory if met with protest.

Key Principle: **Prescription requires the backing of state authority.**

Kasikili/Sedudu Island case, Botswana v Namibia 1999

Facts: Namibia asserted a claim over the Kasikili/Sedudu Island. The island was located in the "main channel" of the Chobe River which was accepted by Botswana and Namibia as determining the boundary between them.

The Namibian claim focused on the Masubia people who originated from Eastern Caprivi in Namibia. Namibia maintained its colonial predecessors had exercised authority over the island through the:

> "modality of 'indirect rule', using the Chiefs and political institutions of the Masubia to carry out the directives of the ruling power, under the control and supervision of officials of that power".

Namibia further maintained this occurred without objection from Botswana, or its predecessor Britain, for almost 100 years until 1984 when a formal claim to the island was made by Botswana.

Held: In establishing Botswana's title to the island the Court considered and denied the Namibian claim which was based on prescription. It denied the Namibian claim that the island members of the Masubia were exercising state authority and state functions on behalf of Namibia by highlighting the evidence produced. That evidence showed the Masubia only used the island intermittently and indeed this use had begun prior to the establishment of any colonial administration in the Caprivi Strip and had continued without being linked to any territorial claims. 1999 ICJ Reports 1045.

Commentary
This case underscores the need for acts which may be regarded
as prescriptive to be carried out publicly and continuously and to
have the endorsement of the state.

Key Principles: **A territory occupied by tribes or peoples with
a social and political organisation was not regarded as** *terra
nullius.* **Such territories were not acquired by occupation.**

Western Sahara case Advisory Opinion 1975

Facts: The General Assembly sought an Advisory Opinion
from the Court as to the status of the Western Sahara. Spain had
colonized the Western Sahara in 1884. The General Assembly
requested Spain to decolonize the Western Sahara pursuant to
Resolution 1514 and further requested Spain to consult with
neighbouring Mauritania and Morocco to determine procedures
for holding a referendum to be conducted under UN supervision. Spain agreed to a referendum in 1975. However Morocco
advanced a territorial claim to the area based on historic title
predating Spain's acquisition. A similar claim was advanced by
Mauritania. At the time of colonisation the Western Sahara was
inhabited by peoples, although nomadic, who were socially and
politically organised in tribes and under Chiefs who were competent to represent them.

Held: See pp.58 and 221 for further discussion.
   In dealing with the status of the Western Sahara, the Court
looked at the term *terra nullius* in the context of the law prevailing at the time. The Court referred to *terra nullius* as a legal
term of art which was utilised in connection with occupation.
Occupation could only give rise to a valid title if the territory in
question was *terra nullius*, i.e. belonged to no one and thus susceptible to acquisition. The Court maintained that state practice
at the relevant time indicated that territories inhabited by tribes
or peoples having a social and political organisation were not
regarded as *terra nullius*. Acquisition of sovereignty in such
instances was acquired not by original title but rather through
agreements concluded with local rulers. Agreements concluded
with local rulers were regarded as providing derivative title to
territory. Occupation in this context was used in a non technical

sense denoting simply acquisition of sovereignty. 1975 ICJ Reports 12.

Key Principle: **The principle *uti possidetis* may not be disregarded when determining boundary disputes.**

Burkina Faso v Mali case 1986

Facts: Reference was made to the ICJ for settlement of a dispute between the two states regarding a certain part of their common frontier. The two states concerned had particularly requested the Court to resolve their dispute on the principle of the intangibility of frontiers inherited from colonisation.

Held: See p.63 for further discussion.

The ICJ articulated the principle of *uti possidetis* as one of respect for the intangibility of frontiers. The Court took it upon itself to emphasise the "exceptional importance" of the principle of *uti possidetis* for the African continent and of course for the two parties involved. The ICJ, although noting the principle was one which appeared to have come from Spanish America, was not a special rule pertaining exclusively to one specific system of law. The Court acknowledged it as a general principle with the obvious purpose of preventing the independence and stability of new states being endangered "by fratricidal struggles provoked by the challenging of frontiers following the withdrawal of the administering power". The ICJ maintained *uti possidetis* as a principle of a general kind logically connected with decolonisation. Looking to Africa, the Court observed that maintenance of the territorial status was often seen as the wisest course and one to be taken account of when interpreting the principle of self determination of peoples. 1986 ICJ Reports 554.

Key Principles: Adopted approach to *uti possidetis* as provided in Burkina Faso v Mali case, see above. Acknowledged *uti possidetis* may be qualified by adjudication and treaty and in principle by acquiescence or recognition.

Case Concerning the Land, Island and Maritime Frontier Dispute, El Salvador v Honduras; Nicaragua intervening 1992

Facts: The dispute between the two parties related to the Gulf of Fonseca, the land around it, the islands within it and the waters off and beyond it.

Held: See p.64 for further discussion.

The Court engaged in a very detailed examination of the six sector land boundaries which were in dispute.

It was acknowledged by the Court that the states themselves could by agreement vary such boundaries and some forms of activity or inactivity might amount to acquiescence in a boundary other than that of 1821. The Court went on to note where the relevant administrative boundary was ill defined or its position disputed:

> "... the behaviour of the two newly independent states in the years following independence may well serve as a guide to where the boundary was, either in their shared view, or in the view acted on by one and acquiesced in by the other".

The Court stated for *uti possidetis uris* the question was not whether the colonial province needed wide boundaries to accommodate its population, but where those boundaries actually were; and post independent effectivites, where relevant, have to be assessed in terms of actual events, not their social origins. The Court emphasised that in instances where the boundary is clearly established the principle of *uti possidetis* applied regardless of an effective display of state functions in the disputed area or any economic inequality which came about as a result of the application of the old boundary. 1992 ICJ Reports 355.

Commentary

It is evident from the Court's decision that it did not consider that applying the principle of *uti possidetis uris* was to freeze for all time the provincial boundaries which as a consequence of independence became international boundaries.

Key Principle: The boundaries of a state established by a treaty concluded in colonial times may establish a valid title, see Land and Maritime Boundary case between Cameroon and Nigeria 2002 ICJ Reports.

Key Principles: The right of self determination arises in limited circumstances and entities within an existing state do not enjoy a right under international law whereby they may secede unilaterally.

Re Reference by Governor in Council Concerning Certain Questions Relating to Secession of Quebec from Canada (1998)

Facts: See p.65 for further discussion.

Held: The Supreme Court held that there existed no such right allowing Quebec to secede unilaterally. The Court recognised that sources of international law establish the right to self determination as belonging to "peoples" in the colonial context, also in instances where there is alien subjugation, domination or exploitation outside a colonial context. (1998) Supreme Court of Canada 161 D.L.R. (4th) 385.

Commentary

This is a case from a domestic jurisdiction, but should be noted as one of the rare instances when a judicial body of a state has been called upon to adjudicate on the exercise and content of the right to self-determination.

Key Principle: The nature of the territory will determine what acts are required to denote sovereignty.

Sovereignty over Pulau Ligitan and Pulau Sipadan (Indonesia/Malaysia) 2002

Facts: The dispute was with respect to the sovereignty over Pulau Ligitan. Indonesia's claim to sovereignty was premised on an 1891 Convention between Great Britain and the Netherlands. Indonesia also advanced an alternative argument that its sovereignty could be established as successor to the Sultan of Bulungan as he had authority over the island.

Malaysia's claim to sovereignty was founded on a series of alleged transmissions of title originally held by the former sovereign the Sultan of Sulu. Malaysia claimed that title passed in succession to Spain, to the US, to Great Britain on behalf of the state of North Borneo, to the United Kingdom of Great Britain and Northern Ireland and finally to Malaysia itself. In the alternative, Malaysia claimed, if the Court were to conclude the islands had originally belonged to the Netherlands, its superior claim would in any event displace any such Netherlands title.

Held: The Court examined the object and purpose of the 1891 Convention and concluded that was the delimitation of boundaries between the parties' possessions within the island of Borneo itself. This the Court based on the wording of the preamble to the 1891 Convention. The Court did not find anything in the Convention to suggest that the parties intended to delimit the boundary between their possessions to the east of the islands of Borneo and Sebatik or to attribute sovereignty over any other islands. The Court concluded that neither the *travaux preparatoires* of the Convention nor the circumstances of its conclusion supported Indonesia's contention that the parties to the Convention had also agreed on an allocation line beyond the east coast of Sebatik.

Regarding title by succession the Court concluded it could not accept Malaysia's contention that there had been an uninterrupted series of transfers of title from the Sultan of Sulu, the alleged original title holder, to Malaysia. The Court denied it had been established with certainty that Ligitan and Sipadan belonged to the Sultan of Sulu nor that any of the alleged subsequent title holders had a treaty based title to these two islands. Accordingly the Court could not find that Malaysia had inherited a treaty based title from its predecessor, the UK.

The Court then turned to Malaysia's alternative argument, namely acquisition of title by way of continuous peaceful possession and administration without objection from Indonesia or its predecessors in title. The Court acknowledged that in the case of very small islands which are uninhabited, or at least not permanently inhabited, there would generally be little overt acts of sovereignty.

The Court then considered the parties' respective claims. It highlighted that Indonesia did not invoke any official acts of either a legislative or regulatory character. Notwithstanding the continued presence of Dutch and Indonesian navies in the waters around Ligitan and Sipadan, there was nothing to suggest the naval authorities considered the islands to be under the sovereignty of either the Netherlands or Indonesia.

In respect of Malaysia, the activities relied upon, although modest in number, were diverse in character and included legislative, administrative and quasi-judicial acts. These acts extended over a considerable time frame and endorsed an intention to exercise state functions in respect of the two islands in the context of the administration of a wider range of islands. Thus the Court concluded that Malaysia held title to Ligitan and Sipadan. 2002 ICJ Reports 625.

Commentary

This case endorses that sovereignty over territory may be established by a variety of means which will depend on the geography of the territory. However in every instance there must be an intention to act as sovereign and this must be evidenced by open public acts.

Key Principle: **The relevance of *uti possidetis uris*.**

Frontier Dispute (Benin/Niger) 2005

Facts: A dispute arose between the parties, the Republic of Benin and the Republic of Niger, as to the whole boundary between them. Benin sought that the boundary would follow the median line of the river Mekrou to a certain point and thereafter the left bank of the river Niger. Benin also sought a declaration that it possessed sovereignty over all islands in the River Niger and in particular the island of Lete.

Niger on the other hand sought a declaration that the boundary between it and Benin followed the line of "deepest soundings" in the river Niger in as far as that line could be established at the date of independence. Niger claimed that line determined which islands belonged to each party and the attribution of islands was to be regarded as final. As to the boundary in the river Mekrou, Niger maintained this was to be established by a line comprising two parts. Regarding the Gaya-Malanville bridges, Niger maintained the boundary should pass through each of these structures. The Court constituted a Chamber to deal with this dispute.

Held: The Chamber noted both parties were in agreement as to the relevance and application of the principle of *uti possidetis uris* for the purpose of determining their common border, namely that as inherited by the French administration. The Chamber emphasised, however, that the consequences of such a determination required to be assessed in relation to present day physical realities and thus it could not disregard the possible appearance or disappearance of a certain island in the stretch concerned. It was emphasised that the effect of the *uti possidetis* principle is to freeze the territorial title and although the examination of post independence documents was permitted, such documents could not lead to any modification of the "photograph of the territory" at the critical date. Modification would be permitted if the documents reflected this was the clear intention of the parties.

The Chamber concluded that neither party provided evidence of title on the basis of regulative or administrative acts during the colonial period. Accordingly the Chamber turned to look at the various activities claimed by the respective parties and decided the claims of the islands in the light of this.

As to the boundary between Benin and Niger the Chamber held it followed the main navigable channel of the river Niger as it existed at the dates of independence.

Regarding the boundary line in the river Mekrou the Chamber acknowledged that contemporary practice as reflected in treaties or conventions defining water course boundaries usually refer to the *thalweg* as the boundary when the watercourse is navigable and to the median line when it is not. The documents presented to the Chamber did not allow the exact course of the *thalweg* to be identified. The Chamber noted the river was not navigable and the median line, rather than the *thalweg,* would provide the legal certainty inherent in the determination of an international boundary. 2005 ICJ Reports 90.

Commentary
The Chamber emphasised the principle of *uti possidetis* as being the determining factor in deciding the territorial boundary. In this particular case it was the boundary which existed at the time the French colony had attained independence. However, it is evident from the decision, the Chamber recognised that the colonial administration that had been exercised over the disputed territory might have to be examined so as to ascertain the frontier. The Chamber therefore recognised that there was an

engagement between *uti possidetis* and the effective display of governmental functions. This had to be examined in the context of efforts to determine the line of the boundary at the critical date as the latter could then be consolidated by the principle of *uti possidetis*.

Key Principle: **Boundary questions are distinct from those arising in title to territorial sovereignty.**

North Sea Continental Shelf cases (Federal Republic of Germany v Denmark); and (Federal Republic of Germany v Netherlands) 1969

Facts: See p.1 for further discussion.

Held: See pp.2, 52, 110 and 119 for further discussion. The Court observed:

> "the appurtenance of a given area, considered as an entirety, in no way governs the precise delimitations of its boundaries, any more than uncertainty as to boundaries can affect territorial rights".

1969 ICJ Reports 3.

Commentary
Notwithstanding this unequivocal statement, a dispute may often raise issues regarding both territorial sovereignty and boundaries. Whether a dispute is to be approached as a sovereignty one or a boundary one may often be one of the points at issue. See also *Burkina Faso v Mali* case (see pp.63, 99) and also *Aegean Sea Continental Shelf* case (see p.207).

6. LAW OF THE SEA

Key Principles: Territorial sea; use of the straight baseline system for determining the breadth of territorial sea is legitimate under international law; determination of the territorial sea is done by the coastal state but subject to international supervision.

Anglo Norwegian Fisheries case (UK v Norway) 1951

Facts: Norway employed the straight baselines method from selected points on its coast to measure the breadth of its territorial sea. The use of this method was justified by Norway as necessary because of the fragmented and highly indented nature of the Norwegian coastline. Use of the straight baseline system meant a greater proportion of water was characterised as Norwegian internal waters than would have otherwise been the case. The UK objected to the use of the straight baselines method and initiated a case before the ICJ.

Held: See pp.10 and 136 for further discussion.

The Court held that the delimitation of the sea area would always be an international matter, although by its very nature the coastal state is the only state competent to measure the territorial waters. The Court recognised a state should be allowed a degree of flexibility in determining the delimitation of the territorial sea so as to give cognisance to practical needs and local requirements. Accordingly the Court upheld the legality of the straight baseline method. Notwithstanding this recognition though, the Court emphasised the base lines should not depart, to any appreciable extent, from the general direction of the coast.

The Court acknowledged that the low watermark had found general acceptance in international law as the means of measuring the breadth of the territorial sea. However in instances where a coast is deeply indented and cut into, or where it is bordered by an archipelago, the baseline becomes independent of the low water mark and can only be determined by means of a geometric construction. The Court highlighted that in such circumstances the line of the low water mark could no longer be put forward as a rule requiring the coast line to be followed in all its sinuosities.

Furthermore it was not possible to speak of an exception when confronted with the high number of derogations that such a rugged coast would demand. The Court acknowledged that the principle that the belt of territorial waters should follow the general direction of the coast, made it possible to fix certain criteria valid for any delimitation of the territorial seas. The Court observed that in order to apply this principle several states had deemed it necessary to follow the straight baseline method and they had done so without encountering objections from other states. Such a method consisted of selecting appropriate points in the low water mark and drawing straight lines between them. This, the Court noted, had been done not only in the case of well defined bays, but also in cases of minor curvatures of the coast line where it was solely a question of giving a simpler form to the belt of territorial waters.

The Court then went on to identify a number of criteria, which although not entirely precise could be instrumental in providing courts with an adequate basis for their decisions and which could be adapted to a number of different factual situations. Among such considerations identified were those of the close dependence of the territorial sea upon the land domain. Indeed the Court identified that certain economic interests peculiar to a region, the reality and importance of which were clearly evidenced by a long usage, were factors which could be taken into account. The Court also maintained that another fundamental consideration was the more or less close relationship existing between certain sea areas and the land formations which divided or surrounded them. In other words, whether certain sea areas lying within the straight baselines were sufficiently closely linked to the land domain to be subject to the regime of its internal waters. The Court held that, in particular with regards to coasts having the geographical configuration of Norway, this should be given particular consideration. The Court also acknowledged that the peculiar geography of the Norwegian coast was such that even before the dispute had arisen the straight baseline method had been consolidated by a constant and sufficiently long practice which had not been opposed by other governments as being contrary to international law. Indeed the Court found the UK had for a period of more than 60 years not contested the Norwegian use of such a method and had only once in a Memorandum of July 27, 1933 made a formal and definitive protest on the point. 1951 ICJ Reports 116.

Commentary
The Court's decision in this case highlighted that the drawing of the territorial sea is not dependent merely on the will of the coastal state as expressed in domestic law but is subject to international supervision. Although it was true the act of delimitation was necessarily a unilateral act, because only the coastal state was competent to undertake it, the validity of the delimitation with regard to other states depended upon international law.

Note too the dissenting opinion of Judge McNair in which he stated that the possession of territorial waters was not optional, dependent on the will of the coastal state, but rather was compulsory.

The Court endorsed the legitimacy of the straight baseline method but did stress that the drawing of baselines should not depart to any appreciable extent from the general direction of the coast.

The Court's judgment is now acknowledged as reflecting customary international law and is also reflected in the 1958 and the 1982 Conventions on the Law of the Sea.

Key Principles: **State sovereignty over its territorial waters; freedom of the high seas; the right of innocent passage.**

Corfu Channel case (Merits) UK v Albania 1949

Facts: See p.152 for further discussion.

Held: See pp.57, 152 and 188 for further discussion.

In respect of the British Royal Navy minesweeping operation carried out in Albanian waters in November 12/13, 1946, the Court considered the submissions of the UK, namely that it was an operation of "extreme urgency" and thereby according to the UK one which could be carried out without anyone's consent. The UK acknowledged that the operation, which had been undertaken, did not have the consent of the International Mine Clearance Organisation. It could not be justified as an exercise of the right of innocent passage and in principle international law did not allow a state to assemble a large number of warships in the territorial waters of another state and carry out minesweeping in those waters.

The UK defence was premised on the suspicious nature of the explosions which had occurred in October 1946 and the issue of responsibility. The UK submitted that its actions constituted a new and special application of the theory of intervention designed to obtain evidence in another state's territory for submission to an international tribunal thereby facilitating the task confronting the international tribunal. The British Government had argued that the evidence could be taken away, leaving no trace of who had been responsible for the mine laying. The UK also submitted that the operation was carried out as a method of self-protection and self-help.

The Court denied claims advanced by the UK and upheld the territorial sovereignty of a state's territorial waters as an extension of its territory. Thus Albania, in turn, as the sovereign state exercising its jurisdiction over its territorial waters, was found to be in breach of its obligations to ensure safe passage to the vessels passing through its territorial waters during peace time.

Nevertheless the Court, whilst acknowledging that the Albanian Government's "complete failure to carry out its duties after the explosions, and the dilatory nature of its diplomatic notes" to be extenuating circumstances, held that irrespective of this, the actions of the British navy constituted a violation of Albanian sovereignty.

The Court also noted that the right of innocent passage exists in customary international law. However this right does not exist during war time. Moreover, in peace time this right does not entitle the one exercising it to engage in such activities as mine sweeping, i.e., the right of passage must be "innocent". 1949 ICJ Reports 4.

Commentary

This case explains the extension of state's territorial sovereignty to its territorial waters. Thus a breach of the sovereignty of territorial waters is treated in the same way as breach of a state's territorial sovereignty. However this also means the state which exercises its sovereignty over the territorial waters must ensure the rights of other states, such as the right to innocent passage, are not infringed.

The right to innocent passage, on the other hand, presumes only such passages which are truly "innocent" in their nature and thus cases, for example, such as in the present would fall outside the scope of this right.

Key Principles: Extension of territorial sovereignty to internal waters and territorial sea; meaning of passage and passage through internal waters.

Nicaragua case (Nicaragua v United States (Military and Paramilitary Activities in and Against Nicaragua) 1986

Facts: See p.4 for further discussion.

Held: See pp.5, 55 and 182 for further discussion.

The ICJ held that the principle of state sovereignty extends to the internal waters and territorial sea of every state. Such sovereignty accords to a coastal state the right to regulate access to its ports. However, the Court went on to declare that "in order to enjoy access to ports, foreign vessels possess a customary right of innocent passage in territorial waters for the purposes of entering or leaving internal waters" (para.214). The ICJ held that the definition of passage provided in Art.18(1)(b) of the UN Convention on the Law of the Sea (1982), represented a codification of customary international law. 1986 ICJ Reports 14.

Key Principles: Delimitation of continental shelf between opposite and adjacent states to be done under customary international law by reference to equitable principles. The aim of such is to ensure that a state has had that continental shelf which is a natural prolongation of its land territory.

North Sea Continental Shelf cases (Federal Republic of Germany v Denmark); and (Federal Republic of Germany v Netherlands) 1969

Facts: See p.1 for further discussion.

Held: See pp.2, 52, 105 and 199 for further discussion. The Court initially held that since the 1958 Geneva Convention on the Continental Shelf was not in force for all parties to the dispute, the matter had to be decided under customary international law.

In respect of the application of the equidistance method of delimitation, the ICJ held that this was not mandatory and that no single method of delimitation was obligatory in every circumstance. The Court acknowledged that in certain circumstances the application of the equidistance-special principle could produce an inequitable result. For example, such would be the case where a state had a concave coast line. The applicable rules of international law were that delimitation should be done by agreement which employed equitable principles and took account of all relevant circumstances so as to maximise for each party those parts of the continental shelf constituting a natural prolongation of its land, territory into and under the sea. In the event of an overlap, the parties involved should decide on a regime of joint use etc. The Court identified that in negotiations between parties such factors which should be taken into account included the general configuration of the coasts of the parties, any special or unusual features, physical and geological structure; natural resources of the continental shelf areas involved, and the element of a reasonable degree of proportionality. 1969 ICJ Reports 3.

Commentary
This decision is one of a series contributing to the international jurisprudence on delimitation. These decisions have influenced the application of the 1958 Geneva Convention on the Continental Shelf and to a large extent the decisions and international practice which has evolved are reflected in the relevant provisions of the 1982 Convention on the Law of the Sea.

Key Principle: **Delimitation of the EEZ and continental shelf.**

Gulf of Maine case (Canada v United States) 1984

Facts: The case came before the ICJ in 1981 as a result of the failure of the US and Canada to effect a joint fisheries management regime in the Gulf of Maine, following the respective extension of both countries of a 200 miles fisheries zone. Canada made such an extension in 1976 and the US in 1977. The Court was requested to determine a single maritime boundary, involving both continental shelf and fisheries jurisdiction. The case was decided by a Chamber of the Court.

Held: The Chamber was of the view that the time was right to consider the problem of asserting the rules of law in the international legal order which governed the matter at issue. The Chamber expressed the view that "rules" and "principles" were essentially one and the same idea as in its view principles clearly meant principles of law extending to include rules of international law. The term "principles" was justified because of their more general and fundamental character. The Chamber acknowledged that "logically" it had to refer primarily to customary international law and that international law would only provide a few basic legal principles laying down general guidelines which could be followed.

In its considerations, the Chamber reviewed the existing law as expressed in the 1958 Geneva Convention on the Continental Shelf, Art.6 and its own jurisprudence on delimitation of a maritime boundary. The Chamber then looked at the relevant provisions of the 1982 Convention on the Law of the Sea, and although noting the Convention had not as yet entered in force, held the relevant provisions as instructive. Accordingly the Chamber looked in particular at Arts 74(1) and 83(1) of the 1982 Convention relating respectively to the delimitation of the EEZ and the continental shelf. Both articles emphasise the use of agreement as the means for determining the delimitation of the EEZ or the continental shelf with the objective of such a settlement procedure being that of achieving an equitable solution. The Chamber noted the text of both articles was singularly concise but highlighted that nevertheless the door had been opened to continuing the development of the relevant law which was already underway in international case law. The Chamber highlighted the symmetry of the two texts which it maintained had to be:

> "most interesting in a case like the present one, where a single boundary line is to be drawn both for the sea-bed and for the superjacent fishery zone, which is included in the exclusive economic zone concept" (para.96).

In the Chamber's words:

> "the identity of the language which is employed, even though limited of course to the delimitation of the relevant principles and rules of international law is particularly significant" (para.96).

The Chamber then proceeded to assess the respective positions of both parties noting the points of disagreement were more numerous than those of agreement. However, notwithstanding this the ICJ noted that the parties had declared that:

> "when considering 'the rules and principles of international law' which, they held, should govern maritime delimitations, that they were at one in believing in the existence of a 'fundamental norm' of international law. According to them [the US and Canada] this norm must apply to any delimitation and, a fortiori, to the drawing of a single maritime boundary like that sought in the Gulf of Maine area" (para.98).

The Chamber then considered the respective positions of both parties with regard to the specific rules of law within the fundamental norm and on consideration rejected all of the contentions put before it.

The Chamber held that each party's reasoning was based on a false premise and that error lay in looking for something which in fact did not exist, namely a set of international rules of law. It was acknowledged that there were principles which might, in certain circumstances, constitute equitable criteria, however that was all and no attempt should be made to raise such principles to the status of established rules endorsed by customary international law.

The Court highlighted the norms regarding the seaward extension of states were new and unconsolidated and were in respect of areas which were until yesterday "zones of the high seas". Hence it would be unrewarding to look to general international law to provide a ready-made set of rules that could be used for solving any delimitation problems that might arise. A more useful course was to seek a better formulation of the fundamental norm which was acknowledged as existing.

The Chamber then proceeded to attempt a more complete and more precise reformulation of the "fundamental norm" and found there were absolutely no conditions of an exceptional kind which might justify any correction of the delimitation line as drawn. The Chamber expressed the view that the delimitation as drawn in compliance with the governing principles and rules of law applying equitable criteria and appropriate methods accordingly had produced an equitable overall result. 1984 ICJ Reports 246.

Commentary
The decision in the case established that a maritime delimitation between states with opposite or adjacent coasts may not be done unilaterally by one state. Delimitation must be effected by way of an agreement pursuant to negotiations undertaken in good faith with the intention of obtaining a positive result. In the absence of such an agreement the matter should be referred to an appropriate third party.

The judgment also endorses that in all instances delimitation should be done by reference to equitable criteria, through the employment of practical methods designed to ensure by cognisance to geographical factors and other relevant circumstances an equitable outcome.

Key Principle: **In delimiting the continental shelf each case is dependent upon on its own particular set of facts.**

Case Concerning the Delimitation of Maritime Areas between Canada and France (St Pierre and Miquelon) (1992)

Facts: The two islands in question lie on the coast of Canada on the west and southwest of Newfoundland. Canada and France had begun negotiations on the delimitation of the Continental Shelf in 1959 and following a 200 nautical mile extension by both France and Canada to their respective fishery zones, the negotiations were expanded in 1978 to include the issue of fisheries jurisdiction.

According to the French, the islands were to be treated like metropolitan territory and accorded the same rights with respect to their continental shelf and EEZ. Thus in practice, on the basis of the French position, the two islands would be entitled to a full 200 miles EEZ and the maritime boundary with Canada was to be determined on the basis of the equidistance principle as measured from the nearest points on the coast of the two islands and of New Finland and Nova Scotia.

Canada on the other hand maintained that France was entitled to no more than a 12 mile territorial sea.

In March 1989 following many years of fruitless negotiations France and Canada concluded a treaty submitting the issue of maritime boundaries to arbitration.

Held: The Court (the Canadian and French Arbitrators dissenting) concluded that neither of the proposed solutions by Canada or France provided even a starting point for the delimitation. The Court endorsed the conclusion in the *Gulf of Maine* case (see above), namely that:

> "it must undertake this final stage of the task entrusted to it and formulate its own solution independently of the proposal made by the Parties" (para.65).

31 ILM 1145 (1992) Court of Arbitration.

Commentary
The decision was favourable to Canada in that the Court's decision resulted in a relatively small area being granted to France. However France was given a corridor out to the edge of the 200 mile fishing zone, situated at least partly in an area not requested by France. Thus the Court appears to have accepted the French assertion that islands warrant as much weight in maritime boundary delimitation as the mainland.

The decision of the Court was apparently based, or compatible with, the following principles:

(1)   the frontal extension of the island;

(2)   non-encroachment or cut-off of the adjacent territory; and

(3)   a perpendicular extension of a maritime area proportional to the relevant coastline.

This judgment in the context of equitable principles endorses that "special circumstances" will be determined on a case by case basis.

Key Principle: **Special circumstances as referred to in Art.6 of the 1958 Geneva Convention and customary international law had become assimilated and had the same end goal namely a resolution determined by reference to equitable principles.**

Maritime Boundary in the Area between Greenland and Jan Meyen (Denmark v Norway) 1993

Facts: The dispute between Denmark and Norway concerned the delimitation of the continental shelf and fishing zone in the area surrounding the Jan Meyen island. The island, belonging to Norway, lies off the coast of Greenland. The Danish claim was based on a single delimitation line corresponding to a 200 mile zone. The Norwegian claim was based on an application of the equidistance principle. Both Denmark and Norway were parties to the 1958 Convention on the Law of the Sea and recognised the Convention's provisions were binding upon them in that the Convention governed how the continental shelf was to be delimited.

Held: In respect of the continental shelf boundary the Court took the median line as a provisional line before examining whether special circumstances demanded any modification of the median line. In looking at special circumstances the Court highlighted the importance of achieving an equitable result.

The fishery zone question fell to be considered under customary international law. Both Denmark and Norway brought a number of circumstances to the Court's notice. However the Court held that neither party had presented these specifically in the context of a possible adjustment or shifting of the median line as provisionally drawn. Denmark, for example, had submitted that the island of Jan Meyen fell within "special circumstances" and should be given no effect on Greenland's 200 mile continental shelf area.

In the light of geophysical and other circumstances the Court held that the median line should be adopted provisionally for both the continental shelf and the fishery zones. The Court concluded the median line as provisionally adopted for both should be modified so that a larger area of maritime space would be granted to Denmark. However the line drawn by Denmark, namely 200 nautical miles from the baselines of eastern Greenland, was seen as being excessive and the consequences inequitable. The Court maintained the delimitation line should be drawn within the area of the overlapping claims between the lines proposed by each party. 1993 ICJ Reports 34.

Commentary
This was the first case in which the ICJ was able to reach a decision on delimitation by reference only to Art.6 of the 1958 Convention. The decision demonstrates that although the equidistant median line will be adopted as the initial provisional delimitation this will be varied if special circumstances demand it.

Key Principles: **Applicable principles and rules of international law for the delimitation of the continental shelf; relationship of 1982 Convention and customary international law.**

Case Concerning the Continental Shelf (Libyan Arab Jamahiriya/Malta) 1985

Facts: The ICJ was asked to determine the principles and rules of international law applicable in the delimitation of the continental shelf between Libya and Malta as well as identifying the circumstances and factors which should be taken into consideration so as to achieve an equitable delimitation.

The states were opposite and not adjacent states. The matter was referred to the ICJ pursuant to a special agreement. Both parties agreed that the matter should be decided by customary international law.

Held: The Court identified one of its tasks as being that of considering the extent to which provisions contained in the 1982 UN Convention on the Law of the Sea reflected rules of customary international law. At the time of the case the 1982 Convention had not yet entered into force; both parties however were signatories to the Convention.

The Court acknowledged the relevant applicable international law for delimiting areas of continental shelf between neighbouring states set the goal as being that of achieving an equitable solution. However as highlighted by the Court, Art.83 of the 1982 Convention is silent on the method to be employed, leaving the method to be determined by states and/or courts. It was further noted that the parties to this particular dispute agreed that delimitation was to be effected in accordance with equitable principles and taking account of all relevant circumstances. The states concerned however were not in agreement on the legal basis of title to continental shelf rights. Thus Libya maintained that the fundamental basis of legal title to the continental shelf areas remained the natural prolongation of the land territory of a state into the sea. Malta on the other hand claimed that continental shelf rights were no longer defined in the light of physical criteria but were controlled by the concept of distance from the coast.

The Court, for its part, maintained the principles and rules pertaining to the EEZ could not be left out in a consideration of the delimitation of the continental shelf. The Court stated that the two institutions were linked together in modern law and cognisance of the legally permissible extent of a state's EEZ should be taken into account in delimiting the continental shelf. The Court characterised the EEZ and its rule on entitlement because of distance as part of customary international law. The Court then acknowledged the continental shelf and EEZ as different and distinct regimes but held the rights flowing from the EEZ were defined by reference to the regime prescribed for the continental shelf. It was further recognised that while there may be a continental shelf without an EEZ there cannot be an EEZ without a corresponding continental shelf. Accordingly the Court stated that for both juridical and practical reasons the distance criterion should now apply to the continental shelf as well as to the EEZ.

The Court refuted Libya's contention that distance from the coast was not relevant and maintained that within 200 miles of the coast natural prolongation was in part defined by distance from the shore. In effect natural prolongation and distance are complimentary and not opposed.

Regarding the relevant circumstances, the Court denied Libya's assertion that the land mass provided the legal justification of entitlement to continental shelf rights. The Court also denied Malta's claim that delimitation should reflect the relative economic position of the two relevant states.

Regarding a state's security or defence interests the Court expressed the view that in the instant case the delimitation which would ensue from the judgment was not so close to the coast of either of the states involved to make these questions a particular consideration.

The Court held the circumstances and factors which were to be taken into account in the present case, so as to achieve an equitable delimitation were:

1) the general configuration of the coasts of the states, their oppositeness and their relationship to each other within the general geographical context;

2) the disparity in the lengths of the relevant coasts of the states and the distance between them; and

3) the need to avoid in the delimitation any excessive disproportion between the extent of the continental shelf areas appertaining to the coastal state and the length of the relevant part of its coast measured in the general direction of the coastlines.

The Court then went ahead and drew a suggested boundary. 1985 ICJ Reports 13.

Commentary
The Court's decision in this case is another instance of a more result oriented, corrective equity approach being favoured. Another such example is that handed down in the following case below.

Key Principle: **Applicable principles and rules of international law for the delimitation of the continental shelf.**

Case Concerning the Continental Shelf Tunisia/Libyan Arab Jamahiriya 1982

Facts: The Court pursuant to the special agreement between Tunisia and Libya was specifically called upon to take account of equitable factors, the relevant circumstances characterising the area and the newly accepted trends evident in the Third UN Conference on the Law of the Sea. The special agreement also sought that the Court should clarify the practical method for the application of these principles and rules.

Held: The Court concluded that given there was just one continental shelf common to both states the criteria of natural prolongation could not be employed to determine an equitable line of delimitation. The Court then turned to the relevant circumstances to be taken into account and identified these as: the area relevant to the delimitation, the general configuration of the coast of the states, the land frontier between the states, economic considerations, and historic rights. The Court then, rejecting the various delimitation methods suggested by both states, indicated the method it saw as being one enabling an equitable solution to be reached in the instant case. 1982 ICJ Reports 18.

Key Principles: **Law applicable to the delimitation of maritime boundary is to be found in customary international law; 1982 Convention on the Law of the Sea reflects customary international law; equidistance line.**

Maritime Delimitation and Territorial Questions between Qatar and Bahrain (Qatar v Bahrain) 2001

Facts: The two states sought the ICJ to draw a single maritime boundary in accordance with international law. The Court indicated the applicable law was customary international law and both states agreed that most of the provisions of the 1982 Convention on the Law of the Sea relevant to their case reflected customary international law (Bahrain had ratified the 1982 Convention whereas Qatar was only a signatory).

Held: The Court observed the concept of a single maritime boundary could encompass a number of functions and in the present case the single maritime boundary would be a result of the delimitation of various jurisdictions. The Court further noted that the concept of the single maritime boundary did not stem from multilateral treaty law but rather from the state practice and it had come about as states wished to establish one uninterrupted boundary line delimiting the various partially co-incident zones of maritime jurisdiction appertaining to them. The boundary which the Court was expected to draw was that which would delimit exclusively the states' territorial seas and thus an area over which the states would enjoy territorial sovereignty. This is what the Court was required to do in the Southern part of the delimitation area which was situated where the coasts of the states were opposite each other and the distance between these coasts was at no point more then 24 nautical miles. However in the North the coasts of the two states were no longer opposite each other but were rather comparable to adjacent coasts. The delimitation was one between the continental shelf and the EEZ of each of the states, areas in which states have only sovereign rights and functional jurisdiction. In drawing the delimiting territorial boundary the Court denied that Bahrain was entitled to employ the method of the straight base lines.

The Court drew an equidistance line for the delimitation of the territorial sea and stated that:

> "the equidistance line is the line every point of which is equidistant from the nearest points on the baselines from which the breadth of the territorial seas of each of the two States is measured" (para.177).

However, the Court then acknowledged that it should be adjusted to take account of special circumstances, namely the existence of a very small uninhabited island under the sovereignty of Bahrain located about midway between the main island of Bahrain and the Qatar peninsula. Thus in the delimitation of the continental shelf and the EEZ the Court initially drew a provisional equidistance line and then considered whether there were any circumstances which would prompt an adjustment of that line.

The Court denied Bahrain's claim concerning the pearl industry and maintained that although important in the past, having effectively ceased to exist, it did not constitute a circumstance which warranted a modification of the equidistance line. The Court did give cognisance to a remote projection of Bahrain's coastline in the Gulf area, as if given full effect the boundary would have been distorted and would have had a disproportionate effect.

The Court then drew a single maritime boundary. 2001 ICJ Reports 40.

Key Principles: **Delimitation of maritime boundaries; the equidistance line; equitable principles/relevant circumstance method; equity in delimiting maritime boundary.**

Land and Maritime Boundary Between Cameroon and Nigeria (Cameroon v Nigeria, Equatorial Guinea intervening) 2002

Facts: The ICJ was asked inter alia to delimit a "single maritime boundary" beyond the limits of the territorial sea that would separate both the continental shelves and EEZ between

Cameroon and Nigeria. The two states are adjacent countries, having a land border that reaches the sea in the south on the Gulf of Guinea.

Held: The ICJ initially determined that Arts 74 and 83 of the UN Convention on the Law of the Sea (1982) were applicable to the current case and reiterated that para.1 of those articles provided that delimitations of continental shelf and EEZ between states with opposite or adjacent coasts must be effected in such a way as to achieve an equitable solution. The Court noted that the parties had agreed that such delimitation should be effected by a single line and stated that the so-called equitable principles/ relevant circumstance method encompassed the applicable criteria, principles and rules for such delimitation. It was held that this method:

> "involves first drawing an equidistance line, then considering whether there are factors calling for the adjustment or shifting of that line in order to achieve an 'equitable result' " (para.288).

The Court referred to its earlier decision in *Qatar v Bahrain* case (see above) about the equidistance line and turned to consider if there were any circumstances which might make it necessary to adjust this equidistance line so as to achieve an equitable result.

The ICJ stressed that delimiting with the aim of achieving an equitable result was not the same as delimiting in equity and stated that "equity is not a method of delimitation, but solely an aim that should be borne in mind in effecting the delimitation" (para.294). The Court noted that the geographical configuration of maritime areas may be taken into account, but in the present case held that the concavity of the coastline did not lie in the area to be delimited and therefore had no impact on the delimitation which the Court had been asked to do.

The Court also stated that the relevant coastline of Cameroon was not longer than that of Nigeria, if it were that could have justified a shifting of the equidistance line in favour of Cameroon.

Finally the ICJ examined the issue of oil concessions and oil wells and stated that these:

> "are not in themselves to be considered as relevant circumstances justifying the adjustment or shifting of the provisional delimitation

line. Only if they are based on express or tacit agreement between the parties may they be taken into account'' (para.304).

The Court ascertained that there were no such agreements between Cameroon and Nigeria.

Consequently the ICJ held that the equidistance line represented an equitable result for the delimitation of the area in respect of which it had been asked to give a judgment. 2002 ICJ Reports 303.

Key Principles: **The first case decided exclusively on basis of convention law as reflected in the UN Convention on the Law of the Sea 1982 Art.74(1) and 83(1); maritime delimitation line should provisionally be equidistance line but that may be modified to take account of relevant circumstances.**

Barbados/Trinidad and Tobago Maritime Delimitation April 11, 2006 Arbitration Tribunal Permanent Court of Arbitration

Facts: The parties were in agreement that in the Western maritime area the delimitation line between their opposite coasts should be the provisional equidistance line. However the two states disagreed on whether the provisional equidistance line should be modified to take into account relevant circumstances. Trinidad and Tobago maintained that the equidistance line should be the delimitation line in the west, whereas Barbados maintained that the line should be adjusted to give cognisance to traditional fishing activities.

In the Eastern area the parties differed in that they did not request delimitation by a single maritime boundary. Barbados requested the Tribunal to determine the single maritime boundary for both the EEZ and the continental shelves of the respective parties. Trinidad and Tobago, however, maintained that the two regimes, namely that of the continental shelf and the EEZ, were separate and distinct and there should therefore be different lines of delimitation for each.

Held: The Arbitral Tribunal held that in this context it would determine a single boundary line for delimiting both the continental shelf and the EEZ to the extent that the claims overlapped. In doing so the Tribunal took notice of the relevant circumstances and adjusted the provisional equidistance line accordingly. The circumstances acknowledged by the Tribunal included regional coasts and their projection, proportionality and regional considerations.

Commentary
It would appear that the Tribunal was seeking to maintain consistency with judicial precedents. The Tribunal showed it was willing to adopt the equity approach of previous decisions and favoured neutral geographical criteria in preference to area specific criteria. Again this appears to reflect the trend in judicial decisions.

Key Principles: **The nationality of ships; the genuine link requirement; the EEZ regime; the right of hot pursuit; use of force when arresting a vessel; prompt release of a vessel.**

The M/V Saiga (No.2) case (St Vincent and the Grenadines v Guinea) International Tribunal for the Law of the Sea (1999)

Facts: The *Saiga*, an oil tanker, was involved in the sale of gas oil as fuel to fishing vessels and on October 27, 1997 it supplied gas oil to Senegalese and Greek flag fishing vessels in the EEZ of Guinea. The next day, while stationed outside the Guinean EEZ, the *Saiga* was boarded and arrested by Guinean patrol boats and taken to Guinea, where the tanker and the crew were detained. St Vincent and Grenadines requested the International Tribunal for the Law of the Sea order the vessel's release. The Tribunal on December 4, 1997 ordered the prompt release of the *Saiga* and its crew. However, by December 17, 1997 the vessel and most of its crew had not been released. On the contrary, its Master was convicted in a Guinean court of the offence of the "illegal import, buying and selling of fuel in the Republic of Guinea". The Master was given a suspended prison sentence and a large fine. The *Saiga* was finally released on March 4, 1998.

The *Saiga* was previously registered as a Maltese tanker, and its six month certificate of provisional registration as a St Vincent and Grenadines ship had expired on September 12, 1997.

Held: The Tribunal first dealt with the preliminary objections raised by Guinea: that St Vincent and Grenadines was not the nationality of the *Saiga*, that there was no genuine link between St Vincent and Grenadines and the *Saiga* and that domestic remedies had not been exhausted.

The Tribunal ruled that Art.91 of the UN Convention on the Law of the Sea (1982) which leaves every state exclusive jurisdiction over the granting of its nationality to ships codifies a well-established rule of general international law. Thus St Vincent and Grenadines was said to be free to decide in its domestic law how and when such nationality is granted. International law recognises several modalities for such granting of nationality. The Tribunal referred to the registration of a vessel in accordance with the domestic legislation, as the most common procedure for merchant ships. However, when considering the criteria and procedures for such registration, the Tribunal reiterated that these matters fell within the exclusive jurisdiction of the flag state.

Nevertheless the Tribunal stated that the nationality of a ship is a question of fact to be determined on the basis of evidence produced. Upon considering the factual evidence produced by St Vincent and Grenadines as well as taking into consideration the fact that St Vincent and Grenadines had always acted as the flag state of the *Saiga*, the Tribunal held that the *Saiga* had the nationality of St Vincent and Grenadines. Moreover, the Tribunal especially noted that Guinea had never previously contested the nationality of the *Saiga*, not even in the earlier proceedings seeking the release of the ship in December 1997.

The next objection raised by Guinea was that there was no genuine link between St Vincent and Grenadines and the *Saiga*, which, according to Guinea, would entitle it to not recognise the nationality of the *Saiga*. The Tribunal held that for the purposes of the UN Convention on the Law of the Sea (1982), the requirement of genuine link had been inserted in order to secure more effective implementation of the duties of the flag state rather, than to establish a criteria by reference to which the validity of the registration of a ship in a flag state could be challenged by other states. Thus the Tribunal rejected this objection of Guinea.

Turning to the merits of the case, the Tribunal examined the question of whether the charge against the *Saiga* by Guinea that it had violated Guinean domestic law by importing gas oil into the customs radius violated the provisions of the UN Convention on the Law of the Sea (1982). The Tribunal made it clear that it had no jurisdiction to examine the domestic law of Guinea. However it stated that it did have jurisdiction to determine whether actions of Guinea by applying its domestic law had conformed to the requirements of the UN Convention on the Law of the Sea (1982). It was established that they did not, since the Convention had clearly defined all circumstances when the coastal state has jurisdiction to apply its customs law and regulations in the territorial sea, contiguous zone and the EEZ and these did not include instances advanced by Guinea.

Since Guinea had argued that the legal basis for its domestic legislation could be found by reference to such rules of international law as "public interest" and "state of necessity", the Tribunal examined whether these might be applicable in the present case. It was stated that only such rules of international law which are compatible with Pt V of the Convention may be invoked and:

> "recourse to the principle of 'public interest', as invoked by Guinea, would entitle a costal State to prohibit any activities in the exclusive economic zone which it decides to characterize as activities which affect its economic 'public interest' or entail 'fiscal losses' for it" (para.131).

The Tribunal held that this would be incompatible with Arts 56 and 58 of the Convention and thereby rejected Guinea's argument.

In examining the second justification invoked by Guinea, namely, the "state of necessity", the Tribunal ruled that Guinea had failed to show that its essential interests were in grave and imminent peril so as to justify its actions.

Consequently it was held that by applying its customs law to a customs radius which included part of the EEZ, Guinea had breached its obligations under the UN Convention on the Law of the Sea (1982).

The Tribunal then examined the claim of St Vincent and Grenadines that Guinea had failed to exercise its right to hot pursuit in the manner consistent with Art.111 of the Convention. Noting that no visual or auditory signals to stop were given and that the alleged hot pursuit was interrupted, the Tribunal held that Guinea stopped and arrested the *Saiga* on October 28, 1997 in circumstances which did not justify the exercise of the right of hot pursuit compatible with the 1982 Convention.

The Tribunal proclaimed that whilst its deliberations had been based on the consideration that the actions of the *Saiga* took place in the EEZ, its findings would have been the same if these would have occurred in the contiguous zone as, for example, the exercise of the right of hot pursuit by Guinea would still have failed to meet the requirements of the UN Convention on the Law of the Sea (1982).

The Tribunal then dealt with the argument advanced by Guinea that when arresting the *Saiga* the use of force was appropriate and justified in the circumstances. The Tribunal stated that:

> "the use of force must be avoided as far as possible and, where force is unavoidable, it must not go beyond what is reasonable and necessary in the circumstances" (para.155).

The Tribunal went on to declare that the normal practice employed for stopping a ship is an auditory or visual signal to stop, using internationally recognised signals. Only in cases where this is unsuccessful may a variety of other actions, like firing shots across the bows of the vessel take place. Thus:

> "It is only after the appropriate actions fail that the pursuing vessel may, as a last resort, use force. Even then appropriate warning must be issued to the ship and all efforts should be made to ensure that life is not endangered" (para.156).

It was established that Guinean patrol boat fired live ammunition to the *Saiga* without any signals or warning, that when the Guinean officers boarded the ship and met no resistance, they still fired indiscriminately on the deck, causing severe injuries to two crew members and used gunfire to stop the engine of the *Saiga*. Consequently, the Tribunal held that Guinea had used excessive force and endangered human life before and after boarding the *Saiga*.

Finally, the Tribunal had to consider whether Guinea had violated its obligations under Art.292, para.4 and Art.296 of the UN Convention on the Law of the Sea (1982) by failing to release the vessel promptly after the Judgment of the Tribunal on December 4, 1997. It was held that while a delay of 80 days could not be considered a prompt release, this delay was caused by various factors of which some could not be attributed to Guinea's failure. Therefore the Tribunal ruled that Guinea had not failed to comply with its Judgment of 4 December 1997.

Guinea was ordered to pay St Vincent and Grenadines a compensation of $2,123,057 US dollars. (1999) 120 I.L.R. 143.

Commentary
This is the first case in which the International Tribunal for the Law of the Sea delivered a judgment on the merits.

Special attention should be paid to the different treatment of the "genuine link" requirement for the purposes of establishing a nationality of a ship in the *Saiga* case and that applied in the *Nottebohm* case for the purposes of establishing a nationality of a person. While the two may appear similar, the "genuine link" requirement for ships was put in place so as to secure more effective implementation of the duties of the flag state.

Key Principles: **The contiguous zone; hot pursuit from the exclusive fishing zone.**

US v Fishing Vessel Taiyo Maru (1975)

Facts: A Japanese fishing vessel was found fishing illegally in the US exclusive fishing zone nine miles offshore and beyond the US territorial sea limit. The vessel was pursued some 68 miles off land on the high seas by the US coast guard vessels and seized.

Held: It was held that the list of purposes for which a contiguous zone may be established as contained in Art.24 of the Convention on the Territorial Sea and Contiguous Zone (1958) is not exhaustive:

"It [Article 24] provides that a costal state 'may' establish a contiguous zone for the purposes of enforcing its customs, fiscal, immigration or sanitary regulations. Although Article 24 only affirmatively recognizes the right of a costal state to create a contiguous zone for one of the four enumerated purposes, nothing in the Article precludes the establishment of such a zone for other purposes, including the enforcement of domestic fisheries law".

Turning to the issue of hot pursuit, the Court held that neither the language used nor the history of the 1958 Geneva Conventions indicated that there had been a willingness by the states parties to limit the right of a coastal state to conduct hot pursuit from an exclusive fishing zone. No.28 395 F.Supp.413 (D.Me.1975).

Commentary
The decision of the Court regarding the right of hot pursuit remains especially important to such countries as the UK, which has an exclusive fishing zone, but not an exclusive economic zone. It is, however, argued that the same principle would also apply in cases of hot pursuit from the exclusive economic zone.

Key Principles: **The right of hot pursuit; punitive damages rarely awarded.**

I'm Alone case Canada v United States (1935)

Facts: The *I'm Alone* vessel was engaged in carrying liquor from Bleless in British Honduras to points on the Gulf of Mexico. Liquor was then transferred to a small craft and smuggled into the US, where it was sold.

The *I'm Alone* was a Canadian registered rum runner and in March 1929 had been sunk on the high seas some 200 miles from the US cost. According to the submission by the US, the *Dexter*, a revenue cutter, had begun pursuit from ten and a half miles from the coast, whereas Canada alleged it was fourteen and a half miles from the coast. In either case pursuit began outside the three mile territorial sea. The *I'm Alone* had originally been sighted and followed by the *Wolcot*, also a US revenue vessel.

Held: The Arbitration Commissioner held that there was a right of hot pursuit and that pursuit in this case had been continuous. However, it was held that the intentional sinking of a foreign registered vessel was contrary both to the treaty between the US and Canada as well as customary international law. What was relevant here was whether in the circumstances, including an assumption that the US Government had a right of hot pursuit, the sinking of the *I'm Alone* was legally justified.

The Commission held that although the US could use necessary and reasonable force so as to board, search, seize and bring into port the vessel, the admitted intentional sinking was unjustified by any provisions of the Convention. If the sinking had occurred incidentally pursuant to an exercise of necessary and reasonable force then "the pursuing vessel might be entirely blameless". However, in the circumstances of the present case the intentional sinking was unjustified both under any conventions provisions between the US and Canada and under principles of international law.

The Commissioners then turned to the issue of damages and found in the light of the facts no compensation should be paid in respect of the loss of the ship or the cargo. However, they characterised the intentional sinking of the ship as an unlawful act, and considered that the US in addition to formally acknowledging the illegality of the act and apologising to the Canadian Government should pay the sum of $25,000 to the Canadian Government as punitive damages. This was to be paid for the benefit of the captain and members of the crew, none of whom were involved in the illegal conspiracy to smuggle liquor into the US or the selling of the liquor within the US. (1953) RIA 1609.

Commentary

This case dealt with issues surrounding the right of hot pursuit and clearly indicates that hot pursuit must be exercised taking account of necessity and reasonable force. The Commission specifically noted that the sinking of the vessel would have only been justified if it was purely incidental. Therefore, since the sinking in this case was intentional, the US was in breach of its obligations. It is thus clear that the circumstances of each case must be examined carefully so as to ascertain whether the right of hot pursuit is exercised diligently. It should also be noted that the right of hot pursuit is now regulated by Art.111 of the 1982 Convention on the Law of the Seas.

7. JURISDICTION INCLUDING IMMUNITIES AND DIPLOMATIC PROTECTION

Key Principles: Nationality as a basis for exercising jurisdiction; real and effective link with the state of nationality necessary; right to diplomatic protection and protection by means of international judicial proceedings only arises when proper nationality link exists between the individual concerned and the state seeking to exercise such rights.

Nottebohm case (Second Phase) (Liechtenstein v Guatemala) 1955

Facts: See p.162 for further discussion.

Held: See pp.51 and 163 for further discussion.

The central question addressed by the ICJ was whether the nationality granted to Mr Nottebohm by Liechtenstein conferred upon it sufficient title to exercise diplomatic protection as against Guatemala and therefore entitling it to seize the Court of a claim in relation to Mr Nottebohm. In answering this question, the ICJ initially reiterated that nationality is the most immediate, far-reaching and in most instances, only has effects within the domain of the state which confers it. The ICJ stated that:

> "Nationality serves above all to determine that the person upon whom it is conferred enjoys the rights and is bound by the obligations which the law of the State in question grants to or imposes on its nationals. This is implied in the wider concept that nationality is within the domestic jurisdiction of the State".

The Court thus concluded that every state has the right to decide how its nationality can be obtained and is free in this domain of its domestic jurisdiction as conferral of nationality at domestic level has no implications for the domain of international law. However, if a state is seeking to exercise diplomatic protection on the basis of nationality, this is a matter, which according to the Court, falls within the domain of international law. Therefore, since nationality is the necessary link between the state and the individual on behalf of whom the state is exercising the diplomatic protection, the question of nationality was of paramount importance in the present case.

The ICJ examined the practice of international arbitration bodies, the courts of third states and the writings of publicists and the relevant practice of states in dual nationality cases and concluded that all of these pointed to a recognition of real and effective nationality:

> "that which accorded with the facts, that based on stronger factual ties between the person concerned and one of the States whose nationality is involved".

While recognising that a state is free to choose how and when nationality is granted for the purposes of its domestic jurisdiction, the ICJ declared that if a state wished to invoke it against another state, nationality had to conform to these requirements of international law. In the words of the Court:

> "a State cannot claim that the rules it has laid down are entitled to recognition by another State unless it has acted in conformity with this general aim of making the legal bond of nationality accord with the individual's genuine connection with the State which assumes the defence of its citizens by means of protection as against other States".

The ICJ described nationality as:

> "a legal bond having as its basis a social fact of attachment, a genuine connexion of existence, interests and sentiments, together with the existence of reciprocal rights and duties. It may be said to constitute the juridical expression of the fact that the individual upon whom it is conferred, either directly by the law or as a result of an act of the authorities, is in fact more closely connected with the population of the State conferring nationality than with that of any other State. Conferred by a State, it only entitles that State to exercise protection vis-à-vis another State, if it constitutes a translation into juridical terms of the individual's connection with the State which has made him its national".

On the other hand, the ICJ stated that diplomatic protection and protection by means of international judicial proceedings are means of defending the rights of the state. Thus, since nationality was the basis for Liechtenstein's claim in affording protection to Mr Nottebohm, the ICJ went on to ascertain whether the nationality conferred by Liechtenstein upon Mr Nottebohm was "real and effective" as required by international law. The ICJ examined the factual situation of Mr Nottebohm and paid special attention to whether:

> "At the time of his naturalization does Nottebohm appear to have been more closely attached by his tradition, his establishment, his interests, his activities, his family ties, his intention for the near future to Liechtenstein than to any other State?".

After careful and detailed assessment of Mr Nottebohm's links to Guatemala and Liechtenstein, the ICJ concluded that the "only links established between the Principality and Nottebohm are the short sojourns" while in case of Guatemala the Court established "existence of a long-standing and close connection". The ICJ thus concluded that Guatemala was under no obligation to recognise the nationality granted to Mr Nottebohm by Liechtenstein and accordingly Liechtenstein was not entitled to extend its protection to Mr Nottebohm. Therefore the claim of Liechtenstein against Guatemala was declared inadmissible. 1955 ICJ Reports 4.

Commentary
This case is the central judgment of the ICJ on the principle of nationality for the exercise of jurisdiction. The ICJ here made a clear distinction between the sphere of domestic jurisdiction and that of international law by declaring that the conferral of nationality is the affair of each individual state and each state is free to decide how and when an individual is granted a nationality. However, in international law, nationality may give rise to rights to the state which has granted such nationality, for example, the right to diplomatic protection, as it was in this case. In such instances it must be established that the nationality in question conforms to the requirements of international law since a state can only expect that other states will respect such a bond if it has been established in conformity with international law. Through the examination of international arbitrators' practice, the judgments of third states, writings of publicists and practice of various countries on the issue of dual nationality, the ICJ concluded that for the nationality to be recognised in international law it must be real and effective. Thus the Court concluded that only real and effective nationality can give rise to a claim by a state under international law. This case clearly shows that the factual circumstances of each individual play the crucial

role in determining whether the nationality in question is real and effective. This case is also significant since the ICJ provided its determination of what constitutes nationality.

Key Principles: **Territorial jurisdiction of a state; subjective and objective territorial jurisdiction.**

SS Lotus case (France v Turkey) 1927

Facts: See p.8 for further discussion.

Held: See pp.9 and 55 for further discussion.

The PCIJ first reiterated that restrictions upon the independence of states cannot be presumed and therefore concluded that states are free to exercise their jurisdiction unless there is a rule of international law which prevents a state from doing so in a particular case. The Court stated that international law certainly prohibited a state from exercising its jurisdiction in the territory of another state and in this sense noted jurisdiction as being territorial.

However, the Court saw no rule of international law which would prevent a state from exercising jurisdiction in its own territory over acts which had occurred elsewhere but for which the state in question cannot rely on any rule of international law expressly permitting it to exercise its jurisdiction. The PCIJ thus stated that:

> "Far from laying down a general prohibition to the effect that States may not extend the application of their laws and the jurisdiction of their courts to persons, property and acts outside their territory, it [international law] leaves them in this respect a wide measure of discretion which is only limited in certain cases by prohibitive rules".

Thus the Court rejected the argument advanced by France, which claimed that the onus was on Turkey to show a positive right in international law which would allow it to exercise jurisdiction over the French officer.

Turning to the specific issue of criminal jurisdiction, the Court came to a similar conclusion by stating that all systems of law adopt the principle of territoriality as a fundamental principle for exercising their criminal jurisdiction. However, the Court noted that it was equally true that all or nearly all states extended their jurisdiction to offences committed elsewhere. The Court concluded that the territoriality of criminal law was not an absolute principle of international law and by no means coincided with territorial sovereignty.

The Court went on to examine the jurisdiction pertaining to vessels on high seas and noted that they are subject to the authority of the state whose flag they are flying which derives from the principle of the freedom of high seas. But, once again adopting the same approach as previously, the PCIJ stated that there was no prohibition on a state from exercising its jurisdiction over acts which had occurred on board a foreign ship on the high seas since the ship on the high seas is assimilated to territory of the state of the flag the ship is flying thus placing a ship in the same position as national territory. Therefore the Court concluded that whatever occurs on the ship in the high seas must be treated as occurring in the territory of a state whose flag the vessel is flying and:

> "If, therefore, a guilty act committed on the high seas produces its effects on a vessel flying another flag or foreign territory, the same principles must be applied as if the territories of two different States were concerned, and the conclusion must therefore be drawn that there is no rule of international law prohibiting the State to which the ship on which the effects of the offence have taken place belongs, from regarding the offence as having been committed in its territory and prosecuting, accordingly, the delinquent".

Thereby the PCIJ concluded that in cases of collision there was no rule of international law which reserved criminal proceedings exclusively to the jurisdiction of the state whose flag is flown and on this basis the claims of France were rejected. 1927 PCIJ Series A No.10.

Commentary

The *Lotus* case is the fundamental case on the issue of state jurisdiction and territorial principle in particular. This case is of significance for the famous dictum of the PCIJ in which the Court stated that unless there was a prohibitive rule of international law which prevented a state from exercising its jurisdiction, it was free to do so. This principle has evolved into a more general tenet of international law pursuant to which no restrictions upon the sovereignty of a state can be presumed. In other words, states are free to do what is not expressly prohibited in international law. This principle has been relied on by the judges in their Separate Opinions in the *Congo Arrest Warrant* case (see below).

The *Lotus* case is also significant for it is the authority of the objective territorial principle in international law: a state is free to exercise its jurisdiction when a crime has been initiated and completed entirely in its territory, but it may also do so when a crime is initiated in its territory (subjective territorial principle) and when the effects of the crime take place in its territory (objective territorial principle).

However it must be noted that the *Lotus* case was decided by the casting vote of the President and many authors have criticised the PCIJ for having adopted an extreme positivist approach in this case, namely, that international law stems from the free will of the sovereign, independent states. Therefore it is important that the dissenting opinions of this judgment are kept in mind, most importantly, that of Judge Moore, who contended that the position adopted by the majority in this case would lead to a scenario, when everybody travelling around would be "taking" the jurisdiction of their state with them and thus any offence would fall under numerous criminal codes.

Key Principles: Domestic jurisdiction; validity of domestic jurisdiction in respect to other states.

Anglo-Norwegian Fisheries case (UK v Norway) 1951

Facts: See p.106 for further discussion.

Held: See pp.10 and 106 for further discussion.

The ICJ ruled that while delimitation of territorial waters is necessarily a unilateral act by one state, since it is only the costal state which is competent to undertake it, the validity of such delimitation in respect to other states will depend upon international law. 1951 ICJ Reports 116.

Commentary

The principle of domestic jurisdiction stems from the wider principle of independence and sovereignty of states as well as from the duty not to interfere in the domestic affairs of another state. Thus, as shown by the *Anglo-Norwegian Fisheries* case, similarly to the position adopted by the ICJ in *Nottebohm* case (see above), while a state is free to act domestically as it wishes, the validity of such actions in respect to other states will depend on the principles of international law. Therefore the extension of domestic jurisdiction in the area of international law will only be valid if that extension conforms to the requirements of international law.

Key Principles: **States are independent and possess territorial sovereignty; principle of domestic jurisdiction.**

Island of Palmas case (Netherlands v United States) 1928

Facts: See p.91 for further discussion.

Held: While this case is most relevant for the international law on territory, the sole arbiter declared that all states are sovereign and independent, having territorial sovereignty. 1928 2R. 1AA 829.

Commentary
Similarly to the findings of the PCIJ in *Lotus* case (see above), Arbitrator Huber in the *Island of Palmas* case derived the principle of domestic jurisdiction from the notion that every state is independent and sovereign and thus possesses territorial sovereignty.

Key Principles: **Private tort action brought by alien against alien accused for acts committed abroad; civil jurisdiction in cases of breach of *jus cogens* norm of international law.**

Filartiga v Pena-Irala (1980)

Facts: See p.41 for further discussion.

Held: See pp.41 and 224 for further discussion.
The case was filed under the terms of the 1789 United States Judiciary Act, also known as the Aliens Claims Tort Act (ACTA), which allows actions in tort for breaches of the laws of nations or a treaty of US. The Court declared that the alleged torture in this case constituted not only a breach of customary international

law, but a breach of a *jus cogens* norm and thus declared that it had jurisdiction despite the fact that both the accused and the victim were Paraguayans and the acts complained of had taken place in Paraguay. 630 F.2d 876 (2d Circ. 1980).

Commentary

Filartiga was the first in the series of cases that have been filed under the ACTA and must be noted for two important reasons. First of all the exercise of jurisdiction in this case can be said to be quasi-universal as while provided for by the national legislation, neither the victims, nor the accused, nor the offence itself had any links with the US. Rather the case fell under the general provision that an alien may bring an action in tort "committed in violation of the law of nations or a treaty of the United States". In this particular case the Court established that the prohibition on torture constituted a prohibition of a *jus cogens* nature and hence established jurisdiction. This case however should be distinguished from the *Congo Arrest Warrant* case (see below) as in the *Filartiga* case both the victim and the accused were present on the US territory.

The second important aspect of this case is the fact that other states have not raised any objections to such an exercise of jurisdiction by the US. In other words, other states have acquiesced to such a US practice. Acquiescence is of course of particular importance when ascertaining the emergence of a rule of international law.

Key Principles: **Private tort action brought by alien against alien accused for acts committed abroad; civil jurisdiction in cases of breach of *jus cogens* norm of international law.**

Sosa v Alvarez-Machain; United States v Alvarez-Machain. 124 S.CT. 2739. United States Supreme Court June 29, 2004

Commentary

This case is one of the latest in the series of cases that have been brought under the 1789 United States Judiciary Act, also known as the Aliens Claims Tort Act (ACTA). The paradigm established in *Filartiga* (see above) was once again reaffirmed.

Key Principles: **Principle of universal jurisdiction; passive personality principle.**

Attorney-General of the Government of Israel v Eichmann 1961

Facts: Adolf Eichmann was the Head of the Jewish Office of the German Gestapo and the administrator in charge of the "final solution", a policy which led to the extermination of millions of Jews during the Second World War. He was found in Argentina in 1960 by agents presumably of the Israeli government and abducted to Israel without the knowledge of the Argentinean government. He was then prosecuted under the Israeli Nazi and Nazi Collaborators (Punishment) Law of 1951 for war crimes, crimes against the Jewish people and crimes against humanity. He was convicted and sentenced to death.

Held: The Court first of all invoked the principle of universal jurisdiction by stating that the crimes Eichmann was accused of were not only crimes under Israeli law, but were the abhorrent crimes "which struck at the whole of mankind and shocked the conscience of nations, are grave offences against the law of nations itself". The Court thus saw that since there is no international court which could try persons accused of such crimes, there was a gap in international law which individual states can fill "to give effect to its criminal interdictions and to bring the criminals to trial". Thus the Court concluded that the jurisdiction to try crimes under international law was universal.

The Court also proceeded to establish its jurisdiction through the so-called protective principle: namely, the protection of its citizens and the vital interests of the state. The argument was raised that at the time when the crimes Eichmann stood accused of were committed there was no Israeli state and thus the state could not claim either the protection of its citizens or of its vital interests. The Court rejected this argument by stating that the legislator, when adopting the 1951 law on the Israeli Nazi and Nazi Collaborators (Punishment) had determined that such vital interests existed and invoked the "linking point" doctrine. Under this doctrine, a legal connection linking the punisher with the punished is required and this gives a right to a state to punish only those persons and acts which concern it more that they concern any other state.

The Court also rejected the argument that since Eichmann had been abducted from Argentina, an act which per se was considered illegal, his trial should not take place. The Court noted the objections by Argentina to the act of the Israeli agents, which had prompted a Security Council Resolution, had been settled between the two countries and invoked examples from various jurisdictions which all supported that the circumstances of the arrest and the mode of bringing the accused into the territory of a state are irrelevant for the trial.

Thus the Court established its jurisdiction in the present case. 1961 36 I.L.R. 5. District of Jerusalem.

Commentary

This case has sparked some controversy amongst international lawyers and Israel has been criticised on the grounds that it would have been more appropriate for the purposes of objectivity and fair trial if Eichmann had been tried elsewhere. Also the fact that Israel invoked the principle of passive personality has received a fair degree of criticism since Israel did not exist as a state at the time when the crimes were committed.

Nevertheless the Eichmann case remains one of the central examples of the exercise of universal jurisdiction, combined with the passive personality principle, in international law. These types of proceedings are inherently complicated and burdensome on states, as such problems as investigating cases and the availability of witnesses are obstacles to overcome. Despite this, there are many countries which have incorporated the principle of universal jurisdiction in their national legislation and have purported to exercise it. For more detailed examination of universal jurisdiction principle see *Congo Arrest Warrant* case (below).

Key Principles: **Relationship between jurisdiction and immunities; immunity of a current senior government official from criminal proceedings in another state; relationship between jurisdictional immunity and individual criminal responsibility; principle of universal jurisdiction.**

Case Concerning the Arrest Warrant of April 11, 2000 (Democratic Republic of Congo v Belgium) 2002

Facts: In April 2000 an arrest warrant *in absentia* was issued by a Belgian investigative judge for Abdulaye Yerodia Ndombasi, a national of the Democratic Republic of Congo (DRC). On the basis of a 1993 Belgian law he was charged with war crimes amounting to grave breaches of the 1949 Geneva Conventions and crimes against humanity allegedly committed in August 1998 in the DRC.

At the time of the issue of the arrest warrant Yerodia was in the DRC, acting as Minister of Foreign Affairs and in November 2000 he became Minister of Education. Belgium transmitted the arrest warrant to the government of the DRC and also to Interpol, which in turn circulated it to other states.

No Belgian nationals were among the victims of the alleged crimes, none of the alleged offences had taken place on Belgian territory, nor was there any other link between Belgium and the accused.

The DRC brought proceedings against Belgium to the ICJ, claiming that Belgium had no jurisdiction in international law to issue and circulate the arrest warrant and that in any case Yerodia had diplomatic immunity as Minister of Foreign Affairs. The ICJ upheld the immunity claim advanced by the DRC, while not dealing with the issue of jurisdiction. Nevertheless several judges gave their separate opinions on the matter of jurisdiction, and these should be considered (see commentary to this case).

Held: The Court first of all determined that in the present case it was only the immunity from criminal jurisdiction and the inviolability of a serving Minister of Foreign Affairs that were before the Court for determination. Noting that none of the conventions invoked dealt with the immunity enjoyed by the Minister of Foreign Affairs, the Court ruled that the case would be decided on the basis of customary international law.

The ICJ went on to declare that immunities accorded to the Ministers of Foreign Affairs "are not granted for their personal benefit, but to ensure effective performance of their functions on behalf of their respective States" (para.53). The ICJ turned to an examination of the duties of Ministers of Foreign Affairs as in the view of the Court the extent of these immunities was determined by the nature of the functions exercised. The Court concluded that the functions of the Ministers of Foreign Affairs are such that "throughout the duration of his or her office, he or she when abroad enjoys full immunity from criminal proceedings and inviolability" (para.54). The Court rejected the distinction advanced between acts performed in "official', capacity and those performed in "private', capacity, as in any case when a

Minister of Foreign Affairs is arrested, he or she is barred from performing the official duties. The ICJ examined the state practice and the practice of various international tribunals, finding no evidence of different practice on the matter.

However, the ICJ made it clear that "jurisdiction does not imply absence of immunity, while absence of immunity does not imply jurisdiction" (para.59). The Court stated that an extension of jurisdiction does not in any way alter the immunities which are accorded under customary international law. Nevertheless, the ICJ also emphasized that:

> "the immunity from jurisdiction enjoyed by incumbent Ministers of Foreign Affairs does not mean that they enjoy impunity in respect of any crimes they might have committed, irrespective of their gravity" (para.60).

The Court went on to state that:

> "Jurisdictional immunity may well bar prosecution for a certain period or for certain offences; it cannot exonerate the person to whom it applies from all criminal responsibility" (para.60).

The ICJ then numerated four instances when the immunity accorded to an incumbent or former Minister of Foreign Affairs is not a bar for criminal proceedings: (i) no criminal immunity is afforded to such persons in their own countries; (ii) if the represented state decides to wave such immunity; (iii) the immunity no longer applies once the person ceases to hold the office and thus can be prosecuted for offences committed prior or after the period of office or for the crimes committed during the period of office but in "private capacity"; and (iv) if that person is subjected to the proceedings by an international tribunal.

The ICJ went on to declare that the very issuance of the arrest warrant in this case violated the immunity accorded to the incumbent Minister of Foreign Affairs by customary international law and thus found Belgium in breach of its obligations under customary international law and requested Belgium to make reparations. 2002 ICJ Reports 3.

Commentary

This case makes a distinction between two types of immunities in international law: immunity *ratione personae* or the personal immunity and immunity *ratione materiae*, the functional immunity. The former extends to any acts that certain classes of officials perform while in office whereas the latter is enjoyed by a state or state official in respect to any official act. The functional immunity in essence is derived from the state immunity as it is based on the premise that a state official enjoys immunity while acting as an agent of that state. However, personal immunity is based on the idea that any act of a state official must be immune from foreign jurisdictions so as to ensure that states enjoy full independence and sovereignty. Since this is a procedural immunity, it only applies to state agents while they are in the office.

The ICJ in the present case stated four instances when a serving and/or former Minister of Foreign affairs may be prosecuted and the third instance according to the Court is the case when a person no longer holds an office, he or she can be tried for acts committed either prior to or after the office term or for acts committed during the office term as long as these were committed in "private capacity". The ICJ has been heavily criticised for this proclamation as in effect the Court here extended the protection of both personal and functional immunity which could lead to a situation in which a former office holder cannot be prosecuted for any offences. After all it is more than likely that the "cloak" of official position would be used for the commission of offences, let alone that some acts, like torture, can only be committed in official capacity. Therefore, by extending both personal and functional immunity to former Ministers of Foreign Affairs, the ICJ has in effect afforded total immunity to such persons, ignoring the principles of customary international law which require lifting of functional immunities for international crimes allegedly committed by state agents, a rule which comes into effect as long as personal immunities are no longer applicable.

The judgment itself did not deal with the issue of jurisdiction, but the Separate Opinions shed some light on the matter and thus should be discussed here. In their Joint Separate Opinion Judges Higgins, Kooijmans and Buergenthal stated that there existed no specific provision which allowed for the exercise of true universal jurisdiction. They pointed out that such universal jurisdiction is commonly read in the provisions of the 1949 Geneva Conventions, which contain *aut dedere aut judicare* (prosecute or extradite) obligations. However, in their opinion, these obligations only oblige the state parties to search for offenders who may be present in their territory. The judges opined that "by the loose use of language" this obligation has been termed "universal jurisdiction" as in reality this is only "an obligatory territorial jurisdiction over persons, albeit in relation to acts committed elsewhere" (para.41). The judges went on to observe that there were no cases of an exercise of "true" universal jurisdiction, but noted that this did not mean that such exercise would be illegal. The famous dictum from the *Lotus* case (see above) was recalled and the judges concluded that there was no rule prohibiting states from exercising their jurisdiction in the way Belgium purported to do in this case. On the contrary, when examining the crime of piracy as a classical example of the crime regarded as the most heinous by the international community, the judges stated that universal jurisdiction over the crime of piracy:

> "was regarded lawful because the international community regarded piracy as damaging to the interests of all. War crimes and crimes against humanity are no less harmful to the interests of all because they do not usually occur on high seas" (para.61).

Thus the judges upheld the legality of an exercise of universal jurisdiction *in absentia*, a sort of quasi-universal jurisdiction, since there was no rule of international law prohibiting it.

This Opinion should be contrasted with the Separate Opinion of the President of the Court, Judge Guillaume, who stated that there is only one true case of universal jurisdiction and that is the case of piracy. In the opinion of the President, the universal jurisdiction invoked in this case was subsidiary universal jurisdiction and he declared that such did not exist in international law. In his opinion, international law had changed since the *Lotus* case (see above) and now the territorial principle in questions of jurisdiction had been strengthened. In his opinion, such universal jurisdiction would cause judicial chaos as any state could prosecute anyone irrespective of where the person was found or where the victims would be or where the crime had been committed. He argued that this would leave the possibility for abuse and "encourage the arbitrary for the benefit of the powerful, purportedly acting as agent for an ill-defined 'international community' " (para.15). Thus he rejected the claim of jurisdiction advanced by Belgium.

Key Principle: **Immunity of Former Head of State in criminal proceedings.**

R v Bow Street Magistrates Ex P Pinochet [2001]

Facts: In 1998 the former Chilean Head of State, Pinochet, was arrested whilst receiving medical treatment in London on the basis of an extradition request by Spain. The charges were, inter alia, of torture and conspiracy to torture. Pinochet came to power after a right wing military coup in 1973 overthrew the left wing Chilean government of President Allende and Pinochet was the Head of State until he resigned in 1990.

Held: The House of Lords ruled that the obligations placed upon the UK by the UN Convention against Torture became part of UK domestic law when the provisions of the Convention were incorporated by s.134 of the Criminal Justice Act 1988, which came into force on September 29, 1988. It was ruled that in accordance with the Convention, all torture wherever committed was then made criminal under the UK law and therefore subject to the jurisdiction of the UK courts. The House of Lords proceeded to examine the cases from various national and international jurisdictions and declared that all confirmed the prohibition of torture as a norm of *jus cogens.*
  The House of Lords then turned to the examination of the applicable immunities and ruled that the absolute prohibition of torture in international law overrides immunity afforded to a former Head of State in criminal proceedings. It was specifically noted that the commission of a crime which is an international crime against humanity and *jus cogens* cannot be done in an official capacity on behalf of a state. Consequently the House of Lords declared that the immunity afforded to former Heads of States did not cover instances of alleged torture since acts of torture cannot constitute official acts of state. [2000] 1 A.C. 147 UKHL.

Commentary
This case represents one of the most important cases on the restrictions on immunity afforded to former state officials. The House of Lords here made it absolutely clear that such immunity would not apply in criminal proceedings about the alleged torture since torture can never be considered to constitute an act

necessary for the functioning of a state and thus cannot be protected by jurisdiction *ratione materiae*.

Key Principles: **State immunity in civil proceedings; immunity of state agents in civil proceedings.**

Al-Adsani v United Kingdom 2001

Facts: The application before the European Court of Human Rights (ECHR) was brought by a dual citizen of the UK and Kuwait after he failed to succeed in proceedings in the UK. He alleged that while in Kuwait in 1991, he was held responsible by the Sheik, a relative of the Emir of Kuwait, for distribution of video tapes containing sex images of the Sheik. Al Adsani alleged that he had been taken to the Kuwait state security prison by the Sheik using the government transport and badly beaten by the security forces. Then, a few days later, he was taken by the Sheik to a royal palace where his head was held underwater in the swimming pool full of corpses and where he suffered severe burns as a result of the Sheik setting fire to a mattress in the cell where he was detained. The victim later received treatment for his burns in London and was also diagnosed as suffering with post-traumatic stress disorder. He also alleged to have received threats from agents of the Sheik and the Kuwaiti Ambassador while in London. Al Adsani brought civil proceedings in the UK against the Sheik and the government of Kuwait claiming damages for the physical injuries and mental harm caused by the attacks in Kuwait and threats in London. The government of Kuwait claimed immunity and the UK courts upheld this claim.

Following this the victim brought proceedings to the ECHR against the UK, claiming breach of Art.3 (prohibition of torture) and Art.6 (right to fair trial). The ECHR unanimously rejected the alleged breach of Art.3 since the UK could not be implicated in any attacks that allegedly took place against the victim. However by nine votes to eight the majority of the ECHR declared that UK had not breached the applicant's rights to fair trial by upholding state immunity claimed by Kuwait.

Held: The ECHR first of all declared that state immunity does not constitute an absolute bar for bringing an action against a state since there is a possibility that a defendant state waives its immunity and in such a case the proceedings would take place. However, the ECHR also noted that an applicant's right to fair trial is not an absolute right and may be limited. In this particular case such limitation was the immunity afforded by the UK to the Kuwaiti state and its officials. The ECHR established that such restriction upon Al Adsani's right to fair trial pursued a legitimate aim of complying with international law to promote good relations between states through the respect of another state's sovereignty.

The ECHR then proceeded to ascertain whether this legitimate aim was proportionate. Initially the Court noted that it was not called upon to decide whether the alleged acts constituted torture, but proclaimed that there was a possibility that these might be so qualified. The ECHR then declared that torture had reached the status of a peremptory norm of international law, but stated that:

"Notwithstanding the special character of the prohibition of torture in international law, the Court is unable to discern in the international instruments, judicial authorities or other materials before it any firm basis for concluding that, as a matter of international law, a State no longer enjoys immunity from civil suit in the courts of another State where acts of torture are alleged" (para.61).

The ECHR thus upheld the position of the UK courts. 2001 34 E.H.R.R. 273.

Commentary

This case must be distinguished from that of *Pinochet* (see above) as it deals with civil and not criminal proceedings. It must also be noted that this case was decided by nine votes to eight and therefore the Dissenting Opinions are of particular importance. Thus Judges Rozakis and Caflish, joined by Judges Wildhaber, Costa, Cabral Barreto and Vajic in their Dissenting Opinion criticised the majority for admitting that the prohibition of torture is a norm of *jus cogens* and failing to draw the necessary consequences of such admission. In their opinion, the hierarchy of norms in this case means that a *jus cogens* prohibition of torture cannot be overridden by a rule of lower hierarchy like state immunity. In their opinion this was the point of error by the majority of the Court.

See also *Jones* case below.

Key Principles: State immunity in civil proceedings; immunity of state agents in civil proceedings.

Jones v Ministry of Interior of the Kingdom of Saudi Arabia [2006]

Facts: An action in damages was brought by four applicants, all UK citizens, who had been falsely accused of involvement in bombings which took place in Saudi Arabia in 2001 and 2002. The four applicants alleged that they were subsequently detained by Saudi officials and held in prison where they were repeatedly subjected to torture. They sought aggravated and exemplary damages from Saudi Arabia's Ministry of the Interior and the Saudi officials allegedly responsible for the mistreatment. Saudi Arabia invoked immunity on its own behalf and on behalf of its officials. The House of Lords upheld the claim of immunity of Saudi Arabia.

Held: The House of Lords declared that there was as yet not enough evidence of state practice which would lead to the conclusion that in cases of torture a state would not enjoy immunity from civil proceedings. It was noted that as long as the very act of torture requires that the alleged actions are performed by a state official, the immunity in civil proceedings still applies. This was contrasted to the criminal proceedings when, as illustrated by the *Pinochet* case (see above), immunity would not apply. The House of Lords concluded that immunity from civil proceedings imposed a restriction upon the UK courts, which the UK itself had chosen to adopt and thus could not abandon at its own discretion. [2006] UKHL 26.

Commentary
The judgment in the *Jones* case follows the reasoning adopted by the ECHR in the *Al Adsani* case (see above) and illustrates that as of yet there is considered insufficient evidence of an emergence of a new rule, one which would remove state immunity in civil proceedings in cases of alleged torture.

Key Principles: **Diplomatic immunity; obligations of the host state.**

US Diplomatic and Consular Staff in Teheran case (United States v Iran) 1980

Facts: On November 4, 1979, several hundred Iranian students and other demonstrators took the US Embassy in Tehran by force in protest at the admission of the deposed Shah of Iran into the US for medical treatment. The Iranian security forces did nothing to either prevent this or address the situation afterwards. The demonstrators seized archives and documents and held 52 US nationals as hostages, of whom 50 were consular staff and two were civilians. The occupation was still ongoing at the time of this judgment and prior to the judgment of the ICJ, in April 1980 US military forces invaded Iran by air, landing in a remote desert area in an attempt to rescue the hostages. The attempt was abandoned due to the failure of military equipment, but no injury was done to Iranian nationals or property.

The US complained before the ICJ that Iran had infringed its various treaty obligations, most notably, the 1961 and 1963 Vienna Conventions on Diplomatic and Consular Relations respectively. The ICJ upheld the US claim and requested Iran take immediate steps to address the ongoing hostage situation and to make reparations to US. Iran refused to participate in the proceedings before the ICJ and thus did not comply with any of the ICJ's requests. The situation was resolved through negotiations between Iran and US in January 1981.

Held: See pp.168 and 210 for further discussion.

The ICJ stated that in accordance with the provisions of the Vienna Conventions of 1961 and 1963, Iran:

> "was placed under the most categorical obligations, as a receiving State, to take appropriate steps to ensure the protection of the United States Embassy and Consulates, their staffs, their archives, their means of communication and the freedom of movement of the members of their staff" (para.61).

The Court went even further and stated that these obligations were not merely contractual obligations of Iran under the said Conventions, but rather were obligations incumbent upon it under general international law. Thus the ICJ declared that it was first the inaction of the Iranian authorities which led to a "clear and serious breaches of its obligations". The Court stated that:

> "The occupation having taken place and the diplomatic and consular personnel of the United States' mission having been taken hostage, the action required of the Iranian Government by the Vienna Conventions and by the general international law was manifest" (para.69).

Moreover, the Court considered that a decree of November 17, 1979 whereby the Ayatollah Khomeini expressly declared that the premises of the embassy and the hostages taken would remain until the US would hand over the former Shah for trial and return his property to Iran as the seal of official government approval to the incident. It thus stated that:

> "this case is unique and of very particular gravity because here it is not only private individuals or groups of individuals that have disregarded and set at naught the inviolability of a foreign embassy, but the government of the receiving state itself" (para.92).

The ICJ declared that Iran had breached its obligations under international law.

The ICJ also made a proclamation on the US invasion. It expressed its sympathy to the US in the face of the inaction of Iranians, but noted that the US invasion was in direct contradiction to Order of the ICJ of December 15, 1979, in which the ICJ requested the parties to take no action which might aggravate the situation. Thus the ICJ considered that irrespective of the motives of the operation, the US action "is of a kind calculated to undermine respect for the judicial process in international relations" (para.93). The Court however noted that the question of the legality of this operation was not before it. 1980 ICJ Reports 3.

Commentary

This is one of the central cases in the jurisprudence of the ICJ on diplomatic immunities and the obligations of a host state. It makes clear that host states do not only have negative obligations, i.e. an obligation not to interfere with the work of the diplomatic missions, but also have positive obligations. In this case, inaction of the Iranian authorities to the attack was considered to constitute a breach of its obligations both under the 1961 and 1963 Vienna Conventions and under general international law.

It is also important to note that the Court found Iran to be in breach not only of its contractual obligations under the two Vienna Conventions, but also under its obligations stemming from general international law.

Key Principle: **Special privileges and immunities of the experts of the UN are such that are necessary for the exercise of their functions.**

Difference Relating to Immunity from Legal Process of a Special Rapporteur of the Commission on Human Rights Advisory Opinion 1999

Facts: See p.85 for further discussion.

Held: See pp.85 and 169 for further discussion.

The ICJ concluded that Special Rapporteurs are entrusted with a mission by the United Nations and this is the decisive element in determining that they are entitled to privileges and immunities as provided by Art.VI, s.22 of the UN Convention on the Privileges and Immunities of the United Nations and its activities. 1999 ICJ Reports 62.

Commentary
The ICJ confirmed that agents of the UN are entitled to such privileges and immunities as are necessary in the course of their actions as experts of the UN. In this particular instance, the provision of immunity arose from the UN Convention on the Privileges and Immunities of the United Nations and its activities. In the case of other international organisations, the relevant agreements concerning the privileges and immunities have to be consulted as there are no general rules in this area.

---

8. STATE RESPONSIBILITY

Key Principle: A state is under an obligation not to knowingly allow its territory to be used for acts contrary to the rights of other states.

Corfu Channel case (Merits), United Kingdom v Albania 1949

Facts: British warships were passing through the Corfu Channel within the territorial sea of Albania when two were heavily damaged by mines. The Corfu Channel straits were within the territorial sea of Albania.

After the incident British warships mine swept the channel. Subsequently the parties submitted two questions to the ICJ. These were whether Albania was responsible under international law for the explosions which had occurred in Albanian waters and whether Albania was responsible for the damage and loss of human life which ensued and therefore under a duty to pay compensation.

The ICJ was also asked whether the UK had violated the sovereignty of Albania and was there any duty incumbent on the UK to provide satisfaction.

Held: See pp.57, 108 and 188 for further discussion.

The ICJ acknowledged there was a generally recognised international custom whereby states in time of peace have a right to send warships through straits which were being used for international navigation between two parts of the high seas, without the prior authorisation of the coastal state provided the passage was innocent. In such circumstances, the coastal state did not have the right to prohibit passage through straits in times of peace.

As to the responsibility of Albania, the Court unequivocally recognised that knowledge of mine laying could not be imputed to the Albanian Government, merely by virtue of the minefield having been discovered in Albanian territorial waters. The Court however stated that international practice was such that the state on whose territory or in whose waters an act contrary to international law had taken place could be called upon to provide an explanation. Such a state could not evade responding to such a request by claiming ignorance as to the circumstances of the act and the identity of the perpetrators. Such a state may be bound to supply particulars of the use it made of the information and enquiry at its disposal.

However, the mere fact of control exercised by a state over its territorial waters did not necessarily mean that the state knew, or ought to have known, of any unlawful act perpetrated therein, nor yet, that it necessarily knew or should have known, the perpetrators. This fact by itself and apart from other circumstances did not give rise to prima facie responsibility nor did it shift the burden of proof. Nonetheless the Court maintained the exclusive territorial control exercised by a state within its frontiers had a bearing upon the methods of proof available for establishing the knowledge a state possessed as to such events.

On the other hand because of such exclusive control another state, namely the victim of the breach of international law, may often be unable to provide direct proof or facts so as to establish responsibility. Accordingly, in the Court's view such a state should be allowed a more liberal recourse to inferences of fact and circumstantial evidence. The Court held that this approach was one recognised by all systems of law with its use being acknowledged by international decisions.

The Court characterised the task before it as that of determining whether by the means of indirect evidence Albania had knowledge of mine laying in her territorial waters, independently of any connivance in that mine laying. Proof could be drawn from inferences of fact provided they left no room for reasonable doubt. The Court then considered a number of issues, such as for example whether the mine laying could be observed from the Albanian coast and concluded from the facts presented that this was not possible.

However, on the facts as presented, the Court held that the laying of the mine field which caused the explosion could not have been accomplished without the knowledge of the Albanian Government. The obligations arising from the Albanian Government's knowledge were not disputed. The obligations incumbent upon the Albanian authorities were enumerated as being: notifying for the benefit of shipping in general the existence of a mine field in Albanian territorial waters; and warning approaching British warships of the imminent danger to which the mine field exposed them. Such obligations were founded on certain general and well recognised principles rather than on the

Hague Convention 1907, No.VIII, which applied in the time of war.

These well recognised principles were identified as elementary considerations of humanity, even more exacting in peace than in war, the principles of freedom of maritime communication and every state's obligation not to knowingly allow its territory to be used for acts contrary to the rights of other states. The failure of the Albanian authorities to prevent the disaster was characterised as a grave omission involving the international responsibility of Albania.

Accordingly, the Court held that Albania was responsible under international law for the explosions which had occurred in Albanian waters and for the damage and loss of human life which resulted from these explosions and that Albania was under a duty to pay compensation to the UK. 1949 ICJ Reports 4.

Commentary
This decision lends some support to the subjective theory of state responsibility, namely there has to be fault for responsibility to be incurred. The decision emphasised that a state is under an obligation to not knowingly allow its territory to be used for acts harmful to other states.

Key Principles: The level of proof demanded for genocide; states can be held responsible for genocide, of a complicity in genocide even in the absence of a conviction, by a competent court, of an individual: need for intent; need for positive characteristics to define the targeted group.

Application of the Convention on the Prevention and Punishment of the Crime of Genocide (Bosnia and Herzegovina v Serbia and Montenegro)

Facts: The case concerned the application of the 1948 Convention on the Prevention and Punishment of the Crime of Genocide (Genocide Convention) and whether the Respondent (Serbia) was in breach of its obligations under the Genocide Convention.

There were a number of stages including the indication of interim measures on two occasions in 1993 (see 1993 ICJ Reports 3 and 1993 ICJ Reports 325).

Yugoslavia then lodged preliminary objections regarding the jurisdiction of the Court. The Court, however on July 11, 1996 rejected these objections and found it had jurisdiction to deal with the case on the basis of Art.IX of the Genocide Convention (1996 ICJ Reports 595). Subsequently Yugoslavia requested a revision of the 1996 judgment maintaining Yugoslavia's membership of the UN amounted to a new fact which was not known in 1996. Yugoslavia further maintained that at the time the Federal Republic of Yugoslavia (FRY) had not been a party to, either the ICJ Statute or, the Genocide Convention. In September 1992, pursuant to General Assembly Resolution 47/1 the UN General Assembly had considered that FRY did not automatically continue in, or succeed to, the membership in the UN of the former Socialist Federal Republic of Yugoslavia. However the Court in 2003 maintained that GA Resolution 47/1 did not affect FRY's right of *locus standi* before the ICJ nor did it affect FRY's position in relation to the Geneva Convention. The Court therefore rejected the application for revision. See international organisations for Court's decision in 1996.

Held: See p.217 for further discussion.

In the instant case it was decided Serbia had violated its obligations under the 1948 Genocide Convention to prevent genocide in Srebrenica. However Serbia had not committed genocide through its organs or persons for whom it was responsible under customary international law; there was no conspiracy to commit genocide or incite the commission of genocide by Serbia nor was Serbia complicit in genocide. Nevertheless the Court held that Serbia had violated its obligations under the Genocide Convention through its failure to transfer a person indicted for genocide and complicity in genocide for trial by the ICTY. The Court's decision also found that Serbia had failed to fully co-operate with the ICTY.

The Court confirmed that Serbia had also failed to comply with provisional measures indicated in April and September 1993 and maintained that Serbia should take immediate and effective steps to ensure full compliance with the its obligations under the Genocide Convention. These obligations being that of punishing acts of genocide as defined by the Geneva Convention and any other acts proscribed by the Convention, the transfer of individuals accused of genocide or any of those other acts for trial to the ICTY, and full co-operation with the ICTY.

The Court held the applicable law was solely Art.IX of the

Convention and the Court's task was limited to ruling on alleged breaches of obligations imposed by the Genocide Convention. However the Court was not to address breaches of other obligations under international law, such as those protecting human rights in armed conflict even if these breaches were obligations under peremptory norms or of obligations which protected essential humanitarian values.

The Court held that states may be held responsible for genocide or for complicity in genocide even if no individual has previously been convicted of the crime by a competent court. The Court observed that for particular acts to be qualified as genocide they must be accompanied by intent to destroy the protected group in whole or in part as such. The Court emphasised the difference between genocide and "ethnic cleansing" and noted whereas ethnic cleansing could be carried out by the displacement of a group or persons from a specific area genocide was defined by a number of positive characteristics—national, ethnic, racial or religious—and not by the lack of them. Accordingly the Court rejected the negative definition of the group advanced by Bosnia and Herzegovina as the non-Serb population and rather pressed the view that for the purposes of the case the group required to be defined as Bosnian Muslims.

Regarding the standard of proof the Court highlighted it was for the applicant to establish the case and that any allegations in respect of the crime of genocide or related acts as enumerated in Art.3 of the Genocide Convention had to be proved by evidence that was fully conclusive. The Court stated unequivocally it required proof at a high level of certainty appropriate to the seriousness of the allegation. The Court also acknowledged that in establishing proof it would make its own determinations of facts based on the evidence presented. However it would accept relevant findings of fact from the ICTY because in the words of the Court such would be "highly persuasive".

As to the factual matrix the Court found there was overwhelming evidence of massive killings throughout Bosnia and Herzegovina which were perpetrated during the conflict. However the Court was not convinced those killings were accompanied by the specific intent by the parties of the perpetrators to destroy, either in all or in part, the group of Bosnian Muslims. The Court acknowledged the killings might amount to war crimes and crimes against humanity but the Court had no jurisdiction to determine whether this was the case.

The Court then turned to examine the facts surrounding the

massacre at Srebrenica and formed the conclusion that the main staff of the army of the Republica Srpska (VRS) had the necessary specific intent to destroy in part a group of Bosnian Muslims. Specifically Bosnian Muslims of Srebrenica and accordingly acts of genocide were committed by the VRS in or around Srebrenica from about July 13, 1995. The Court also concluded that Bosnian Muslims were systematically victims of massive mistreatment, beatings, rape and torture causing serious bodily and mental harm during the conflict. However it was of the view the specific intent to destroy the protected group was not conclusively established. Similarly the Court concluded that although alleged acts of deliberately inflicting on the group conditions of life calculated to bring about its physical destruction, in whole or in part, had occurred, again there was not sufficient evidence to demonstrate the necessary specific intent. The Court further found there was insufficient evidence to establish steps had been taken to impose measures to prevent births within the protected group or that there had been a forcible transfer of children of the protected group to another group.

The Court held that Bosnia Herezgovina had failed to demonstrate there was any overall plan to commit genocide on the part of Serbia or that the very pattern of the atrocities committed, over many communities over a lengthy period, focused on Bosnian Muslims was such to demonstrate the necessary specific intent to destroy the group in whole or in part.

Turning to the question of responsibility, the Court held that in light of the information available to it that the acts of those who committed genocide at Srebrenica could not be attributed to Serbia under the rules of international law of state responsibility. In particular the Court concluded the acts of genocide could not be attributed to Serbia as having been committed by persons or entities who could be classified as organs or agents of the respondent. The Court could also not establish the massacres had been committed on the instructions or under the direction of the respondent or that the respondent exercised effective control over the operations in the course of which the massacres were committed.

The Court also considered the question of complicity in genocide. It was evident to the Court that the Srebrenica atrocities were committed with resources the perpetrators had by way of a general policy of aid and assistance by FRY. However what was not conclusively established was that FRY had supplied aid to the perpetrators of the genocide in full awareness that the aid supplied would be used to commit genocide. Thus a very specific condition necessary for the legal responsibility of Serbia had not been fulfilled.

Regarding an obligation to prevent genocide the Court stated the obligation was one of conduct and not one of results. The responsibility was not incurred simply because genocide had occurred and responsibility would only be incurred if the state manifestly failed to take all measures to prevent genocide which were within its power and which might have contributed to preventing the genocide. The Court further noted that a state would only be held responsible if genocide had actually been committed and thus considered Serbia's conduct only in connection with the Srebrenica massacres. It was sufficient for the state however to be aware, or should normally have been aware of, the serious danger that acts of genocide would be committed. The Court concluded Serbia federal authorities should have made the best efforts within their power to try and prevent the "tragic events taking shape" and avert the atrocities which were committed. Accordingly the Court held Serbia had violated its obligations to prevent genocide in such a manner so as to engage its international responsibilities under Art.1 of the Geneva Convention.

In respect of the obligation to punish perpetrators of genocide the Court maintained, pursuant to Art.6 of the Convention, states have an obligation to co-operate with "such international penal tribunal as may have jurisdiction" in the relevant matter. Thus the Court concluded the ICTY was such an international penal tribunal.

Finally on the question of reparation the Court addressed Bosnia and Herzegovina's request for reparation and stated it had not been shown the genocide in Srebrenica would in fact have been averted if FRY had attempted to prevent it. Thus financial compensation for the failure to prevent the genocide was not an appropriate form of reparation. The Court accordingly concluded that the most appropriate form of satisfaction would be a declaration in the operative clause of the judgment that the respondent had failed to comply with its obligation to prevent the crime of genocide.

A similar finding was made by the Court with respect to the respondent's failure to transfer to the ICTY persons accused of genocide. Judgment of February 26, 2007.

Commentary
The decision taken shows a willingness on the part of the Court to accept evidence previously before, and accepted by, another judicial body.

The ICJ in this case also made a very important proclamation regarding the obligations of a state party to the Genocide Convention: there is an obligation to prevent genocide and failure to comply with this obligation entails state responsibility.

It should also be noted that although the facts and events, which were the subject of the merits of the case occurred when Serbia and Montenegro constituted a single state, the Republic of Montenegro had not acquired the status of respondent in the case. Serbia had accepted continuity between Serbia and Montenegro and the Republic of Serbia and had assumed responsibility for its commitments derived from international treaties concluded by Serbia and Montenegro. Montenegro, however, did not claim to be "the continuator" of Serbia and Montenegro. In other words the Republic of Montenegro did not continue the legal personality of Serbia and Montenegro.

Key Principles: **Breach of an international obligation, the obligation to make reparation; the nature of the damages which may be claimed for and how that compensation is to be calculated.**

Chorzow Factory case (Claim for Indemnity case), (Germany v Poland) (Merits) (1928)

Facts: See p.25 for further discussion.

Held: The PCIJ held that it is a principle under customary international law that any breach of an engagement involved an obligation to make a reparation. The estimate as to the damage caused by the unlawful act only takes into account the value of the property rights and interests which have been affected and property rights and interests of the owner, who is the person on whose behalf compensation is claimed. This was held to be an accepted principle in the jurisprudence of arbitration tribunals. However, such a principle excluded from the calculation of damages injury resulting for third parties from the unlawful act but did not exclude from the damages the amount of debts and other obligations for which the injured party was responsible. The Court acknowledged that in the particular instance the

Polish action was contrary to the 1922 Geneva Convention on Upper Silesia but it was not expropriation. If it had been expropriation it could have been rendered lawful by payment of fair compensation. The Court acknowledged that if it had been only compensation that was due to the German Government then compensation would be limited to the value of the undertaking at the moment of this possession plus interest to the day of payment. The Court maintained there was an established principle in international practice, which was reflected in the decisions of the tribunals, that reparation must, as far as possible, wipe out all the consequences of the illegal act and re-establish the situation which would, in all probability, have existed if the unlawful act had not been committed. Restitution in kind was said to be the aim of reparation but if this was not possible, payment of a sum corresponding to the value which a restitution in kind would bear was required. There should also be an award, if need be, of damages for loss sustained which would not be covered by restitution in kind or payment in place of it.

Regarding the principles which would be utilised to determine the amount of compensation due for an act contrary to international law, the Court stated that if reparation consisted in the payment of a sum of money, the Court could decide the method of such payment. The Court would determine to whom the payment should be made, in what place, at what moment and whether it should be by way of a lump sum or instalments. (1928) PCIJ Series A No.17.

Commentary

This case endorses that reparation is required under international law for a breach of an international obligation. It also states the object of reparation should be to wipe out, as far as is possible, the consequences of the illegal act and return the injured party to the situation it would have been in had the breach of international law not taken place. If this is not possible then compensation is to be awarded. Compensation takes account of material loss and may also take account of loss of profits in so far as that can be established.

Furthermore the Court established that reparation is the indispensable compliment of a failure to comply with a treaty and there is no requirement that this be stated as such in the relevant treaty.

Key Principles: A breach of an international law obligation engages state responsibility; legal consequences of such a breach; breach of *erga omnes* obligation and legal consequences thereof.

Legal Consequences of the Construction of a Wall in the Occupied Palestinian Territory Advisory Opinion 2004

Facts: See p.61 for further discussion.

Held: See pp.62, 187, 212 and 219 for further discussion.

The ICJ established that Israel had breached its various obligations under international law and thus declared that such breaches engaged Israel's responsibility under international law. The Court then examined the legal consequences of such a breach and observed Israel was obliged to comply with its obligations under international law and most importantly was obliged to respect the right of the Palestinian people to self-determination. The Court highlighted that Israel should put an end to the violations, cease the construction works and all associated acts. Moreover, referring to the PCIJ judgment in the *Factory at Chorzow* case (see above), the ICJ opined that Israel was obliged to make reparation for damage caused to all natural or legal persons concerned.

Furthermore, since Israel was in breach of an *erga omnes* obligation, the ICJ stated this imposed certain obligations upon other states. Thus other states were found to be under an obligation not to recognise the illegal status resulting from the construction of the wall, not to render any assistance in maintaining such illegal situation, to see that any impediment to the exercise of the Palestinian people of their right to self-determination from the construction of the wall was brought to an end, and to ensure Israel's compliance with its obligations under human rights and humanitarian law treaty obligations.

Finally, the ICJ also expressed the view that both the General Assembly and the Security Council should consider further action in order to bring an end to the illegal situation resulting from the construction of the wall. 2004 ICJ Reports 134.

Commentary

The significance of this Advisory Opinion is two-fold. First the ICJ endorsed the long standing principle that a breach of an international obligation engages state responsibility and imposes a duty to make reparations. Moreover, in the case when an *erga omnes* obligation is violated, an obligation is incumbent not only upon the guilty state, but upon all states since the protection and due observance of an *erga omnes* obligation is of interest to all states.

What is particularly interesting about this Advisory Opinion is that the ICJ also made suggestions, albeit very broad and general ones, as to what the two primary UN organs, namely, the Security Council and the General Assembly, should do in such a situation.

Key Principles: **A state can only espouse a claim on behalf of a national; nationality gives a right to diplomatic protection; nationality for the purposes of diplomatic protection must conform to the requirements of international law.**

Nottebohm case, Lichtenstein v Guatemala 1955

Facts: Nottebohm, a German by birth, had gone, in 1905, to Guatemala where he had set up his business and residence. In the years after 1905 he sometimes went to Germany on business. He also visited his brother, who since 1931 had lived in Lichtenstein.

In 1939 Nottebohm went to Lichtenstein to visit his brother and made an application for Lichtenstein naturalisation. In his application he sought dispensation from the requirement of at least three years residency in the Principality and applied for the proceedings to be initiated and concluded without delay. In accordance with Lichtenstein naturalisation law Nottebohm would lose his former nationality as a result of naturalisation. On receipt of his Lichtenstein passport Nottebohm returned to Guatemala and resumed his life there.

In December 1951, Lichtenstein initiated proceedings before the ICJ claiming restitution and compensation on behalf of Nottebohm for acts contrary to international law taken against him and his property by Guatemala. Guatemala argued that the claim was inadmissible before the Court and challenged the standing of Lichtenstein to act on Nottebohm's behalf. The Court was confronted with the question as to whether the nationality conferred on Nottebohm by Lichtenstein could be validly invoked against Guatemala and whether Lichtenstein could exercise diplomatic protection on behalf of Mr Nottebohm.

Held: See pp.51 and 131 for further discussion.

The Court held it was the prerogative of every sovereign state to determine the rules relating to the acquisition of nationality and each state could confer nationality by naturalisation in accordance with its own legislation. However the Court acknowledged that it was not concerned with the legal system of Lichtenstein but rather with the rules of international law regarding the right of a state to exercise protection and thus come before the Court.

The Court ruled that while conferral of nationality was an exclusive domain of Lichtenstein's domestic legislation, when it was invoked as a basis for a claim by Lichtenstein in international law, it had to conform to established principles of international law.

After a detailed examination of the facts the Court concluded that the nationality conferred by Lichtenstein did not conform to the requirements prescribed by international law and concluded that Guatemala was under no obligation to recognise the Lichtenstein nationality conferred upon Nottebohm. Consequently Lichtenstein could not afford diplomatic protection to Mr Nottebohm. 1955 ICJ Reports 4.

Commentary

This case illustrates that while a state has a right to exercise its diplomatic protection over its nationals and a right to bring international claims on behalf of its nationals', these rights are limited by the provisions of international law. In this particular case, the ICJ declared that while conferral of nationality lies within the exclusive competence of each state, if a state wishes to exercise diplomatic protection in the international arena, the conferral of nationality must conform to the requirements established by international law. In other words, a state is free to confer its nationality upon whom it wishes but the conferral of nationality will be challenged if a state seeks to espouse a claim at the international level and the conferred nationality does not conform to the rules established in international law.

The *Nottebohm* case is in line with the acknowledgement that it is the bond of nationality which confers the right of diplomatic protection and diplomatic protection is limited to a state's own nationals see also *Panevezys–Saldutiskis Railway case, Estonia v Lithuania* (1939) PCIJ Series A/B No.76

Key Principle: **An individual cannot deprive his/her state of nationality from extending diplomatic protection against breaches of international law.**

North American Dredging Company Claim (1926)

Facts: The case arose by way of an agreement between the North America Dredging Company and the Government of Mexico. The agreement was to the effect that the company was to be considered as Mexican and all issues arising from the contract would be subject to Mexican law. The company was to be deprived of any rights as a foreigner in Mexico and under no circumstances was there to be any US diplomatic intervention in any matter relating to the contract.

The North American Dredging Company claimed damages for a breach of the contract by the Mexican Government while the US acting on behalf of the company claimed damages against Mexico.

The matter was then referred to the Mexico/US General Claims Commission.

Held: The General Claims Commission held it did not have jurisdiction and required reference be made to Mexican law. However the General Claims Commission observed that an individual could not deprive his national state of its undoubted right of affording diplomatic protection because its Government frequently has a larger interest in maintaining the principles of international law than in recovering damages for one of its citizens. (1926) 4 RIAA 26.

Commentary

This recognises the principle that in taking up a claim on behalf of an individual, a state is in reality seeking respect for its own right that its national, when abroad, would be treated in a particular manner.

The General Claims Commission emphasised that diplomatic

protection is prompted by an injury to the national state rather than by injury to the individual national.

What the General Claims Commission was confronted with here was the operation of the so called Calvo Clause. A Calvo Clause was frequently inserted in contracts whereby individuals agreed not to invoke the assistance of their national Government in matters arising from the contract. A Calvo Clause prescribed exhaustion of local remedies.

Key Principles: **A right of a state of nationality to bring claims on behalf of its citizens; punitive damages.**

Lusitania case, United States v German, Mixed Claims Commission (1923)

Facts: In May 1915 a German U boat torpedoed the *Lusitania*, a British liner. The incident took place off the coast of Ireland during the time when America was neutral. The German Government acknowledged liability in respect of damage sustained by American nationals, some 128 of whom died.

Held: The Mixed Claims Commission acknowledged that in both civil and common law a violation of private rights involving injury gave rise to a remedy and that the remedy should be commensurate with the injury received and should be capable of monetary damages. The basis of the damage was not the physical or mental suffering of the deceased, his/her loss or the loss to his/her estate, but the losses resulting to the claimants from his/her death.

The Commission held that it was not concerned with the punishment of a wrongdoer but only with the straightforward question of fixing the amount which would afford compensation for the wrong done. It was noted that legal representatives had failed to provide the Commission with any instances of money being awarded where exemplary punitive or vindictive damages had been assessed against one sovereign nation in favour of another presenting a claim on behalf of its nationals. The Commission held that Germany must make compensation and reparation for all losses sustained by the American nationals and that compensation should be full, adequate and complete. (1923) 7R. IAA 32.

Commentary
This case illustrates the reluctance of international bodies to award punitive damages and the emphasis is on reparation.

Key Principles: **Obligation to exhaust local remedies; no need to exhaust if appeal to higher court would be of no use; a state will have no claim on behalf of its national if local remedies have not been exhausted.**

Ambatielos Arbitration, Greece v United Kingdom (1956)

Facts: Mr Ambatielos, a Greek national, had his claim against the UK, taken up on his behalf by the Greek Government. The claim arose out of Mr Ambatielos' contract with the UK in respect of the purchase of certain ships.

Held: The Arbitration Commission endorsed that exhaustion of local remedies is a well established rule in international law. Since this rule was not disputed by either party, the onus of proof was on the UK to demonstrate that domestic remedies existed within the UK legal system and that these had not been utilised. The Greek Government contended the contrary and maintained that the remedies which were available to Mr Ambatielos under UK law were ineffective and thus the exhaustion of the local remedies rules was not applicable.

The Commission characterised local remedies as including not only those of courts and tribunals, but also the use of all procedural facilities which are available to individuals under municipal law. The Commission emphasised that it was the whole apparatus of legal protection, as provided by domestic law, and that this apparatus had to be put to the test before a state, acting on behalf of one of its nationals, could prosecute the claim on the international plane.

The Commission then expressed the view the non-employment of certain procedural means could only be accepted as constituting a gap in the exhaustion of local remedies if use of these procedural means was essential to establishing the claimant's case before the municipal courts.

In the case of Mr Ambatielos one such failure had been to call a certain witness whom he subsequently alleged was essential to his case. However, under UK law the calling of such witnesses as identified by Mr Ambatielos was not prohibited. Accordingly the Commission expressed the view it was not concerned with whether Mr Ambatielos was right or wrong in acting as he did, that was not the question to be determined, and the decision which he had taken had been at his own risk.

As to Mr Ambatielos' failure to make use of, or exhaust, his appeal rights, the Greek Government argued that once the Court of Appeal had decided not to admit the evidence of the witness who Mr Ambatielos was now maintaining was essential to his case, would have made proceeding with the general appeal futile. The reason the Court of Appeal had refused to admit the evidence of the crucial witness, was one of evidence and it would not give leave to invoke further evidence which could have been adduced at the original trial.

The Arbitration Commission stated that the failure of Mr Ambatielos to exhaust the local remedy at the first instance by not calling the relevant witness was the reason why it was futile for him to prosecute his appeal. Consequently the Commission held that Mr Ambatielos by his own actions, namely by failing to exhaust his opportunities in the Court at first instance, had made his appeal pointless. Accordingly, he could not rely on this fact so as "to rid himself of the rule of exhaustion of local remedies". (1956) 12 RIAA 83.

Commentary
Exhaustion of local remedies is a fundamental principle of international law, its purpose is to allow the state which allegedly has breached an obligation to rectify and afford the means of redress.

The decision also underscores that local remedies encompasses not just the legal institutions such as courts and tribunals but extends to the entire system of legal protection as provided by domestic law. The decision nevertheless acknowledges that the non-exhaustion of local remedies will not be an obstacle to a claim if it is apparent in the circumstances of the case there was no further justice to exhaust. Consequently if a person has failed to exhaust domestic remedies, his/her state of nationality will not have a legal standing to pursue a claim on behalf of the national concerned. However it is only necessary to exhaust those local remedies which could affect the final outcome of the case.

Key Principles: State responsibility; responsibility for the acts of its agents.

US Diplomatic and Consular Staff in Teheran case (United States v Iran) 1980

Facts: See p.149 for further discussion.

Held: See pp.149 and 210 for further discussion.

The ICJ divided the events into two phases. It first considered the initial seizure of the Embassy by the demonstrators and noted there had been no suggestion that the people involved in the attack acted on behalf of Iran or had any official status as recognised agents or organs of Iran. The ICJ maintained the actions:

> "might be considered as itself directly imputable to the Iranian State only if it were established that, in fact, on the occasion in question the militants acted on behalf of the State, having been charged by some competent organ of the Iranian State to carry out a specific operation" (para.58).

The Court found no such indication in respect of the attack itself.

However, when turning to an examination of the subsequent developments, the ICJ declared that state responsibility of Iran was engaged with what it called "seal of official government approval", which the Court saw stemming from a decree of November 17, 1979 of the Ayatollah Khomeini. In that he expressly declared the premises of the Embassy and the hostages would remain as they were until the US handed over the former Shah for trial and returned his property to Iran. The Court held that the:

> "approval given to these facts by the Ayatollah Khomeini and other organs of the Iranian State, and the decision to perpetuate them, translated continued occupation of the Embassy and detention of the hostages into acts of that State. The militants, authors of the invasion and jailers of the hostages, had now become agents of the Iranian State for whose acts the State itself was internationally responsible" (para.74).

Thus, having established the responsibility of Iran, the ICJ went on to order Iran to make reparations to the US. 1980 ICJ Reports 3.

Commentary
In this case the ICJ made a distinction between the acts of a state and its agents and other acts, which cannot be attributed to the state. The case illustrates when state responsibility may be engaged. Clearly, once state responsibility on the international scene has been engaged, the obligation to make reparations follows.

Key Principles: **A state is responsible for the actions of its agents, also judicial bodies; state responsibility for the conduct of its organs is a rule of customary international law.**

Difference Relating to Immunity from Legal Process of a Special Rapporteur of the Commission on Human Rights Advisory Opinion 1999

Facts: See p.85 for further discussion.

Held: See pp.85 and 151 for further discussion.
   The ICJ confirmed the principle of state responsibility for the actions of its agents and stated that "According to a well-established rule of international law, the conduct of any organ of a State must be regarded as an act of that State". The ICJ went on to affirm this was a principle of customary international law. 1999 ICJ Reports 62.

Commentary
This case is primarily important for what it says regarding the privileges and immunities of a UN expert. However in this Advisory Opinion the ICJ also confirmed that if actions of a state's court lead to a breach of a state's obligations under international law, international responsibility would be incurred.

Key Principle: **A state will be held liable for the conduct of its officials, even when these officials act contrary to orders.**

H Youmans Claim, US v Mexico, General Claims Commission (1926)

Facts: A disturbance had taken place in a Mexican town following an argument between an American national, Connelly, the engineering manager of a tunnel construction project and a labourer. The house in which Connelly lived was surrounded by a mob of 1,000 people. In the house with Connelly were two other Americans. Connelly's employer, on hearing of the attack, went to the Mayor of the town and requested protection for the Americans. The Mayor was unable to quell the mob, returned to his office and ordered troops to be sent to disperse the mob and end the attack on the Americans. However, on arrival, the troops rather than affording protection opened fire on the house and one of the Americans was killed.

Connelly and his colleague, Youmans, were forced to leave the house as it was set alight by the mob and in doing so they were killed by the troops and members of the mob. A claim was made by Youman's son on the basis that the Mexican Government had failed to act with due diligence in affording protection to his father.

The participation of the soldiers was highlighted. It was argued that the Mexican Government should not be held responsible for the wrongful acts of the 10 soldiers and one officer concerned, because they had been ordered by the highest official in the locality to protect the American citizens.

Held: The General Claims Commission held that it was a well recognised rule of international law that a Government was not responsible for the malicious acts of soldiers committed in their private capacity. It was acknowledged that certain cases coming before international tribunals may have revealed some uncertainty as to whether the acts of soldiers should properly be regarded as private acts, for which there was no liability on the state or acts for which the state should be held responsible. However, the General Claims Commission concluded that the participation of the soldiers in the murder of Youman and his colleagues could not be regarded as acts of soldiers committed in their private capacity, when at the time of the commission of these acts the men in question were on duty under the immediate supervision of and in the presence of a commanding officer. It was held that soldiers inflicting personal injuries or committing wanton destruction or looting always act in disobedience of some rules laid down by superior authority. The General Claims Commission observed there could be no liability whatever for such mistakes if the view was taken that any acts committed by soldiers in contravention of instructions were always to be considered as personal acts. (1926) 4 RIAA 110.

Commentary

This case illustrates that the responsibility of a state for the acts of its officials is engaged also in instances when the officials in question trespass their competencies or orders given. This arises from the presumption that when acting in an official capacity, a state official represents a state and therefore when such an official disobeys an order, it is assumed that state has so disobeyed thus engaging its responsibility. In other words, state officials are regarded as an "extension of a state".

Key Principles: **Espousal of claims by a state on behalf of a company; principle of genuine connection; diplomatic protection on behalf of a company.**

Barcelona Traction case, Belgium v Spain 1970

Facts: See p.10 for further discussion.

Held: See pp.11, 26 and 220 for further discussion.

The Court acknowledged the wrong done to a company frequently causes prejudice to its shareholders, but the mere fact that the damage is sustained by the company and shareholders does not imply that both are entitled to claim compensation. Whenever a shareholder's interests were harmed by an act done to the company, it is to the company the injured shareholder must look for possible redress. Although two separate entities may have suffered from the same wrong, the Court held that only one entity had had its rights infringed. The Court continued that the position of the company rested on a positive rule of both municipal and international law.

The Court highlighted the Belgium Government had advanced the proposition that it was inadmissible to deny the shareholders' national state a right of diplomatic protection merely on the ground that another state possesses a corresponding right in respect of the company itself. The Belgian Government argued that there existed no rule of international law denying the national state of the shareholders the right of exercising diplomatic protection. However, the Court noted that by emphasising the absence of any expressed denial of the right conversely implied the admission that there was no rule of international law expressly conferring such a right on the shareholder's national state.

The Court highlighted that international law may not in some fields provide specific rules in particular cases. In this particular instance, the company which had sustained the consequences of the unlawful acts had rights which were expressly vested in it but no such right was expressly provided by the shareholders in respect of these acts. The Court highlighted the position of the company rested on a positive rule of both domestic and international law. The shareholder may have certain rights conferred by municipal law but in the circumstances of the Barcelona Traction Co reference could only be made to the silence of international law and in any case such silence scarcely admitted of an interpretation in favour of the shareholder. The Court dismissed any parallel between the situation in the *Reparations* case (see p.83), namely where one person is in possession of two separate bases of protection, each of which is valid. The Court stated there was no such parallel present between foreign shareholders and a company as in the instant case.

The Court looked at the position in domestic law and recognised the "lifting of the veil" was an exceptional one allowed by domestic law and could be equally admissible on the international plane. However, in this particular instance although from an economic point of view the company had been paralysed, the corporate entity of the company had not ceased to exist, nor had it lost its capacity to take corporate action. It had not lost competence in law in defence of its own rights and the interests of the shareholders. A precarious financial situation could not be equated with the demise of the corporate entity. What was important was the company's status in law, not its economic conditions, nor even the possibility of it being practically defunct. Only in the event of the legal demise of the company would the shareholders be deprived of the possibility of a remedy available through the company. Only if they became deprived of all such possibility would an independent right of action for the shareholders and their company arise.

The Court considered what it termed a lack of the capacity of the company's national state to act on its behalf. In other words, whether in law Canada was the national state of the Barcelona Traction Co. The Court stated that in allocating corporate entities to states, whereby diplomatic protection could be afforded, international law was based on an analogy with the rules governing the nationality of individuals even albeit to a limited extent. The Court acknowledged that traditionally the right to extend diplomatic protection to a corporate entity was a right of the state under the laws of which the corporate entity was incorporated and in whose territory it had its registered office. That, the Court stated, was established by long practice and by numerous international instruments.

The Court then looked at the practice of states but noted that in the field of the diplomatic protection of corporate entities no absolute test of the "genuine connection" had found general acceptance. Such tests that had been applied were of a relative nature and sometimes the links of one state had to be weighed against the links of another. The Court in the particular case before it, on both the legal and factual aspects, was of the opinion that there was no analogy with either the issues raised or the decision given in the *Nottebohm* case.

In this particular case Canada was the country in a position to afford diplomatic protection and indeed the Canadian Government had made representations to the Spanish Government and these representations could not be considered as anything other than an exercise of diplomatic protection in respect of Barcelona Traction. The Court acknowledged the Canadian Government had ceased to act on behalf of Barcelona Traction but it had done so by its own free will. There was no legal impediment which prevented it from exercising diplomatic protection. The Court emphasised the state must be viewed as the sole judge to decide whether its protection is to be granted, the extent to which it is to be granted and when that protection will cease. Thus it is a discretionary power, the exercise of which may be determined by considerations of a political or other nature unrelated to the particular case. Whatever the reason the fact that a state of nationality may cease to exercise such diplomatic protection cannot in itself constitute a justification for the exercise of diplomatic protection by another Government. That would only be legitimate if there was some independent and otherwise valid ground.

However the Court stated in an appeal for diplomatic

protection, as in other areas of international law, it was necessary that the law be applied reasonably. Nevertheless the Court dismissed the suggestion that considerations of equity might call for the possibility of protection of the shareholders in question by their own national state. The discretionary nature of diplomatic protection was such that considerations of equity would not require more than the possibility for some protector state to intervene, whether it be the national state of the company, based on a general rule of diplomatic protection, or in a secondary capacity the national state of the shareholders claiming protection.

The Court then considered the adoption of the theory of diplomatic protection of the shareholders, but concluded that by opening the door of competing diplomatic claims this would create an atmosphere of confusion and insecurity in international economic relations. This would be intensified as companies are engaged in international activity and the shares of companies are widely scattered and frequently change hands. The Court maintained the essence of a secondary right of protection would only come into existence at the time when the original rights cease to exist.

The Court therefore dismissed the submission that the right of protection which lies with the national state of a company was not extinguished simply because the national state had chosen not to exercise that right. Thus it was not possible to accept that in such circumstances the national states of shareholders enjoy a right of protection, secondary to the company's state of nationality.

The Court held that to reconcile the discretionary power of the company's national state, with a right of protection for the shareholders' national state, would be particularly difficult if the former state had concluded with the state which had caused injury to the company, an agreement providing the company compensation which the foreign shareholders found inadequate.

This would be the case if, after such an agreement had been concluded, the national state of the foreign shareholders could, in turn, put forward a claim based on the same facts.

Thus in this particular case, it was concluded that the Barcelona Traction Co, as a company was never reduced to a position of impotence form which it could not have approached Canada, the state of nationality, to ask for diplomatic protection. There was nothing to prevent, in the Court's view, Canada, if it wished, from continuing to grant diplomatic protection to the company.

Accordingly, the decision of Canada to cease extending diplomatic protection did not provide Belgium with a right of intervention on behalf of the shareholders. 1970 ICJ Reports 3.

Commentary
The Court in this case expressed the view that no absolute test of the "genuine connection" had been accepted in international law in respect of companies. A company's state of nationality enjoyed the right to bring the claim, and in this particular instance the fact the company was still in existence meant the state of nationality retained that right. The state of the shareholders' nationality did not enjoy a residual right of protection which was triggered when the state of the company's nationality chose not to exercise its espousal a claim on behalf of the company. Only in the event of the company no longer existing might a claim be advanced by the shareholder's state of nationality. This case establishes that the norm is a right of protection lies with the company's state of nationality. A company's nationality is normally decided as being the state wherein it is registered. The guidelines as set out here have been followed, for example by the UK in the Rules Regarding International Claims.

ENVIRONMENT

Key Principles: **A state has a responsibility to protect other states from injurious acts originating within its jurisdiction. A Tribunal may apply, as the appropriate law—domestic as well as international—and practice, in resolving a dispute.**

Trail Arbitration United States v Canada (1931–41)

Facts: In 1896 a smelter was started near Trail in British Columbia. The smelter was acquired in 1906 by the Consolidated Mining and Smelting Company of Canada Ltd. The company continued to operate the smelter and from 1925 until at least 1937 the sulphur dioxide emitted from the smelter caused damage in the State of Washington in the US.

Initially, attempts were made to resolve the problem by means of an investigation by an International Joint Commission, however these were unsuccessful and in 1935 Canada and the US negotiated a specific arbitration agreement.

The Tribunal was confronted with a number of questions including whether the damage caused by the Trail smelter in the State of Washington had occurred since the first day of 1932 and if so, what indemnity should be paid. In the event of an affirmative answer to question one, should Trail smelter be required to refrain from causing damage in the state of Washington in the future, and if so, to what extent? What measure of regime, if any, should be adopted or maintained by Trail smelter and what indemnity or compensation, if any, should be paid on account of any decision or decision rendered by the Tribunal?

Issues raised by the Tribunal included the extent to which the questions should be answered on the basis of law, as followed in the US, or on the basis of international law.

Held: The Tribunal looked at a number of decisions from US domestic law and international law and concluded that these decisions, taken cumulatively provided an adequate basis for the Tribunal's conclusions. Under the principles of international law, as well as US domestic law the Tribunal found no state had the right to use or permit the use of its territory in such a manner so as to cause injury by fumes to the territory of another, or to the properties or to persons within that territory. This was the case when serious consequences ensued and injury was established by clear and convincing evidence.

The Tribunal held that Canada was responsible in international law for the conduct of Trail smelter and it was Canada's duty to see that this conduct was in conformity with Canada's obligations under international law.

Accordingly, the Tribunal held that as long as the conditions in the Columbia River valley prevailed, Trail smelter should refrain from causing any damage, through the emission of fumes, in the State of Washington. (1931–41) 3 RIAA 1905.

Commentary

The Tribunal in this case utilised the principle of state responsibility to determine Canada's obligations. The use of state responsibility became standard when dealing with matters of the environment until the precautionary approach was adopted. The precautionary approach was recognised as being more suitable for dealing with issues relating to the environment, particularly as it emphasised preventing damage. In contrast, state responsibility could only be utilised after the damage had occurred. It may also be noted that the Tribunal acknowledged that US domestic law reflected general rules of international law.

Key Principle: **Further endorsement that a state has a responsibility to protect other states from injurious acts perpetrated from within its territory.**

Lake Lanoux Arbitration, France v Spain 1957

Facts: A dispute arose between France and Spain over the use of Lake Lanoux. France proposed it be used for hydroelectric purposes, but Spain objected that a hydroelectric scheme would interfere with the flow of the boundary waters contrary to an agreement concluded between the two states in 1866.

Held: The Arbitration Tribunal initially found in favour of France to the effect that the hydroelectric scheme would not breach the 1866 Treaty. The Tribunal then discussed the conduct that was expected from France towards Spain in putting this scheme into operation. Spain had argued that prior agreement to the proposed scheme was demanded from both parties.

The Tribunal held that to require states to agree, before jurisdiction in a certain field could be exercised, was to place a restriction on the sovereignty of a state. Such a restriction could only be admitted on the basis of clear and convincing evidence. Although the Tribunal noted such restrictions had become a reality in some instances, it was held that in general in international practice these were the exception rather than the norm. International judicial decisions had been slow to recognise such restrictions, especially when to do so involved a fetter on the territorial sovereignty of a state, as it would in the instant case.

It was acknowledged that states were perfectly conscious of the importance of the interests brought into play by the industrial use of international rivers and of the necessity to reconcile these interests by mutual concessions. The only way to reach compromise was to conclude agreements on an increasingly comprehensive basis.

It was noted that whilst international practice was encouraging states to conclude such agreements, international practice did not go so far as permitting more than the rule that states could utilise the hydraulic power of international water courses only on condition of a prior agreement between the interested states. Such a rule could not be established as a custom, even less as a general principle of law.

As to how interests could be safeguarded, the Tribunal stated that if the method necessarily involved communications, it could not be confined to purely formal requirements, such as taking note of complaints, protests or representations made by the downstream state.

The Tribunal held that the upstream state was, according to the rules of good faith, under an obligation to take into consideration the various interests involved, and to afford them satisfaction compatible with its own interests, and to show it was genuinely concerned with reconciling the interests of the other riparian state with its own.

The upstream state had procedurally a right of initiative and was not obliged to involve the downstream state in the elaboration of its schemes. If, in the course of discussions, downstream states were to submit a scheme, the upstream state must examine such schemes, but it retained the right to give preference to the solution contained in its own scheme provided account was taken in a reasonable manner of the downstream state.

In the particular case, the Tribunal held that France had maintained throughout that the solution was to divert the waters with full restitution. In making this choice France was exercising its right. The development works of Lake Lanoux were on French territory, the financing of and the responsibility for the enterprise fell upon France, and France alone was the judge as to which works of public utility which were to be executed on her own territory.

Spain, on the other hand, could not invoke a right insisting on a development of Lake Lanoux based on the needs of Spanish agriculture. In effect, the Tribunal held that if France were to renounce all of the works envisaged on her territory, Spain could not demand that other works in conformity with her wishes be carried out. Spain could only argue for her interests to be reflected within the framework of the scheme as decided upon by France. The Tribunal then turned to consider whether this requirement had been fulfilled. Notwithstanding the fact the parties had failed to reach agreement, the Tribunal held that France had sufficiently involved Spain in the preparation of the development scheme. 1957 12 RIAA 218.

Commentary

The Lake Lanoux decision highlights, as indeed did the *Trail Smelter* (see above) and the *Corfu Channel* (see pp.49 and 72), that customary international law, as it existed prior to 1971, was inadequate for dealing with the increasing problem of trans-boundary environmental issues, either in general or with pollution in particular. The instances highlight that the concept of state responsibility was utilised to afford compensation after the damage had actually occurred. Since 1972 the increasing emphasis in dealing with environmental issues has been on a precautionary principle approach.

Key Principle: **A state is responsible for the injurious consequences of acts which have taken place within its territory.**

Gut Dam Arbitration (1969)

Facts: The Gut Dam was built by Canada with the consent of the US across their international boundary on the St Lawrence River. The dam raised the water levels of Lake Ontario during the years 1947 and 1952 and caused considerable damage to the property owners on the US shore of the lake. Attempts made to sue Canada and the US government in the US courts proved unsuccessful.

A Foreign Claim Settlement Commission was authorised by US statute to investigate the Gut Dam claims, but before any decisions were handed down, the US and Canada agreed to establish an International Arbitral Tribunal to determine the claims of the US citizens.

Held: The Tribunal held in a number of preliminary decisions in favour of the US and Canada agreed to pay to the United States $350,000 in full settlement of all claims.

Commentary

The decisions in the above cases commencing with that in the *Trail Smelter* case (see above) underscore an obligation on states not to cause trans-boundary environmental damage. This principle has subsequently been reflected in international declarations and in international jurisprudence. Such declarations include Principle 21 of the Stockholm Declaration 1971 and

Principle 2 of the Rio Declaration 1992. The Trail Smelter principle was endorsed by the ICJ in the *Nuclear Test* case. 8 ILM 118 (1969).

9. USE OF FORCE

Key Principles: The right to self-defence is a customary rule of international law; the elements of the right to self-defence: necessity and proportionality.

Caroline Incident

Facts: In 1837, during the Canadian rebellion, the rebels managed to gain considerable support from Americans despite the attempts of the American authorities to prevent this. The rebel forces conducted attacks against passing British ships from the Navy Island in Canadian waters. *The Caroline* was an American ship that was supplying the rebels and was seized and destroyed by the British on the night of 29–30 December. During the British attack on the ship, two Americans were killed. The incident was followed by a correspondence between the British and American authorities which dealt with the legality of the attack in great detail.

Held: The right to self-defence is triggered by a necessity for self-defence. The necessity must be "instant, overwhelming, leaving no choice of means, and no moment for deliberation". Moreover, when such necessity exists, the actions taken in accordance with such necessity must not be unreasonably excessive as "the act, justified by the necessity of self-defence, must be limited by the necessity, and kept clearly within it". 29 B.F.S.P. 1137–1138, 30 B.F.S.P. 195–6.

Commentary
The Caroline incident remains the cornerstone of the international law on the right to self-defence as a rule of customary international law. In the correspondence which the incident precipitated two basic principles for the exercise of this right to self-defence were laid down: (a) necessity: the right to self-defence must be initiated by "instant, overwhelming, leaving no choice of means, and no moment for deliberation" necessity. It is a requirement that a right to self-defence must be exercised only when it is necessary, i.e. when a state has been attacked. This means that the right to self-defence is a last resort and a state, exercising this

right, must have no other option other than to engage its right to self-defence as opposed to exercising this right for punitive or retaliatory purposes. Moreover, (b) the self-defence must be proportionate to the act that triggered the right to self defence and thus the right to self-defence is limited as its aim must be to halt and repel an attack. However this does not necessarily mean that the state exercising its right to self-defence is only allowed to use the same weapons as the attacking state, for example. This means that the self-defence must be proportionate to the attack that triggered the necessity for self-defence. Both of these principles were elaborated by the ICJ in the *Nicaragua* case (see below), which is undoubtedly the seminal international law case in studies on the use of force. It is worth noting here that the ICJ in the *Nicaragua* case recognised these two elements as essential pre-requisites for the exercise of right to self-defence.

Regarding the time element of the exercise of the right to self-defence, many arguments have been raised about the condition of "leaving ... no moment of deliberation". This has been taken by some commentators as meaning that the right to self-defence must be exercised imminently after the necessity for it has been triggered. A right to self-defence cannot be exercised legally if an unjustifiable length of time has lapsed between the attack and the act of alleged self-defence. As to what constitutes a justifiable time the best answer to this, perhaps, is that just as the issue of whether the requirements of necessity and proportionality of self-defence are met, the time element can only be decided on the merits of each individual case.

Key Principles: **Prohibition of the use of force is a *jus cogens* rule; right to self-defence as a rule of customary international law; components of the right to self-determination: necessity and proportionality; collective self-defence; what constitutes an "armed attack"; principle of non-intervention and counter measures.**

Nicaragua case (Nicaragua v United States (Military and Paramilitary Activities in and against Nicaragua)) 1986

Facts: See p.4 for further discussion.

Held: See pp.5, 55 and 110 for further discussion.

Initially it was held that the international law on the use of force was not covered by the provisions of the UN Charter exclusively, and the ICJ specifically noted that Art.51 of the UN Charter refers to an "inherent" right to self-defence, thus pointing to the right of self-defence as a rule of customary international law. It was thus concluded that customary international law continues to exist alongside treaty law on the use of force. However, when examining the specific prohibition on the use of force as contained in Art.2(4) of the UN Charter, the ICJ held that this rule is not only a principle of customary international law, but constitutes a *jus cogens* norm.

Turning to the issue of self-defence, the ICJ first of all noted that the right to self-defence constituted an exception from the general prohibition on the use of force. The ICJ noted that the right to self-defence is a rule of customary international law, and then elaborated on its content. The principles deriving from the *Caroline* incident (see above) were affirmed as essential requirements for the exercise of the right to self-defence. Thus for the right of self-defence to arise, an armed attack must have already taken place against the state which is claiming the right to self-defence and self-defence must conform to the principles of necessity and proportionality. The ICJ made a distinction between individual self-defence and collective self-defence, stating that in the latter case self-defence must still conform to the requirements of necessity and proportionality.

However, for the right to self-defence to arise, an armed attack must occur. The ICJ ruled that not every action can be considered as constituting an armed attack and stated that:

"it may be considered to be agreed that an armed attack must be understood as including not merely action by regular armed forces across an international border, but also 'sending by or on behalf of a State of armed bands, groups, irregulars or mercenaries, which carry out attacks of armed force against another State of such gravity as to amount to' (*inter alia*) an actual armed attack conducted by regular forces, 'or its substantial involvement therein.' (...) The Court sees no reason to deny that, in customary international law, the prohibition of armed attack may apply to the sending by a State of armed bands to the territory of another State, if such operation, because of its scale and effects, would have been classified as an armed attack rather than as a mere frontier incident had it been carried out by regular armed forces. But the Court does not believe that the concept of 'armed attack' includes not only acts by armed bands where such acts occur on a significant scale but also assistance to rebels in the form of the provision of weapons or logistical or other support. Such assistance may be regarded as a threat or use of force, or amount to the intervention in the internal or external affairs of other States" (para.195).

The ICJ also made a distinction between armed attack and a mere frontier dispute on the basis of "circumstances and motivations", but did not elaborate on these requirements in any more detail.

Turning to the issue of collective self-defence, the ICJ ruled that a state which is a victim of armed attack must itself form and declare the view that it has been attacked and therefore for the right to collective self-defence to arise, the victim state must request help from other states. Thus:

> "The Court concludes that the requirement of a request by the State which is the victim of the alleged attack is additional to the requirement that such a State should have declared itself to have been attacked" (para.199).

The ICJ examined Art.51 of the UN Charter, which deals with the right to self-defence and concluded that when exercising this right, states must report to the Security Council immediately. While noting that the right to self-defence in customary international law does not contain such an obligation of immediate reporting, the ICJ held that:

> "if self-defence is advanced as a justification for measures which would otherwise be in breach both of the principle of customary international law and of the Charter should be respected. Thus for the purpose of enquiry into the customary law position, the absence of a report may be one of the factors indicating whether the State in question was itself convinced that it was acting in self-defence (...)" (para.200).

Finally, the ICJ examined the principle of non-intervention and referred to the *Corfu Channel* case (see below). The ICJ reaffirmed that this principle "involves the right of every sovereign State to conduct its affairs without interference" and the ICJ recognised this right to be part of customary international law (para.202). This then led the ICJ to consider the question of counter measures as an exception to the prohibition of non-intervention: if one state breaches the principle of non-intervention against another state, is a third state justified in taking such action by way of counter measures against the first state which would otherwise constitute an intervention in its internal affairs? The Court observed that a right to employ counter measures:

"would be analogous to the right of collective self-defence in the case of armed attack, but both the act which gives rise to the reaction, and that reaction itself, would in principle be less grave" (para.210).

However the ICJ refrained from elaborating on the issue of counter measures generally and declared that "States do not have a right of 'collective' armed response to acts which do not constitute 'armed attack' (. . .)" (para.211). 1986 ICJ Reports 14.

Commentary

The *Nicaragua* judgment was the first pronouncement of the ICJ on the law on the use of force and to date it remains as one of the most authoritative statements on the matter. The judgment has been heavily criticised, especially so by the US writers, who were unhappy about the ICJ's brevity in its treatment of the issue of collective self-defence and disagreed with its approach to the customary international law. It should also be noted that two dissenting judges, Judge Ruda and Judge Oda, disagreed with the majority of the ICJ on the treatment of collective self-defence. The former felt that the ICJ should not have addressed the issue of self-defence at all since it had established that there was no armed attack, while Judge Oda felt that the ICJ had been far too brief on such a controversial topic as self-defence. Irrespective of these opinions, the *Nicaragua* judgment is the seminal decision on the law on the use of force and there are six main points that may be extracted from the decision.

First of all the ICJ declared that the prohibition on the use of force, as contained in Art.2(4) of the UN Charter constitutes a *jus cogens* norm of international law. This was contrasted to Art.51 of the UN Charter, which deals with the right to self-defence: while the right to self-defence was recognised to be a rule of customary international law, Art.51 was said not to be a perfect mirror of this customary rule since it required the state invoking the right to self-defence to inform the Security Council about this immediately.

Secondly, turning to the nature of the prohibition on use of force, the ICJ declared that there are exceptions to this and one of these exceptions is the right to self-defence, which can be individual or collective. The ICJ reaffirmed the two basic principles of self-defence: there must be an armed attack and the self-defence in response to this armed attack must conform to the principles established in the *Caroline* incident: necessity and proportionality. It is clear that in order to ascertain the legality of the exercise of the right to self-defence, these concepts must be unwrapped in the light of the circumstances of each individual case.

Thirdly, the ICJ elaborated on the meaning of "armed attack" by stating that the sending of armed bands or irregulars as opposed to regular army, could constitute an armed attack, if the scale and effects of such an operation would allow it to be classified as an armed attack and not just a frontier incident. The ICJ unfortunately did not elaborate on what would be the distinguishing features between an armed attack and a frontier incident. It only stated that such a distinction could be made on the basis of surrounding circumstances and motivations. The lack of any further elaboration on the distinction between the two has attracted considerable criticism. However it appears that the ICJ was attempting to draw a distinction between fully-fledged armed attacks and incidents where there has been no intention to carry out an armed attack, like accidental incursions or instances when orders are trespassed. In any case, the ICJ made a clear declaration that mere assistance to rebels, when a state is providing rebels with weapons or logistical or other support does not amount to armed attack, but could only be considered as a threat or use of force or intervention in internal or external affairs of the state. This is perhaps another of the more controversial points of the judgment, but nevertheless state practice conforms to this view.

Fourthly, the state against which the armed attack is directed must believe and declare that it has been attacked.

Fifthly, turning to the issue of collective self-defence, the ICJ declared that the victim state must issue a request and thus collective self-defence cannot be exercised in the absence of such a request. The ICJ specifically noted that Art.51 of the UN Charter inserts an additional requirement to the customary rule of self-defence: the obligation to report to the Security Council immediately. Thus, every case of collective self-defence must comply with the same requirements as individual self-defence: there must be an armed attack, the state must believe and declare it has been attacked and the response must conform to the principles of necessity and proportionality. In the case of collective self-defence there is also an obligation to report to the Security Council and while this requirement is not part of customary international law, the ICJ declared that:

"the absence of a report may be one of the factors indicating whether the state in question was itself convinced that it was acting in self-defence" (para.200).

Sixthly and finally, the ICJ reaffirmed the principle of non-intervention as elaborated in *Corfu Channel* case (see below) by stating that this principle involves the right of every state to conduct its internal affairs without outside interventions. However, on the issue of counter measures, the ICJ was brief and did not elaborate further. It did state, however, that there is no right of collective armed response to acts which do not constitute armed attacks. Consequently it is clear that the right to self-defence, both individual and collective, only exists when there has been an initial armed attack. For elaboration on the legality of counter measures see *Gabcikovo-Nagymaros Project* case below.

Key Principle: **The right to self-defence in Art.51 cannot be employed in arguing necessity to defend a state against the territory it has occupied and exercises control over.**

Legal Consequences of the Construction of a Wall in the Occupied Palestinian Territory Advisory Opinion 2004

Facts: See p.61 for further discussion.

Held: See pp.62, 161, 212 and 219 for further discussion.

Since Israel had claimed that the construction of the wall was necessary in order to prevent the violent attacks emanating from the occupied territories and thus constituted a legitimate exercise of self-defence by Israel, the ICJ examined the content of Art.51 of the UN Charter. The Court concluded while Art.51 indeed allows self-defence, it allows such self-defence only in the case of an armed attack by one state against another state. In the present case, since Israel was not claiming that the attacks were imputable to another state, Art.51 was not applicable. Moreover, the ICJ observed that Israel was exercising control over the occupied territory from which the threat originated, as Israel had itself argued. Thus the ICJ distinguished the situation from that described in the Security Council Resolutions 1368 (2001) and 1373 (2001) and declared that Israel had no right to self-defence in the instant circumstances of the case. 2004 ICJ Reports 134.

Commentary

This opinion is of particular significance in the contemporary context of a threat of terrorism as it provides important guidelines as to the ICJ's interpretation on the right to self-defence in case of terrorist attacks. The ICJ drew a distinction between the circumstances of the case and those of the September 11, 2001 attacks on the United States. In the present instance the ICJ paid special attention to the fact that the alleged threat of attacks was not originating from a different state, but rather from a territory under the control of Israel. Thus the Court concluded that Israel could not claim its right to exercise self-defence.

Key Principle: **Respect for territorial sovereignty and non-intervention in affairs of other states.**

Corfu Channel case (Merits) United Kingdom v Albania 1949

Facts: See p.152 for further discussion.

Held: See pp.57, 108 and 152 for further discussion.

The ICJ rejected the claim advanced by Britain that its mine sweeping activities were carried out on the basis of the theory of intervention: intervention to secure possession of evidence to be submitted to an international tribunal. It was stated that:

> "The Court can only regard the alleged right of intervention as the manifestation of a policy of force, such as has, in the past, given rise to most serious abuses and such as cannot, whatever be the present defects in international organisation, find a place in international law. Intervention is perhaps still less admissible in the particular form it would take here; for, from the nature of things, it would be reserved for the most powerful States, and might easily lead to preventing the administration of international justice itself."

The ICJ went on to reject the argument of self-protection or self-help advanced by Britain, stating that respect for territorial sovereignty is an essential foundation of international relations. 1949 ICJ Reports 4.

Commentary
The principle of non-intervention remains a basic tenet of international law as it rests on the principle of the sovereign equality of all states. It is important to note this principle especially in the light of Art.2(4) of the UN Charter which prohibits a threat or use of force against "territorial integrity or political independence of any state, or in any other manner inconsistent with the purposes of the United Nations". The ICJ in the *Nicaragua case* (see above) declared the principle of non-intervention described in the *Corfu Channel* case as a norm of customary international law and referred to it as "a corollary of the principle of sovereign equality of States" (para.202 of the *Nicaragua* judgment).

Key Principles: **The right to self-defence is a rule of customary international law, but must be exercised (1) in response to an armed attack and (2) be necessary and proportionate.**

Oil Platforms case (Merits) Iran v United States 2003

Facts: During the Iran-Iraq war, a number of merchant ships were attacked in the Persian Gulf which led the US and other countries to provide naval escorts for the ships flying their flags. Despite this, however, the *Sea Isle City*, a Kuwaiti tanker, flying the US flag for escort purposes, was hit by a missile in Kuwaiti waters in October 1987. In April 1988, the warship USS *Samuel B. Roberts* was damaged by a mine while on escort duty in international waters. Following each of these incidents, the US attacked Iranian oil platforms after the lapse of three and four days respectively, claiming to exercise its right to self-defence.

Iran claimed that the US attacks were in breach of the 1955 USA-Iran Treaty of Amity, Economic Relations and Consular Rights.

Held: The ICJ reaffirmed that the right to self-defence is a rule of customary international law and stated that for this right to arise there must have been an armed attack carried out by Iran against the US. Having examined the particular circumstances, the ICJ concluded that there was no armed attack: the *Sea Isle City* was hit in the Kuwaiti waters by a missile which was not directed at the ship flying the US flag, but any ship in these waters, while the *Samuel B. Roberts* was damaged by a mine in the waters where mines had been laid by both belligerents of the Iran–Iraq war. The ICJ did accept that the evidence presented that Iran is responsible for this particular mine was "highly suggestive" but decided it was not conclusive. Therefore it was held that:

> "The Court does not exclude the possibility that the mining of a single military vessel might be sufficient to bring into play the 'inherent right of self-defence'; but in view of all the circumstances, including the inconclusiveness of the evidence of Iran's responsibility for the mining of the USS *Samuel B. Roberts,* the Court is unable to hold that the attacks on the Salman and Nasr platforms have been shown to have been justifiably made in response to an 'armed attack' on the United States by Iran, in the form of mining of the USS *Samuel B. Roberts"* (para.72).

The ICJ went on to examine the other two requirements for the exercise of the right to self-defence, namely necessity and proportionality. First of all, the argument by the US that it had considered in good faith that these attacks were necessary and states should be allowed a measure of discretion in their good faith application of measures taken to protect their essential security interests was rejected by the ICJ. The Court stated that the requirement of international law that the measures taken allegedly in self-defence must have been necessary for that purpose is strict and objective and does not allow any room for a measure of discretion. Thus, turning to an examination of the issues of necessity and proportionality, the ICJ stated that one aspect that must be considered was "the nature of target of the force used avowedly in self-defence" (para.74). Noting that it was not convinced about the significance of the military presence and activity on the oil platforms, the ICJ concluded that the attacks were not necessary to respond to the two incidents. The Court particularly noted the fact that the US did not complain to Iran about the military activities on the platforms in marked contrast to its repeated complaints about mine-laying and attacks on neutral shipping. Such a pattern of actions led the ICJ to the conclusion that the US itself did not consider the attack on oil platforms as "necessary".

Finally, on the point of proportionality, the ICJ again turned to an examination of the US actions and determined that the attack on oil platforms took place within the remit of the wider operation "Operation Praying Mantis". The Court saw it impossible to assess the proportionality of the two attacks without looking at the operation as a whole. It was thus concluded that:

> "As a response to the mining, by an unidentified agency, of a single United States warship, which was severely damaged but not sunk, and without loss of life, neither 'Operation Praying Mantis' as a whole, nor even that part of it that destroyed the Salman and Nasr platforms, can be regarded, in the circumstances of this case, as a proportionate use of force in self-defence" (para.77).

2003 ICJ Reports 161.

Commentary

This judgment addresses some crucial aspects on the legality of self-defence. The ICJ first reaffirmed the right to self-defence and restated the circumstances when and how this right can be exercised: in response to an armed attack, strictly adhering to the principles of necessity and proportionality. Any advances on allowing states a measure of discretion in deciding how to respond were strictly rejected.

Secondly, the ICJ engaged in a detailed examination of the facts thereby showing that setting precise definitions of what may constitute an armed attack is impossible. In this case the existence of an armed attack, or rather lack of it, was decided on a purely factual basis, but the ICJ did refer to its judgment in the *Nicaragua* case where an armed attack was described as the "most grave" form of the use of force. The factual circumstances of this case did not reach this "most grave" threshold.

Thirdly, on the points of necessity and proportionality, the ICJ again turned to a detailed examination of the facts surrounding the case. The past behaviour of the US led the ICJ to the conclusion that the attack on oil platforms was not considered as "necessary" by the US itself. Also the gravity of the US response was seen as disproportionate.

Key Principle: **Legality of reprisals.**

Naulilaa case (Responsibility of Germany for damages caused in the Portuguese colonies in the south of Africa) (Portugal v Germany) (1928)

Facts: Germany conducted a military raid on Naulilaa and outposts in the Portuguese colony of Angola, following the mistaken killing of three German nationals there. The Portuguese claimed compensation from Germany before the arbitration tribunal. One of the central questions was what constituted reprisals and their legality in international law.

Held: The Tribunal held that reprisals are acts of self-help which the victim state may employ in response to a prior act which was contrary to the law of nations, but only if the victim state's demand for reparations has not been satisfied. Reprisals must be proportionate to the offence committed since their aim is to impose on the offending state reparation or the return to legality. (1928) 2 RIAA 1011.

Commentary
Reprisals are acts which per se would be illegal, but can be justified if the three conditions laid down in the *Naulilaa* case are satisfied: existence of a prior illegal act; unsatisfied demand by the victim state and proportionate response to the prior illegal act. However, today it has to be borne in mind that reprisals are subject to the general prohibition on the use of force and the rules governing self-defence. Any reprisals involving the use of force today must conform to the same rules governing the use of force in international law. As the ICJ held in the *Legality of the Threat or Use of Nuclear Weapons* case (see below), armed reprisals undertaken during peace time are considered unlawful unless exercised in the framework of the right to self-defence and conform to the requirements of legality of self-defence, i.e. armed attack, necessity and proportionality.

Key Principles: **Legality of threat of and use of force; legality of threat and use of nuclear weapons; legality of reprisals.**

Legality of the Threat or Use of Nuclear Weapons case
Advisory Opinion 1996

Facts: See p.7 for further discussion.

Held: See pp.7, 56 and 200 for further discussion.

ICJ first of all noted that Art.2 (4) of the UN Charter prohibits use or threat of use of force and the only exceptions to this general prohibition are found in Art.51, which allows self-defence and Art.42, which empowers the Security Council to authorise a use of force. Since the question posed to the ICJ concerned the legality of use or threat of use of nuclear weapons specifically the ICJ observed that no illegal weapons may used under the two exceptions provided for in the UN Charter.

Turning to the issue of self-defence, the ICJ reiterated that the requirements of necessity and proportionality of self-defence are rules of customary international law. The Court specifically addressed the issue of proportionality in case of nuclear weapons by stating that:

> "it suffices for the Court to note that the very nature of all nuclear weapons and the profound risks associated therewith are further considerations to be borne in mind by States believing they can exercise a nuclear response in self-defence in accordance with the requirements of proportionality" (para.43).

The ICJ addressed the issue of threat of use of force and stated that threat of use of force is illegal if the envisaged use of force itself would be illegal. Thus:

> "if it [threat of use of force] is to be lawful, the declared readiness of a State to use force must be a use of force that is in conformity with the Charter" (para.47).

The ICJ turned to an examination of the threat of use of nuclear weapons in the specific and noted that many states had employed the policy of deterrence by possessing nuclear weapons. The mere possession of weapons was not recognised as a threat and the ICJ stated that the intention to use nuclear weapons must be credible to constitute a "threat" in the meaning of Art.2(4) of the UN Charter. Whether that is so would depend on the specific circumstances of each case.

The ICJ then turned to an examination of the law on armed conflict to establish whether nuclear weapons are legal, making a link between the law on use of force and law of armed conflict. However, upon the examination of the existing treaty law and the customary international law, the ICJ found lack of agreement among the states in their treatment of nuclear weapons. The Court noted that there appeared to be a trend towards a general prohibition of nuclear weapons, but concluded that as yet no uniform view had been formed. By seven votes to seven, with the casting vote of the President, the ICJ stated that it was unable to:

> "conclude definitively whether the threat or use of nuclear weapons would be lawful or unlawful in an extreme circumstances of self-defence, in which the very survival of a State would be at stake" (para.105).

1996 ICJ Reports 226.

Commentary

This is an Advisory Opinion, which contains important views of the ICJ regarding the issues of threat and/or use of force. The ICJ made it clear that a threat to use force would be illegal if the use of force itself would be illegal. In other words, it would have to comply with the requirements of self-defence or be authorised by the Security Council. Furthermore, it is clear from the Advisory Opinion that the ICJ considers the type of weaponry to be a part of the proportionality requirement in the case of self-defence. Moreover, the ICJ also made a link between the law on use of force and the law of armed conflict by stating that any use of force which meets requirements of necessity and proportionality of self-defence, must still comply with the law of armed conflict to be legal. Therefore, if a State should employ arms or warfare prohibited by law of armed conflict, it could not justify such a use of force by the two exceptions to the general prohibition on the use of force.

However the ICJ was unable to reach a definitive answer to the question posed and noted the difference between states who possess nuclear weapons and employ the policy of deterrence and other states, who argue in favour of total prohibition of nuclear weapons. The Court concluded that this tension between the two groups of states had prevented the formation of *opinio juris* on the matter. Nevertheless, the ICJ suggested that the best way of reconciling these two positions in its view would be complete nuclear disarmament and unanimously agreed that states are obliged to pursue in good faith and bring to conclusion negotiations leading to nuclear disarmament.

The ICJ in this Advisory Opinion also upheld the *Naulilaa* case principle that the reprisals undertaken in time of peace are unlawful unless they form part of lawfully exercised self-defence.

Key Principle: **The legality of counter measures.**

Gabcikovo-Nagymaros Project case (Hungary v Slovakia) 1997

Facts: See p.15 for further discussion.

Held: See p.16 for further discussion.

The ICJ elaborated on the legality of counter measures and stated that for a counter measure to be legal in international law it must first of all be taken in response to a previous international wrongful act of another state and must therefore be directed against that state. Secondly the Court stated that the injured state must have called upon the state who had committed the wrongful act to discontinue the act in question or to make reparations for it. Furthermore, the counter measure must fulfil the requirement of proportionality: "the effects of the counter-measure must be commensurate with the injury suffered, taking account of the rights in question" (para.85). Finally, the purpose of the counter measure must be to induce the wrongdoing state to comply with its obligations and therefore the counter measure must be reversible.

The Court then applied this test to the actions of Czechoslovakia and declared that the counter measures taken by Czechoslovakia did not fulfil the proportionality criteria. This failure came about through Czechoslovakia unilaterally assuming control of a shared resource thus depriving Hungary of its right to an equitable and reasonable share of natural resources. The ICJ declared that it was therefore not necessary to establish whether Czechoslovakia had complied with the last requirement of the legality of counter measures. 1997 ICJ Reports 7.

Commentary
In this case the ICJ elaborated on the content and showed the application of the legality criteria for counter measures in international law. A four-step test was established: (i) there must be an initial wrongful act in response to which a counter measure is taken; (ii) before taking the counter measure, the injured state must call on the state who has committed the wrongful act to discontinue it or make reparations for it; (iii) the countermeasure must be proportionate; and (iv) since the aim of the counter measure is to make the wrongdoing state to comply with its obligations under international law, the counter measure must be reversible.

For use of force as counter measure see *Nicaragua* case above.

Key Principles: **Measures of collective security; peacekeeping may be authorised even though it is not explicitly mentioned in the UN Charter.**

Certain Expenses of the United Nations case, Advisory Opinion 1962

Facts: The General Assembly requested an Advisory Opinion from the ICJ after some UN members failed to pay their membership fees, on the grounds that the expenses of certain UN peacekeeping missions were not legitimate expenses of the UN. The argument was that expenditures pursuant to GA Resolutions relating to operations undertaken in the Congo (ONUC) and in the Middle East (UNEF) did not amount to expenses of the UN within the terms of Art.17(2) of the UN Charter. Those members who refused to pay did so on the grounds that the operations related to activities which were ultra vires to the General Assembly and not activities authorised by the Security Council.

Held: The ICJ upheld the legality of the UN peacekeeping missions even though the UN Charter does not mention these measures specifically. The ICJ endorsed the right of the Security Council to authorise use of military force even in the cases when agreements mentioned in Art.43 of the UN Charter have not been concluded. Moreover, the Court concluded that:

"expenditures [relating to peacekeeping missions] must be tested by their relationship to the purposes of the United Nations in the sense that if an expenditure were made for a purpose which is not one of the purposes of the United Nations, it could not be considered an 'expense of the Organisation'."

The two peacekeeping missions at the centre of the Advisory Opinion were found to correspond to the aims and purposes of the United Nations as stated in the Charter and therefore the expenses related to these missions were established as expenses of the organisation. 1962 ICJ Reports 151.

Commentary

In 1950 the General Assembly, being concerned over the inability of the Security Council to act in cases when there was a threat to international peace and security due to the veto powers of its permanent members, passed the *Uniting for Peace Resolution*. This Resolution provided the possibility for emergency meetings when the Security Council is unable to act due to the veto being exercised by one of the permanent members. The General Assembly may recommend collective measures for the maintenance of international peace and security, including the use of force, when the situation is such that there is a threat to or breach of international peace and security. This is precisely what the General Assembly did and the legality of such peacekeeping missions was upheld in the Advisory Opinion by the ICJ. Since then it has been the Security Council which has authorised the deployment of the peacekeeping missions.

It should also be noted that this Advisory Opinion deals with the peacekeeping missions and does not specifically mention operations taken in accordance with Art.42 of the UN Charter. However it is generally accepted that the same line of reasoning would apply to Art.42 operations too.

10. JUDICIAL SETTLEMENT OF INTERNATIONAL DISPUTES

Key Principles: An international dispute is a disagreement on a point of law or fact, a conflict of legal views of interest between two persons. If there are two versions of a treaty possessing equal authority, but one version is of larger scope than the other, the Court is required to adopt the more limited interpretation which simultaneously is in conformity with both versions and accords with the intentions of the parties. A state which espouses a claim on behalf of one of its nationals is in effect exercising its own right.

Mavrommatis Palestine Concession case 1924

Facts: An action was initiated by the Greek Government against the British for an alleged refusal by the Palestinian Authorities (under British Mandate) to recognise the rights which Mr Mavrommatis had acquired under contracts. These contracts Mr Mavrommatis had entered into with the Ottoman Empire which was the predecessor sovereign in Palestine.

Held: See p.50 for further discussion.
    The Court ruled that although initially the dispute was one between a private person and a state, once it had been taken up by the Greek Government the dispute became one between two states and it entered the domain of international law. It was in this context that the Court gave its definition of an international dispute. The Court then continued that in taking up the claim on behalf of one of its own nationals, the state was in reality asserting its own right. Therefore PCIJ held that it was irrelevant from an international standpoint where the dispute originated from, as once a state had taken up a case on behalf of one of its subjects before an international tribunal, the state became the sole claimant. 1924 PCIJ Reports Series A No.2 12.

Commentary
This decision highlights that states are the primary subjects of international law and a state, when taking up a claim on behalf

of one of its own subjects, is in effect exercising a sovereign right of its own.

Key Principles: **States are under an obligation to enter into negotiations. Such negotiations should be undertaken with a view to arriving at an agreement. The obligation on states is to conduct themselves so that the negotiations are meaningful. Meaningful means that a negotiating state cannot insist upon its own position without contemplating a modification.**

North Sea Continental Shelf cases (Federal Republic of Germany v Denmark) and (Federal Republic of Germany v Netherlands) 1969

See pp.1, 52, 105 and 110 for further discussion.
  1969 ICJ Reports 3.

Key Principle: **The ICJ can only exercise jurisdiction over a state with its consent.**

East Timor case (Portugal v Australia) 1995

Facts: This case came before the ICJ by way of Art.36(ii) of the ICJ Statute whereby Portugal made an application against Australia. Portugal alleged that Australia had not respected the rights of Portugal when, as the administering power of East Timor, it entered into an agreement with Indonesia in 1989, and that by doing so Australia had failed to respect the right of the East Timor people to self-determination.

Held: See pp.61 and 223 for further discussion.
  The Court held that to give a judgment, as requested by Portugal, would in effect constitute a determination that Indonesia's continued presence in East Timor was unlawful and as a consequence East Timor would not have a treaty making power in matters relating to the continental shelf resources (the treaty in question related to the limitation of the continental shelf between East Timor and Australia). The ICJ declared that it could not give

a judgment in the absence of Indonesia since such a judgment would in essence determine the rights and obligations of Indonesia. To give such a judgment without Indonesia being a party to the proceedings would run contrary to the well-established principle of international law embodied in the ICJ Statute that the Court may only exercise jurisdiction over a state with the state's consent. 1995 ICJ Reports 90.

Commentary

The Court thus endorsed what had been said previously in *Monetary Gold Removed from Rome in 1943* 1954 ICJ Reports 32.

This case underlines the well-established principle in the practice of the ICJ that the Court will not exercise jurisdiction in the absence of a party's consent. Given that the proceedings in this case were initiated between Portugal and Australia, but in effect concerned the rights and obligations of Indonesia, the ICJ declared that giving a judgment would run counter to the said principle.

Key Principle: **Consent to the Court's jurisdiction need not be expressed in any particular form.**

Corfu Channel (Preliminary Objections) 1948

Facts: The United Kingdom made a unilateral application to the ICJ and maintained that the Court had jurisdiction by virtue of Art.36(I) of the ICJ Statute. The United Kingdom maintained the matter was one which had been specially provided for in the Charter of the UN. The UN had recommended to both parties that the dispute be referred to the ICJ. The Albanian Government had accepted the invitation and the conditions laid down by the Security Council. The United Kingdom also maintained that members of the UN agreed to accept and carry out decisions of the Security Council in accordance with the UN Charter. Albania had accepted the invitation of the Security Council to take part in discussing the dispute and had accepted the condition laid down by the Security Council. That condition contained in the invitation to participate in discussions was:

> "that Albania accepts in the present case all the obligations which a Member of the United Nations would have to assume in a similar case."

Albania had been informed of the application by the Court Registry and had responded by a letter of July 2, 1947. However Albania subsequently filed a preliminary objection to the Court's jurisdiction.

Held: The Albanian letter of July 2, was accepted as being a voluntary and indisputable acceptance to the Court's jurisdiction. The Court did this by reference to the wording of the letter in which Albania "fully accepts the recommendation of the Security Council" and accepted the "jurisdiction of the Court for this case". The Court held that while the consent of the parties confers jurisdiction on the Court, neither the Court Statute nor the Court's rules require this consent be expressed in any particular form. 1948 ICJ Reports 15.

Key Principle: **That conditions regarded as integral to a state's reservations contained in a compulsory acceptance of the ICJ's jurisdiction are conditions that must be complied with, either in the case of determination or modification.**

Nicaragua case (Jurisdiction and Admissibility) (Nicaragua v United States) 1984

Facts: In 1946 the United States (US) had made a declaration under Article 36(ii) of the ICJ Statute, making the termination of the ICJ's jurisdiction over the US conditional upon receiving six months notice. In 1984 the US made a declaration limiting its acceptance of the Court's jurisdiction. Jurisdiction was excluded in disputes with any Central American state or arising out of or related to events in Central America, stating that any such disputes were to be settled in a manner to which the parties would agree.

This provision was, notwithstanding the terms of the 1946 declaration, to take effect immediately and to remain in force for two years. The US was prompted to make this declaration in 1984 once it was evident that the dispute with Nicaragua was to be brought before the Court.

Held: The Court recognised that declarations accepting the compulsory jurisdiction are ones that states may or may not make and that states may also make such declarations with or without a condition, without a time limit for their duration. A state may also limit the ICJ's jurisdiction to disputes arising after a certain date.

The effect of such declarations is that although they are unilateral acts they establish a series of bilateral engagements with other states which accept the same obligation of compulsory jurisdiction. The Court declared that in finding the common ground, the conditions, reservations and time limit clauses are taken into account.

In the instant case the ICJ held that the six months' notice clause formed an important and integral part of the US declaration and it constituted a condition that had to be complied with in case of either termination or modification of the said declaration. Consequently, the 1984 notification that the withdrawal from the Court's jurisdiction on matters relating to Central America was to take immediate effect, would not override the US obligation to submit to the compulsory jurisdiction of the Court. 1984 ICJ Reports 392.

Commentary
The judgment of the ICJ, and in particular its findings regarding the jurisdiction, led the US on October 7, 1985 to give six months' notice in accordance with its 1946 declaration, thus terminating the US acceptance of the ICJ's jurisdiction.

Key Principle: **Declarations including a reservation contained in the declaration will be interpreted in a natural and reasonable way.**

Fisheries Jurisdiction, Spain v Canada case 1998

Facts: Spain initiated proceedings against Canada alleging that Canada had violated the international law of navigation and fishing of the high seas as well as the right of exclusive jurisdiction of the flag state over its ships on the high seas. The case arose following the apprehension on the high seas of a Spanish registered fishing boat by a Canadian patrol boat.

Held: The Court held that it is for each state to decide upon the limitations it places upon its acceptance of the ICJ's jurisdiction. Decisions or reservations, do not by their terms, derogate from a wider acceptance already given. There is no reason to interpret conditions or reservations restrictively and all elements in a declaration made under Art.36(ii) should be read together and interpreted accordingly; a declaration accepting the Court's jurisdiction is an act of state sovereignty. It establishes a consensual bond and the potential for a jurisdictional link with other states which have made a declaration pursuant to Art.36(ii).

The interpretation of declarations, however, is not identical to that established for the interpretation of treaties by the 1969 Vienna Convention of the Law of Treaties. That Convention is only to apply to the extent that it is compatible with the *sui generis* character of the unilateral acceptance of the Court's jurisdiction. Although a unilateral sovereign act, the Court acknowledged, the intention of the depositing state is important. Relevant words of the declaration including any reservation contained in the declaration are to be interpreted in a natural and reasonable way with due regard to the intention of the state concerned, at the time of its acceptance of the compulsory jurisdiction of the Court. That intention can be deduced not only from the text of the relevant clause, but also from the context in which the clause is to be read and an examination of the evidence regarding, for example the purposes intended to be served.

The Court highlighted that reservations from the Court's jurisdiction may be made by states for a variety of reasons and noted that there was a fundamental distinction between the acceptance by a state of the Court's jurisdiction and the compatibility of particular acts with international law. Acceptance of the Court's jurisdiction requires consent, whereas compatibility of particular acts with international law may only be required when the Court has dealt with the merits of the case, after establishing its jurisdiction.

This was the response to the Spanish contention that in the case of doubt, reservations contained in declarations should be interpreted consistently with the law and any interpretation inconsistent with the Statute of the Court; the Charter of the UN; or with general international law should be held inadmissible. However, the Court maintained that nowhere in its previous case law had it been suggested that interpretation in accordance with legality, under international law of the matter exempted from the jurisdiction of the Court, was a rule governing the interpretation of such reservations. 1998 ICJ Reports 432.

Commentary
In this particular case the Court applied the Canadian reservation and concluded that the dispute fell within the terms of the reservation as contained in Canada's declaration. Accordingly the Court found it had no jurisdiction to deal with the merits of the case.

Note: It is important that the reservation to a declaration be interpreted in a manner compatible with the effects sought by the reserving state. Note too, that although the ICJ may be precluded from exercising jurisdiction by virtue of Art.36(ii) the Court may nevertheless enjoy jurisdiction on another basis such as a clause in a treaty subsisting between the parties to a dispute. See *Appeal relating to the jurisdiction of the International Civil Aviation Organisation Council* case 1972 ICJ Reports 46.

Key Principles: **The effect of reciprocity in the case of declarations under Article 36(ii) of the ICJ Statute; obligation to exhaust local remedies.**

The Interhandel case Switzerland v US 1959

Facts: Switzerland initiated proceedings against the US before the ICJ in 1957, following unsuccessful legal proceedings in the US domestic forum. However, the US objected to the Court's jurisdiction on the grounds that even if a dispute before the Court arose at a date subsequent to the US declaration of 1946, it arose before July 28, 1948, the date of the entry into force of the Swiss declaration accepting the ICJ's jurisdiction.

The US maintained that the reciprocity principle was such that between the US and Switzerland the Court's jurisdiction was to be limited to disputes arising after July 18, 1948 only. To do otherwise would be to give retrospective effect to compulsory jurisdiction of the Court. It was also contented with regard to disputes arising after August 26, 1946 (the US acceptance date) but before July 28, 1948 that Switzerland, as a respondent, could have invoked the principle of reciprocity and claimed that in the same way as the US was not bound to accept the Court's jurisdiction with respect to disputes arising before its acceptance,

Switzerland too could not be required to accept the Court's jurisdiction in relation to disputes arising before its acceptance.

Facts and situations which have led to a dispute must/may not be confused with the dispute itself.

The case against the US by Switzerland was for the restitution of the assets of Interhandel, a Swiss company, in the US. The assets had been taken since 1942 by the US on the grounds that Interhandel was German and enemy controlled. This was contended by Switzerland and in 1948, following a number of years of negotiation, Switzerland asked the US to return Interhandel's property this the US refused to do.

Held: The Court held that the effect of reciprocity in the case of declarations made under Art.36(ii) was to enable a party to invoke a reservation to that acceptance which it had not expressed in its own declaration but which the other party had expressed in its declarations. The effect of reciprocity is to enable the state which has made the wider acceptance of the jurisdiction of the Court to rely upon the reservations to the acceptance laid down by the other party. There the effect of reciprocity ends. The effects of reciprocity do not allow a state to rely upon a restriction which the other party has not included in its own declaration. The Court rejected the preliminary objection of the United States.

The Court held that although Interhandel's assets had been seized in 1942, and although the disagreement between the parties, Switzerland and the US, over the issue of whether Interhandel was enemy or non-enemy, occurred before 1946, the dispute itself between the two parties occurred, in the Court's opinion, when the US refused Switzerland's request to return Interhandel's assets in July 1948.

The Court stated that local remedies must be exhausted before resort could be made to the international forum. The Court held that exhaustion of local remedies was a well-established principle in customary international law and that the forum state of the violation should have been given the opportunity to provide redress within its own domestic legal system. 1959 ICJ Reports 6.

Commentary
In this particular case, it was held that even though 10 years had lapsed, there were still viable domestic remedies to be exhausted.

Key Principles: Effect of a reservation; automatic self-judging reservation.

Norwegian Loans case, France v Norway 1957

Facts: The case involved national bonds issued before the First World War by Norway and two Norwegian banks. The bonds were owned by French nationals and initially contained clauses that France claimed, expressly promised and guaranteed payment in gold. Subsequently, Norway passed legislation providing for the payment of the bonds with Bank of Norway notes which were not convertible into gold. France took up the claim of its nationals and proposed, inter alia, that the dispute be referred to the ICJ. Norway, however, maintained that the bondholders' claims were exclusively within the jurisdiction of the Norwegian Court and these claims were solely matters of domestic law.

France initiated proceedings before the ICJ, whereas Norway contested the ICJ's jurisdiction, claiming that it could rely on the reservation contained in the French declaration. The French declaration, accepting the Court's jurisdiction, contained the reservation that the Court's jurisdiction was excluded in matters which "are essentially within the national jurisdiction, as understood by the Government of the French Republic". The Norwegian declaration did not contain such a reservation, however Norway maintained that it had a right to rely upon a reservation entered by France.

Held: The Court held that as the case had been brought on the basis of Art.36(ii) the jurisdiction of the Court depended upon the declarations made by the respective states on the basis of reciprocity. Jurisdiction was conferred upon the Court only to the extent to which the declarations coincided. The Court held that on the basis of a comparison between the two declarations, the French declaration reflected an acceptance of the Court's jurisdiction within narrower limits than did the Norwegian declaration. Thus, the Court held that the common will of the parties was as it existed within the narrower limits as indicated by the French reservation. Therefore Norway was exempted from the compulsory jurisdiction of the Court, if the dispute in question was understood by Norway to be essentially within its national jurisdiction. The validity of the reservation was not questioned and according to the Court, it was clear that France had fully maintained its declaration, including the reservation, and that Norway relied upon that reservation. 1957 ICJ Reports 9.

Commentary

The French reservation was of a type known as the automatic self-judging reservation, whereby a state making the reservation may decide for itself whether the matter falls within its domestic jurisdiction or is one of international law. However, the Court explicitly stated that it did not regard it as necessary to examine whether the French reservation was consistent with the undertaking of a legal obligation and compatible with Art.36(vi) of the Statue which provides that in the event of a dispute as to whether the Court has jurisdiction the matter is one to be settled by the Court itself.

Such reservations are contrary to the spirit of the ICJ's own Statute and could undermine the authority of the Court.

Key Principle: **Provisional measures demand "irreparable prejudice to the rights in issue".**

Aegean Sea Continental Shelf case (Greece v Turkey) Provisional Measures 1976

Facts: In this instance Greece made a request for interim measures to prevent Turkey from undertaking further exploratory measures within the area in dispute. Furthermore, a request was made for interim measures to prohibit any further military conduct which could represent a threat to peaceful relations.

Held: The Court held that the required proof to grant the provisional measures did not exist. The Court stated that granting provisional measures demands "irreparable prejudice to the rights in issue".

The Court in fact found that it did not have jurisdiction to hear the dispute. 1976 ICJ Reports 3.

Commentary

This case shows that provisional measures will be granted by the ICJ only in cases in which there is real risk of irreparable damage to the rights which are at stake in the particular proceedings.

Since this threshold was not reached in the present case, the request for provisional measures was not granted.

Key Principle: **An order of provisional measures is legally binding.**

La Grand case, Germany v United States 2001

Facts: The La Grand brothers, both German nationals, had moved to the US as young children with their mother, a German national, and had made the US their permanent home. The brothers were sentenced to death following their conviction for murder in 1984. Pursuant to the Vienna Convention on Consular Relations 1963, Art.36(i)(a), the brothers had a right to Consular access and to be informed of this right. However, they were not officially informed of the right by the United States until 1998. German representations to halt the executions were unsuccessful and one of the brothers was executed in 1999. On the day before the scheduled execution of the other brother, Germany filed an application to the ICJ instituting proceedings against the US, alleging a breach of the Vienna Convention, Art.36(i)(a), and made a request for provisional measures.

The ICJ indicated provisional measures, namely that the execution should not be carried out while the case was pending. However, the second brother was executed on the same day the Court indicated provisional measures.

Held: The Court looked at Art.41 of the ICJ Statue and considered both the French and English versions of the text. It was held that from the object and purpose of the ICJ's Statute, as well as from the terms of Art.41, when read in their context of the Statute, the power to indicate provisional measures entails that such measures should be binding. This arises from the need for such interim measures to be based on necessity when circumstances call for such measures to safeguard and avoid prejudice to the rights of the parties. The Court held that the contention that provisional measures indicated under Art.41 might not be binding was contrary to the object and purpose of Art.41.

The Court also looked at Art.94 of the UN Charter to ascertain whether that provision precluded attributing a binding effect to orders indicating provisional measures (Art.94 requires member states to comply with the decision of the ICJ in any case to which they are parties). The Court considered the interpretation to be attributed to the decision and held this could refer not only to the Court's judgments, but to any decision rendered by the Court thereby including any order for provisional measures. The Court thus held that orders on provisional measures under Art.41 have binding effects. 2001 ICJ Reports 466.

Commentary
The decision in the *La Grand* case unequivocally acknowledged the binding effect of an order for provisional measures. Such an order is legally binding and if not complied with can give rise to a claim against the offending state under international law.

Key Principle: **Interim measures will be ordered only if the Court is satisfied that it has at least prima facie jurisdiction to determine the merits of the case.**

Application of the Genocide Convention case, Order for Provisional Measures 1993

Held: The Court held that although the ICJ did not have to be finally satisfied that it had jurisdiction on the merits of the case, interim measures should not be ordered unless there would appear to be at least prima facie support for the Court having jurisdiction. 1993 ICJ Reports 3.

Key Principle: **A political dimension of a dispute does not prevent the ICJ from the exercise of its jurisdiction.**

Competence of the General Assembly for the Admission of a state to the United Nations case Advisory Opinion 1950

Facts: See p.17 for further discussion.

Held: See pp.17 and 81 for further discussion.

The Court declared that it cannot refuse to give an Advisory Opinion just because the question posed has some political aspects. 1950 ICJ Reports 4.

Commentary

This is one of the first instances when the ICJ rejected the argument that it should not exercise jurisdiction in cases containing a political dimension, be that either Advisory Opinions or contentious cases. (See cases below).

US Diplomatic and Consular Staff Tehran case (United States v Iran) 1980

Facts: See p.149 for further discussion.

Held: See pp.149 and 168 for further discussion.

The Court held that legal disputes occur between sovereign states and by their very nature are likely to occur within a political context. The Court emphasised that often a legal dispute may only be but one element in a wider and long standing political dispute between the relevant states. However, the Court maintained that there was no basis for denying its jurisdiction just because of the presence of a political element. There was no basis for this in the Court's jurisprudence, nor in the Charter of the UN or the statute of the ICJ. The ICJ held that if the Court were to accept such a restriction this would be a far reaching and unwarranted restriction upon the role of the Court in the peaceful solution of international disputes.

The Court acknowledged that whereas UN Charter Art.12 forbids the General Assembly from making any recommendations when a dispute or situation is before the Security Council there is no such restriction placed on the Court, either in its own statute or that of the UN since the Court is the principal judicial organ of the UN and its primary task is to resolve any legal disputes. Resolving disputes and legal questions is important and may also be a decisive factor in promoting the peaceful settlement of international disputes. 1980 ICJ Reports 3.

Commentary

This case is illustrative of the long standing approach adopted by the ICJ whereby it has consistently refused to accept that a political dimension of a dispute may preclude the Court from exercising its jurisdiction.

The WHO Regional Offices case (Interpretation of the Agreement of March 25, 1951 between the WHO and Egypt) Advisory Opinion 1980

Facts: See p.83 for further discussion.

Held: The ICJ stated that:

> "in situations in which political considerations are prominent it may be particularly necessary for an international organisation to obtain an advisory opinion from the Court as to the legal principles applicable with respect to the matter under debate" (para.33).

1980 ICJ Reports 73.

Commentary

This opinion confirms the ICJ approach whereby the existence of a political dimension to a dispute is not considered as a bar to the ICJ exercising its jurisdiction. In this opinion the ICJ went even further and declared that it is especially important for the Court to exercise its jurisdiction in cases when a dispute has a political dimension so as to provide parties with the guidance about the applicable legal principles.

Legality of the Threat or Use of Nuclear Weapons case Advisory Opinion 1996

Facts: See p.7 for further discussion.

Held: See pp.7, 56 and 193 for further discussion.
The Court affirmed that:

> "the political nature of the motives which may be said to have inspired the request and the political implications that the opinion given might have are of no relevance in the establishment of its jurisdiction to give such opinion" (para.13).

1996 ICJ Reports 226.

Commentary
This opinion reaffirms the approach of the ICJ in refusing to accept that any political implications that its judgment or advisory opinion may have bar it from exercising jurisdiction.

Legal Consequences of the Construction of a Wall in the Occupied Palestinian Territory Advisory Opinion 2004

Facts: See p.61 for further discussion.

Held: See pp.62, 161, 187 and 219 for further discussion.

The ICJ rejected the argument advanced that it should not exercise its jurisdiction in this case because of the "political" character of the question posed to the Court and referred to its long-standing jurisprudence on the matter (see the cases above). 2004 ICJ Reports 134.

Commentary
This opinion is the latest confirmation by the ICJ that it will exercise its jurisdiction over disputes which may have political implications.

Key Principle: **Example of an instance in which the Court refused to give an Advisory Opinion because to do so would have been tantamount to handing down a decision; a state may not be required to submit to dispute settlement mechanisms without having given its consent.**

Eastern Carelia case (1923)

Facts: An Advisory Opinion was requested by the League of Nations Council as to whether the USSR was in breach of its obligation imposed under a treaty subsisting between Finland and the USSR. The treaty in question concerned the area of Eastern Carelia. The Council of the League of Nations requested the Advisory Opinion as to whether that treaty and its annexe amounted to an obligation of an international nature which

Russia was required to discharge to Finland. The USSR, which incidentally was not then a member of the League, refused to appear before the Court.

Held: The Court expressed the view that to deliver an opinion on the proposed question would have a bearing on the actual dispute. The Court observed:

> "it was a fundamental principle of international law that no state could be compelled to submit a dispute to settlement without its consent".

The Court also observed the USSR possessed information that was essential to the determination of the opinion. (1923) PCIJ Series B No.5.

Commentary
This is the only occasion when an Advisory Opinion has been refused on the grounds that to do so would in effect be making a decision over an issue in dispute between the parties.

Key Principle: **Competence of the ICJ to review acts of the UN Security Council.**

Case Concerning Questions of Interpretation and Application of the Montreal Convention Arising out of Arial Incident at Lockerbie (Provisional Measures) Libya v the UK 1992

Facts: In January 1992 the Security Council, responding to a request from the US, the UK and France, adopted Resolution 731 urging Libya, inter alia, to respond to the request of the three states to extradite two Libyan nationals for trial in Scotland. This was in the wake of an aircraft being destroyed by a bomb over the town of Lockerbie, in Scotland, on December 21, 1988 when all on board were killed. Some of the victims were nationals of France, the US and the UK.

Libya also initiated proceedings against both the US and the UK under the 1971 Montreal Convention for the Suppression of Unlawful Acts Against the Safety of Civil Aviation, Art.14. Pursuant to Art.14 a convention party may unilaterally request the reference of a dispute concerning the interpretation or application of the Convention to arbitration. If agreement of a Tribunal is not made within six months of the request then a state may unilaterally refer the case to the ICJ. Libya, however, did not wish to wait six months. The ICJ was asked, by Libya, to declare that it had complied with its obligations under the Montreal Convention by:

1)   taking the required steps to investigate the case and prosecute the two Libyans; and

2)   the UK had breached the Convention by seeking to force Libya to return the alleged offenders and by not providing assistance for the Libyan proceedings.

Libya also applied to the Court for provisional measures.

The Security Council, subsequently, adopted Resolution 748 pursuant to Chapter VII of the UN Charter requiring Libya to return the alleged offenders and imposing sanctions against Libya for not doing so. This Security Council Resolution was also passed at the request of the US, UK and France. This was the second of two resolutions adopted by the Security Council, the earlier one being Resolution 731.

The request for interim measure was refused on the basis of Resolution 748.

Held: The Court declined to order interim measures of protection against the UK and the US because Resolution 748 had made a determination pursuant to Chapter VII of the UN Charter. This meant that in effect Libya was requesting interim protection contrary to British and US rights which the Security Council had deemed to be in need for protection. In other words, in declining the order for interim measures the Court deferred to the Security Council.

Although the Court itself in its judgment did not deal with the issue of the Court's competence to consider the legality of Security Council Resolutions a number of judges gave individual opinions in which they addressed this particular issue.

One such opinion was the dissenting opinion of Judge Weeramanatry in which he stated:

"this case has raised as perhaps no case has done in the past, certain questions of importance and interest concerning the respective functions of this Court and the Security Council ..."

Judge Weeramanatry recognised that the ICJ was not, within the UN system, vested with the review or appellate jurisdiction which may be found vested in the highest court within the domestic legal system. However he went on to say:

> "as a judicial organ, it will be the Court's duty from time to time to examine and determine from a strictly legal point of view matters which may at the same time be the subject of determination from an executive or political point of view by another principal organ of the United Nations ..."

What made the particular case before the Court of special importance was the fact the Court and the Council had been approached "by opposite parties to the dispute, each claiming a form of relief consistent with its own position". Judge Weeramanatry considered the respective roles of the Court and the Council and made reference to the *travaux preparatoires* of the UN Charter. He highlighted the history of the UN Charter was such so as to endorse that a clear limitation on the plenitude of the Security Council's powers is that those powers must be exercised in accordance with the well established principles of international law. 1992 ICJ Reports 3.

Commentary

Security Council Resolution 748 imposed an obligation upon Libya to extradite the alleged offenders whereas the 1971 Montreal Convention allows a state to use discretion and make a choice.

What may be extracted from this dissenting opinion of Judge Weeramanatry is the suggestion that the ICJ has competence, although admittedly the circumstances are as yet undefined, to adjudicate on the extent of the powers of the Security Council and the legality of any acts which may be called into question. The decision in the case was regarded by some as an abdication of the Court of its judicial role. However the Court has not consistently maintained such a differential role. For instance in the case *Concerning Armed Activities on the Territory of the Congo (Congo v Uganda) (Provisional Measures)* July 1, 2000, interim measures were ordered notwithstanding the Security Council having passed a Resolution demanding a cessation of hostilities. Note, however, that the difference here was that the Security Council demanded interim measures but in the Lockerbie case the Security Council had made a finding under Chapter VII of the UN Charter and determined the rights of the UK and the US should be protected.

See also *Legal Consequences of the Construction of a Wall in the Occupied Palestinian Territory Advisory Opinion* 2004 ICJ Reports 134 in which the Court made it unequivocally clear that when it is validly seized of an issue pursuant to the terms of its statute and the UN Charter it will not be dissuaded from considering the matter which is under consideration by the General Assembly or the Security Council.

11. HUMAN RIGHTS

Key Principles: The level of proof demanded for genocide; states can be held responsible for genocide, and of a complicity in genocide even in the absence of a conviction by a competent court of an individual; need for intent; need for positive characteristics to define the targeted group.

Application of the Convention on the Prevention and Punishment of the Crime of Genocide (Bosnia and Herzegovina v Serbia and Montenegro)

Facts: See p.154 for further discussion.

Held: See p.155 for further discussion.

The Court held that before acts may be characterised as genocide it must be evident that there is an intention to destroy the protected group either in whole or in part as such, *dolus specialis*. The Court distinguished between genocide and "ethnic cleansing" and commented on the legal significance of the latter term. The Court at para.190 observed that the term "ethnic cleansing" was not included in the Genocide Convention. Indeed, as was highlighted by the Court, efforts to include in the genocide definition, namely "measures intended to oblige members of a group to abandon their homes in order to escape the threat of subsequent ill treatment" had been rejected by the drafters of the Genocide Convention. The Court continued that ethnic cleansing could:

"only be a form of genocide within the meaning of the Convention, if it corresponds to or falls within one of the categories of acts prohibited by Article II of the Convention. Neither the intent, as a matter of policy, to render an area 'ethnically homogeneous', nor the operations that may be carried out to implement such policy, can *as such* be designated as genocide: the intent that characterizes genocide is 'to destroy, in whole or in part' a particular group, and deportation or displacement of the members of a group, even if effected by force, is not necessarily equivalent to destruction of that group, nor is such destruction an automatic consequence of the displacement" (para.190).

The Court, however, acknowledged that in certain circumstances acts described as "ethnic cleansing" could constitute genocide provided that is they were accompanied by the requisite *dolus specialis*. The Court further acknowledged that acts of "ethnic cleansing" could occur in parallel to acts prohibited by Art.II of the Genocide Convention and could also be "significant as indicative of the presence of a specific intent (*dolus specialis*) inspiring those acts". The Court held that although genocide demanded "substantial" destruction of the group, it nevertheless could occur where there is intent to destroy a "targeted" group within a geographically limited area as in the instance of the destruction of the Bosnian Muslims of Srebrenica. ICJ February 26, 2007.

Commentary

The decision in this case has ramifications beyond the states actually involved. The decision will contribute to the substantive body of law on the interpretation of the Genocide Convention and to the development of international law generally.

On the issue of responsibility, Art.I of the Genocide Convention was interpreted as imposing a direct obligation on Contracting Parties to prevent genocide, an obligation from which it could be inferred that states and not only individuals are prohibited from committing genocide as well as all other acts enumerated in Art.III. However several of the judges maintained a contrary stance and expressed the opinion that only individuals could commit the "crime of genocide". Some judges acknowledged that states would incur international responsibility for genocide if the acts in question perpetrated by individuals could be attributed to the state. On the other hand, other judges expressed the view that the Genocide Convention provided for the punishment of individuals so that attributing genocide to the state could be avoided.

The decision also illustrates a willingness on the part of the Court to accept evidence previously before, and accepted by, another judicial body. The case shows the interaction between the ICJ and the ICTY: the ICJ in this case accepted fact findings and judgments of the ICTY thus underlining the importance of respecting the ICTY and endorsing that the ICTY is an integral part of the UN human rights protection system. See also *Palestinian Wall* case below.

Key Principles: The human rights obligations that a state has undertaken extend to its occupied territories; derogations to human rights treaties must be proportionate and necessary for the aim to be achieved.

Legal Consequences of the Construction of a Wall in the Occupied Palestinian Territory Advisory Opinion 2004

Facts: See p.61 for further discussion.

Held: See pp.62, 161, 187 and 212 for further discussion.

The ICJ first of all observed that since Israel had been the occupying power of the Palestinian territories for the previous 37 years and had been exercising territorial jurisdiction over the area, the obligations it had undertaken under human rights treaties extend to the occupied territories.

In examining Israel's obligations under the international human rights treaties to which it is a party, the ICJ declared the protection afforded by human rights instruments, did not cease in the case of armed conflict unless a derogation had been made in the appropriate accepted manner. The ICJ, in this context, referred to General Comment No.27 of the Human Rights Committee and reinforced the view contained therein, namely that any derogation must pursue a legitimate aim; must be proportionate; and necessary for the achievement of that aim. The ICJ went on to examine the measures, namely the construction of the wall and the related activities, and concluded that the:

> "wall, along the route chosen, and its associated regime infringe a number of rights of Palestinians residing in the territory occupied by Israel, and the infringements resulting from that route cannot be justified by military exigencies or by the requirements of national security or public order" (para.137).

The Court concluded that Israel was in breach of its obligations under, inter alia, the 1966 ICESCR. 2004 ICJ Reports 134.

Commentary

This part of the Advisory Opinion is significant since the Court engaged in the interpretation of Israel's obligations under specific human rights treaties, and in doing so it referred to the Human Rights Committee, thus underlining the authority of this body.

Moreover, the Court also made a strong pronouncement that an occupying power cannot restrict the human rights of those in the occupied territory. In this case, since Israel was exercising territorial jurisdiction over the Palestinian occupied territory, the Court extended the applicability of the human rights treaties to which Israel is a party.

Key Principle: **Successor states are bound by the human rights obligations undertaken by the states they succeed.**

Case Concerning the Application of the Convention on the Prevention and Punishment of the Crime of Genocide (Bosnia and Herzegovina v Yugoslavia)

See pp.21 and 88 for further discussion. (Preliminary Objections) 1996

Key Principles: **Obligations** *erga omnes;* **prohibition of genocide; protection from slavery and racial discrimination as examples of** *erga omnes* **obligations.**

Barcelona Traction case (Belgium v Spain) (2nd Phase) 1970

Held: See pp.10, 11, 26 and 171 for further discussion.

The ICJ defined the meaning of *erga omnes* obligations and stated that these:

> "derive, for example, in contemporary international law, from the outlawing of acts of aggression, and of genocide, as also from the principles and rules concerning the basic rights of the human person, including protection from slavery and racial discrimination" (para.32).

1970 ICJ Reports 3.

Commentary
The definition of *erga omnes* provided by the ICJ in this case has become one of the most important and well-known statements of the Court on the issue of *erga omnes* rules. However the Court also gave examples of such *erga omnes* rules, which is important for international human rights law. It should be noted the list provided by the ICJ in this case is by no means exhaustive but merely illustrative.

Key Principles: **Principle of self-determination as a rule of customary international law; possible outcomes of self-determination; exercise of self-determination.**

Western Sahara case Advisory Opinion 1975

Facts: See p.98 for further discussion.

Held: See pp.58 and 98 for further discussion.
   The ICJ upheld the principle of self-determination of all peoples and noted its particular importance in bringing an end to colonial situations.
   Three possible outcomes for non-self-governing territories were distinguished:

   (i) emergence as a sovereign and independent state;

   (ii) free association with an independent state; and

   (iii) integration with an independent state.

The ICJ however emphasised that the main factor determining the choice between these three options must be the freely expressed will of the peoples concerned. The Court acknowledged that in the past the UN General Assembly had not consulted the peoples concerned on some occasions, but sought to make a distinction between those instances and the current one by maintaining that:

> "those instances were based either on the consideration that a certain population did not constitute a 'peoples' entitled to self-determination or on the conviction that a consultation was totally unnecessary, in the view of special circumstances".

Consequently the ICJ ruled that a full exercise of the principle of self-determination in the colonial context required consultation with the peoples concerned and that such peoples must have been given the opportunity to freely express their will.

The ICJ also recognised the principle of self-determination as a part of customary international law. 1975 ICJ Reports 12.

Commentary

This case is significant for international human rights law as it deals with one of the most significant and controversial collective rights, the right of peoples to self-determination.

This Advisory Opinion makes it clear that in the colonial context the right to self-determination constitutes a part of customary international law and sets out the ways this right can be exercised. See also *Namibia* Advisory Opinion below.

Key Principle: **Principle of self-determination is part of customary international law.**

Legal Consequences for states of the Continued Presence of South Africa in Namibia (South-West Africa) Notwithstanding Security Council Resolution 276 Advisory Opinion 1971

Facts: See p.18 for further discussion.

Held: See pp.18, 57 and 82 for further discussion.
The ICJ declared that:

"the subsequent development of international law in regard to non-self-governing territories enshrined in the Charter of the United Nations, made the principle of self-determination applicable to all of them" (para.52).

Thus the ICJ upheld the right of the peoples of Namibia to self-determination. 1971 ICJ Reports 16.

Commentary

In this Advisory Opinion the ICJ made it clear that the principle of self-determination is not just a political concept, but rather a legal one. The ICJ upheld its applicability in the context of colonial territories and trusteeships and declared that the exercise of this right involved the right of the concerned peoples to decide freely on their future. See also *Western Sahara* Advisory Opinion above.

Key Principles: **The right to self-determination is an obligation *erga omnes*; content of the right to self-determination.**

Case Concerning East Timor (Portugal v Australia) 1995

Facts: See p.199 for further discussion.

Held: See pp.161 and 199 for further discussion.

The ICJ ruled that the right to self-determination as evolved from the UN Charter and the practice of the UN is an *erga omnes* obligation and constitutes one of the essential principles of contemporary international law.

The ICJ also made it clear that the right to self-determination includes sovereignty over the natural resources of the country and may provide criteria for the resolution of disputes. 1995 ICJ Reports 90.

Commentary

The importance of the case for international human rights law is two-fold. Firstly the ICJ held that the right to self-determination of peoples is not just a right arising from customary international law, but constitutes an *erga omnes* obligation. Moreover, the circumstances of this case allowed the ICJ to make a further proclamation on the content of the right to self-determination: such aspects as sovereignty over natural resources and the applicable criteria for the resolution of disputes are also affected.

Secondly, in marked contrast to the *Western Sahara* and *Namibia* cases, this was not an Advisory Opinion but rather a judgment by the ICJ thus strengthening the claim that the right to self-determination is truly a rule of customary international law and an *erga omnes* obligation.

Key Principle: **Prohibition of torture is a rule of the law of the nations.**

Filartiga v Pena-Irala (2d Cir. 1980)

Facts: See p.41 for further discussion.

Held: See pp.41 and 137 for further discussion.

Having examined the sources from which customary international law is derived, namely the practice of states, judicial opinions and the work of jurists, the Court held that torture was prohibited by the law of nations. The prohibition was clear and unambiguous and admitted no distinction between the treatment of aliens and citizens. The Court compared a torturer to a slave trader and a pirate and named such to be the enemies of mankind. The Court recognised torture as a breach of a *jus cogens* norm. 630 F. 2d 876 (2d Circ. 1980).

Commentary

This case is an important example of the way domestic courts may establish jurisdiction for grave violations of human rights that have occurred elsewhere. In this case the US Court established its jurisdiction after finding that the prohibition of torture is a norm of *jus cogens*.

Key Principles: **Prohibition of torture is non-derogable; evidence obtained by torture is inadmissible in UK courts; burden of proof; threshold of burden of proof.**

A & Others v Secretary for the Home Department [2005]

Facts: The proceedings were initiated by 10 applicants who, with the exception of two, were certified and detained by the UK for an indefinite period of time in December 2001 under the Anti-Terrorism, Crime and Security Act 2001. Their appeal for release to the SIAC was dismissed. The applicants argued the evidence relied upon for the issue of their detention certificates had been obtained by torture administered by another state. This argument was rejected both by the Commission and the Court of Appeal and the case was brought before the House of Lords. The

House of Lords was composed of seven Law Lords as opposed to the usual five, highlighting the importance of the case.

Held: See p.38 for further discussion.

The House of Lords first addressed the issue of admissibility of evidence obtained by torture. It was held that from its earliest days the common law of England rejected the use of torture. This hostility towards the use of torture was inspired by the inherent unreliability of confessions or evidence produced through the practice of torture and by the belief that it degraded all those who lent themselves to the practice. The prohibition of torture was said to require states to do more than just avoid the practice of torture. Thus Lord Bingham maintained:

> "It would indeed be remarkable if national courts, exercising universal jurisdiction, could try a foreign torturer for acts of torture committed abroad, but could nonetheless receive evidence obtained by such courts." (para.35).

While recognising the immense difficulties faced by security and intelligence forces in the current climate of terrorism threats, Lord Bingham characterised the prohibition of torture as a non-derogable right. Therefore it was unanimously held that evidence obtained by torture irrespective of where obtained or by whom, is inadmissible in judicial proceedings in the UK.

The House of Lords then turned to the issue of the burden of proof. It was recognised that in cases like this the appellant may not know the name or identity of the author of an adverse statement relied on against him and may not see the statement or know what the statement says. Thus, while rejecting the idea of a presumption of torture, the House of Lords unanimously maintained that the appellant must ordinarily advance some plausible reason why evidence may have been procured by torture. It is then the task of the SIAC to initiate or direct such inquiry as necessary to make a fair judgment on whether the evidence has, or whether there is a real risk that it may have been, obtained by torture.

Finally, the House of Lords dealt with the issue of the threshold of the burden of proof. The majority of the House decided that in cases of doubt where it cannot be shown by the Secretary of State that the evidence has indeed been obtained by the use of torture, such evidence should be allowed. [2005] UKHL 71.

Commentary

This case illustrates the consequences of a total prohibition on torture: no evidence obtained by such means can be admissible in UK courts. It should be noted that this also conforms to the practice of the Human Rights Committee as expressed in its General Comment No.7 (para.12).

Moreover, the House of Lords not only unanimously rejected admissibility of such evidence, but also reversed the burden of proof. Thus, a duty was imposed on a state to show that no torture has been used in cases when a plausible argument has been advanced by an applicant that particular evidence against him/her has been obtained under torture.

Note: Below are selected findings of the Human Rights Committee. They are not judicial decisions but constitute the Human Rights Committee's jurisprudence on how the Articles of the ICCPR should be interpreted. These are also supplemented by General Comments which the Human Rights Committee has issued from time to time.

The following is only a selection of what may be regarded as important examples and as such are not intended to be comprehensive or exhaustive. In addition to the Human Rights Committee reference has also been made, for illustrative purposes only, to the views of other Treaty created bodies: the Committee against Torture; the Committee on the Elimination of all Forms of Racial Discrimination; and the Committee on the Elimination of Discrimination against Women.

The Human Rights Committee was established pursuant to Art.28 of ICCPR and the First Protocol (the Optional Protocol) provided for the right of individual communication.

Key Principles: **The concept of "victim"; Optional Protocol 1 of the ICCPR, Art.1, and a person may only be a victim if actually affected, no provision for *actio popularis*.**

(Mauritian Women case) Shirin Aumeeruddy-Cziffra and 19 other Mauritian Women v Mauritius (1981)

Facts: Twenty Mauritian women claimed the enactment of the Immigration (Amendment) Act, 1977, and the Deportation (Amendment) Act, 1977, by Mauritius constituted discrimination based on sex against Mauritian women, violation of the right to found a family and home, and removal of the protection of the courts of law, in breach of Arts 2, 3, 4, 17, 23, 25 and 26 of the International Covenant on Civil and Political Rights. The women claimed to be victims of the alleged violations and submitted that all domestic remedies had been exhausted.

The women claimed that prior to the enactment of the laws in question foreign men and women married to Mauritian nationals enjoyed the same residence status. In other words, foreign spouses of both sexes had the right protected by law to reside in the country with their Mauritian husbands or wives. The women contended that, under the new laws, foreign husbands of Mauritian women lost their residence status in Mauritius and had to apply for a "residence permit" which, apparently, could be refused or revoked at any time by the Minister of the Interior. The new laws, however, did not affect the status of foreign women married to Mauritian husbands who retained their legal right to reside in the country.

The women further contended that under the new laws foreign husbands of Mauritian women could be deported under a ministerial order which was not subject to judicial review.

Mauritius submitted that both acts had been passed following certain events in which some foreigners (spouses of Mauritian women) were suspected of subversive activities. Mauritius also maintained however, that the women did not allege that any particular individual had been the victim of any specific act in breach of the provisions of the ICCPR. Mauritius claimed the communication was aimed at obtaining a declaration by the Human Rights Committee that the Deportation Act and the Immigration Act, as amended, were capable of being administered in a discriminatory manner in violation of Arts 2, 3, 4, 17, 23, 25 and 26 of the ICCPR.

As far as the allegation of a violation of Art.25 of the ICCPR was concerned, Mauritius argued that if a citizen of Mauritius chose to go and live abroad with her husband because he was not entitled to stay in Mauritius, she could not allege she was thus denied the right to take part in the conduct of public affairs and to have access on general terms of equality to public service in her country. Mauritius maintained there was nothing in the law preventing the woman from exercising her Art.25 rights, although she might not be in a position to exercise the said rights as a consequence of her marriage and of her decision to live with her husband abroad.

Mauritius argued the exclusion of a non-citizen was lawful (the right to stay in a country not being one of the rights guaranteed by the provisions of the ICCPR) and such an exclusion (based on grounds of security or public interest) could not be said to be an arbitrary or unlawful interference with the family life of nationals in breach of Art.17 of the ICCPR.

The women claimed they were not concerned primarily with the rights of non-citizens (foreign husbands) but with those of Mauritian citizens (wives). They alleged that:

(a) female citizens unlike male citizens did not have an unrestricted right to married life in their country if they married a foreigner;

(b) the law, being retroactive, prevented female citizens from taking part in public life and restricted, in particular, the right of one of the women in this respect;

(c) the "choice" to join the foreign spouse abroad was only imposed on Mauritian women and that only they were under an obligation to "choose" between exercising their political rights guaranteed under Art.25 of the ICCPR, or to live with their foreign husbands abroad;

(d) the female citizen concerned might not be able to leave Mauritius and join her husband in his country of origin for innumerable reasons (e.g. health);

(e) by rendering the right of residence of foreign husbands insecure, Mauritius was tampering with a female citizen's right to freely marry and found a family.

Of the 20 women, 17 were unmarried and the remaining three were married to foreign husbands who had lost residence status following the coming into force of the Immigration (Amendment) Act, 1977. In the case of Mrs. Aumeeruddy-Cziffra, one of the three married women, more than three years had elapsed since her husband applied to the Mauritian authorities for a residence permit. However no formal decision had been taken. If her husband's application were to receive a negative decision, she would be obliged to choose between either living with her husband abroad and giving up her political career, or living separated from her husband in Mauritius and continuing to participate in the conduct of public affairs of that country.

Held: Pursuant to Art.1 of the Optional Protocol to the ICCPR, the Human Rights Committee only possesses a mandate to consider communications concerning individuals who are alleged to be themselves victims of a violation of any of the rights set forth in the ICCPR. The Committee based its views on the fact a distinction had to be made between the different groups of the authors of the communication. It was thus concluded that a person can only claim to be a victim in the sense of Art.1 of the Optional Protocol if he or she is actually affected.

However, no individual can in the abstract, by way of an *actio populari*, challenge a law or practice claimed to be contrary to the ICCPR, if the law or practice has not already been concretely applied to the detriment of that individual. It must in any event be applicable in such a way that the alleged victim's risk of being affected is more than a theoretical possibility. The Human Rights Committee found there had been a violation of Arts 2 (1) and 3 of the ICCPR, in conjunction with Art.17(1) for the three women who were married. (1981) 1 Selected Decisions H.R.C. 67.

Commentary
This opinion is the leading one on the interpretation of the notion of "victim". There is no provision for an action *actio popularis* in the ICCPR and if the alleged violation has not occurred to the detriment of the individual the likelihood of such must be more than an abstract possibility. In the present case only the three married women were in such a position.

The victim must be a natural person and not an artificial one, e.g. a company. However an NGO is competent to bring a claim on behalf of an individual provided the individual concerned has given authorisation or in the absence of authorisation there are grounds explaining the absence, e.g. the person may be in prison or deceased.

Key Principle: **Only individuals have a standing before the Human Rights Committee under Protocol I.**

S.M. v Barbados (1994)

Facts: The author of the application, sole owner and shareholder of a Barbadian company, submitted a complaint alleging that he had been denied a fair and public hearing in a case which involved an insurance claim on behalf of his company.

Held: The Committee held the true "victim" in this case was the company and not the author of the application. Special note was made of the fact that all the domestic remedies referred to by the applicant were brought in the name of the company rather than that of the author. Accordingly the complaint was declared inadmissible as pursuant to Art.1 of the Optional Protocol, namely only individuals may submit a communication. (1994) Communication No.502/92.

Commentary

This case illustrates that the right of complaint under the Optional Protocol belongs to individuals and consequently companies cannot be "victims" of a violation within the term as employed in the Optional Protocol. This case, however, should be contrasted with the *Singer* case, see below.

Key Principle: **Only individuals have the right to bring communications to the Human Rights Committee.**

Singer v Canada (1994)

Facts: Mr Singer had a stationery and printing business in Quebec and his clientele was predominantly English speaking. According to the laws of Quebec outdoor advertising in a language other than French was prohibited. This, in Mr Singer's opinion, amounted to a breach of his right to freedom of expression. Canada, in turn, challenged his communication by arguing that it was not Mr Singer but rather his company, Allan Singer Ltd, which was the victim. Therefore, according to Canada, the communication should be declared inadmissible.

Held: The Human Rights Committee declared the communication admissible by stating that:

> "the Covenant rights, which are at issue in the present communication, and in particular the right to freedom of expression, are by their nature inalienably linked to the person. The author has the freedom of impart information concerning his business in the language of his choice. The Committee therefore considers that the author himself, and not only his company, has been personally affected by the contested provisions of Bills Nos. 101 and 178" (para.11.2).

(1994) Communication No.455/91.

Commentary

The distinction between the *S.M.* case (above) and the *Singer* case is not very clear. In this case it appears the Committee formed the view that the restrictions on Singer's company's commercial expression naturally impacted upon his own rights to freedom of expression. Therefore the aspect of personal impact may be the determining factor, whilst the extent of such an interpretation is still unclear, after all there are many instances when restrictions upon the rights of a company may impact upon the personal rights of shareholders. An interesting question is whether the reasoning of the Committee would have been the same if Singer had been a large multinational company and not a small family business.

Key Principle: **Group of individuals may bring communications if each of them has been personally and similarly affected.**

Ominayak, Chief of the Lubicon Lake Band v Canada (1990)

Facts: The communication alleged a breach of Art.27 ICCPR, viz the minority rights of Lubicon Lake Band, a group of native Canadian indigenous people and their Chief.

Held: The Committee declared the communication admissible by stating that while the Optional Protocol provided a complaint procedure for individuals:

> "there is, however, no objection to a group of individuals, who claim to be similarly affected, collectively to submit a communication about alleged breaches of their rights" (para.32.1).

(1990) Communication No.167/84.

Commentary

Whilst the right to bring communications before the Committee belongs to individuals, this opinion shows that in instances when a certain violation similarly affects a number of individuals, they are entitled to bring a communication together and it will be admitted by the Committee.

Key Principle: No "potential victims" or "hypothetical victims" may bring communications under the Optional Protocol.

Bordes and Temeharo v France (1996)

Facts: The communication alleged breaches of the right to life and freedom from interference in the family life of the two authors. They claimed that these rights had been violated by France's underground detonation of nuclear bombs in the South Pacific in 1995. France, showing evidence of the apparent safety of the tests, argued that the authors could not submit that the risk to which they might have been exposed through the nuclear test:

> "would be such as to render imminent a violation of their rights under articles 6 and 17 of the Covenant. Purely theoretical and hypothetical violations, however, do not suffice to make them 'victims' within the meaning of the Optional Protocol" (para.3.6).

Held: The Human Rights Committee agreed with France and declared the case inadmissible:

> "It [the Committee] recalls that for a person to claim to be a victim of a violation of a right protected by the Covenant, he or she must show either that an act or omission of a State party has already adversely affected his or her enjoyment of such right, or that there is a real threat of such result" (para.5.4).

(1996) Communication No.645/95.

Commentary
In this case the authors failed to show that the French actions of nuclear testing had affected their personal rights. The Committee characterised the authors' allegations that such tests could cause further deterioration of the geological structure of the atolls as "highly controversial even in concerned scientific circles" (para.5.6) and maintained that it was unable to ascertain either the validity or correctness of such allegations. It is thus clear that the Committee will not accept communications which fail to show that the alleged action or failure to act has had a concrete impact on individual's rights. This case should be contrasted with *Toonen* (see below).

Key Principle: If a "potential victim" can show that his/her rights are breached by the very existence of a law, the communication will be admissible.

Toonen v Australia (1994)

Facts: The author brought a communication alleging that the Tasmanian laws which criminalised sexual relationships between consenting males, violated his rights under the ICCPR. It should be noted that the law had not been enforced for many years, but the author claimed the very existence of such a law had a stigmatising effect and thus made him a "victim" within the meaning of the Optional Protocol.

Held: The Committee agreed with the author that he could be deemed to be a victim within the meaning of the Optional Protocol. Although the law in question had not been enforced by the authorities for many years and it had not been enforced against the author in particular, the Committee claimed that:

"the author had made reasonable efforts to demonstrate that the threat of enforcement and the pervasive impact of the continued existence of these provisions on administrative practices and public opinion had affected him and continued to affect him personally, and that they could raise issues under articles 17 and 26 of the Covenant" (para.5.1).

(1994) Communication No.488/92.

Commentary
This case should be contrasted to the *Bordes* and *Temeharo* cases (see above) as here, while the law in question had not been enforced against the author, because he was capable of showing the direct impact it had on his rights protected under the Covenant, the communication was declared admissible.

Key Principles: **Extraterritorial application of the ICCPR: state party is responsible for the actions of its agents abroad.**

Lopez Burgos v Uruguay (1981)

Facts: The communication was brought by a wife of a victim, who claimed her husband had been kidnapped in Buenos Aeries, Argentina, by Uruguayan security and intelligence forces, aided by Argentine paramilitaries. She alleged that he was detained in Buenos Aeries for about two weeks and then secretly and illegally transferred to Uruguay, where he was detained incommunicado for three months.

Held: Since the alleged kidnapping took place in Buenos Aeries, Argentina, the Committee had to examine whether the communication conformed to the requirements of Arts 1 and 2 of the Optional Protocol. In finding in the affirmative and declaring the communication admissible, the Human Rights Committee emphasised that Art.2(1) of the ICCPR placed an obligation upon all state parties to guarantee the rights of all individuals "within their territory and subject to its jurisdiction". This, in the opinion of the Committee:

> "does not imply that the State party concerned cannot be held accountable for violations of rights under the Covenant which its agents commit upon the territory of another State, whether with the acquiesce of the Government of that State or in opposition to it" (para.12.3).

(1981) Communication No.52/79.

Commentary
This case illustrates that the ICCPR may have an extraterritorial application, especially in the cases when state agents act abroad.

Key Principles: **The burden of proof; reversal of burden of proof.**

Bleier v Uruguay (1982)

Facts: The author of the original communication, the daughter of the alleged victim claimed that her father, Eduardo Bleier, had been arrested without a court order in Montevideo, Uruguay, at the end of October 1975. However, the authorities did not acknowledge his arrest and held him incommunicado at an unknown detention place. The victim's detention had, however, been indirectly confirmed.

The author also alleged her father was subjected to particularly cruel treatment and torture because of his Jewish origin. At the time of the submission of the communication the author assumed her father was either being detained incommunicado or had died as a result of torture. The author further maintained since her father's arrest, owing to the uncertainty, there had been a complete disruption of her family life.

The author claimed the following provisions of the ICCPR had been violated by the Uruguayan authorities in respect of her father: Arts 2, 3, 6, 7, 9, (1) (2) (3) (4) and (5), 10, 12 (2), 14, 15, 17, 18, 19, 25 and 26.

Uruguay, for its part, failed to co-operate with the Human rights Committee which the Committee interpreted as:

"13. The failure of the State party to address in substance the serious allegations brought against it and corroborated by unrefuted information cannot but lead to the conclusion that Eduardo Bleier is either still detained, incommunicado, by the Uruguayan authorities or has died while in custody at the hands of the Uruguayan authorities."

Uruguay accused the Human Rights Committee of acting in "ignorance of legal rules relating to presumption of guilt" and contrary to "ethics".

Held: The Human Rights Committee maintained:

"With regard to the burden of proof, this cannot rest alone on the author of the communication, especially considering that the author and the State party do not always have equal access to the evidence and that frequently the State party alone has access to relevant information. It is implicit in article 4 (2) of the Optional Protocol that the State party has the duty to investigate in good faith all allegations of violation of the Covenant made against it and its authorities, especially when such allegations are corroborated by evidence submitted by the author of the communication, and to furnish to the Committee the information available to it. In cases where the author has submitted to the Committee allegations supported by substantial witness testimony, as in this case, and where further clarification of the case depends on information exclusively in the hands of the State party, the Committee may consider such allegations as substantiated

in the absence of satisfactory evidence and explanations to the contrary submitted by the State party." (para.13.3)

The Human Rights Committee held there had been breaches of
the ICCPR Arts 6, 7, 9 and 10 (1). (1982) 1 Selected Decisions
H.R.C. 109.

Commentary

This decision highlights that lack of co-operation and failure to
reveal information to which the state would have access may
infer guilt on the part of the alleged defaulting state. In this case
the Committee reversed the burden of proof so that the author
had to show a plausible case had occurred and it was then up to
Uruguay to rebuff the accusations.

   This is a common sense approach, especially in the cases when
a person is being held incommunicado by state authorities as in
this case and where the author had no means of actually proving
that her father was held by the state.

Key Principle: **When derogating from its obligations under
the ICCPR, the state party must provide the nature of emergency and the scope of the derogation for such a derogation to
be valid.**

Silva v Uruguay (1981)

Facts: The communication was brought by a number of victims
who alleged their rights under the ICCPR had been violated by
the 1976 executive decree which banned them from engaging in
"any activity of a political nature, including the right to vote, for
a term of 15 years". Uruguay argued that it had given a notice of
derogation under Art.4 of the ICCPR which would allow it to
issue such a decree.

Held: The Human Rights Committee initially examined the
notice of derogation by Uruguay and highlighted that the note
expressed a state of emergency existed in the country which
according to Uruguay was a matter of universal knowledge. The
Committee, however, noted the notice was silent as to the nature
and the scope of the derogation. It was observed that the right of
a state party to derogate from certain obligations it has

undertaken under the ICCPR is limited to those circumstances when it is strictly necessary. Thus, while acknowledging the sovereign right of every state party to declare a state of emergency, the Committee held that a mere invocation of exceptional circumstances could not constitute a legitimate excuse relieving a state of the obligations it had undertaken when ratifying the ICCPR. The Committee maintained that when entering a derogation, a state party is duty-bound to give a sufficiently detailed account of the relevant facts justifying the derogation. The absence of such an account means the Committee is unable to conclude that valid reasons exist for the state's departure from the normal regime and its obligation to apply the normal regime prescribed by the ICCPR. Thus the derogation by Uruguay was held to be inapplicable. (1981) 1 Selected Documents H.R.C.65.

Commentary

This communication illustrates the preparedness of the Human Rights Committee to scrutinise the notices of derogations entered by the states parties under Art.4 of the ICCPR. It also clearly indicates the limitations of such derogations: a state party must show in sufficient detail the facts justifying the derogation and must provide an account of the nature and scope of the derogation. Failure to do so will lead the Committee to ignore the derogation and the normal regime of the ICCPR will be applicable.

Key Principles: **Derogation from the ICCPR is only allowed in strictly defined circumstances; non-exhaustion of domestic remedies is not a bar if the remedy is unreasonably prolonged.**

Weinberger Weisz v Uruguay

Facts: The communication to the Committee was initiated on behalf of Ismael Weinberger by his brother. Ismael Weinberger was a journalist who was arrested at home in January 1976 without an arrest warrant and held incommunicado for some ten months. The Uruguayan authorities denied his detention until June 1976. In addition to severe torture, he was tried and, according to his brother, he did not have a fair and public hearing and was only provided with legal counsel after approximately ten months in detention. The judgment against him was not made public. In all it was maintained Arts 2, 3, 7, 9, 10, 12, 14, 15, 25 and 26 of the ICCPR had been violated. Pursuant to Art.4(2) ICCPR no derogation may be made to Arts 7 and 15.

Initially Uruguay objected to the admissibility of the communication on three grounds:

(a) the case had been considered by the Inter American Commission on Human Rights but the case had been shelved when the complaint had been withdrawn;

(b) the date of the alleged violation of human rights preceded the date of the entry into force for Uruguay of the ICCPR and the Optional Protocol; and

(c) domestic remedies had not been exhausted (the state party enclosed an annex listing the domestic remedies in the Uruguayan legal system).

Uruguay maintained that the victim had been arrested for participating directly in subversive activities. His brother, on the other hand, maintained that his arrest was precipitated by his having provided information on trade union activities to an anti-government newspaper.

Held: The Human Rights Committee initially declared the communication admissible and maintained that it was not barred from considering the case since the matter was no longer under consideration by the Inter American Commission on Human Rights. Although the arrest of Ismael Weinberger preceded the date of the entry into force for Uruguay of the ICCPR and the Optional Protocol, the alleged violations continued beyond that date and thus the violation was continuous. The Committee further claimed that were no further domestic remedies available for the alleged victim to pursue.

Turning to the merits of the case, the Committee noted that Uruguay had failed to submit copies of any court orders or decisions relevant to Mr Weinberger's case. Accordingly the Committee decided to base its views on the facts which had been presented to it and which had either been essentially confirmed by Uruguay or were uncontested, except by denials of a general character providing no particular information or explanation.

The Committee held that apart from reference to prompt security measures, Uruguay had failed to make any submissions of fact or law justifying its derogation from the ICCPR.

Additionally, the Committee expressed the view that some of the facts raised issues under non-derogable articles. The Human Rights Committee acknowledged that the legislation of many countries deprived criminal offenders of certain political rights. The Committee went on that:

> " ... , article 25 of the Covenant only prohibits 'unreasonable' restrictions. In no case, however, may a person be subjected to such sanctions solely because of his or her political opinion (arts. 2 (1) and 26)." (para.15)

The Committee maintained with regard to the instant case that deprivation of the right to engage in political activities for 15 years was without justification. The Committee found that Uruguay had violated a number of articles in the ICCPR in particular:

> Arts 7 and 10(1), because of the severe treatment which Ismael Weinberger received during the first 10 months of his detention;
>
> Art.9(3), because he was not brought promptly before a judge or other officer authorised by law to exercise judicial power and because he was not tried within a reasonable time;
>
> Art.9(4), because recourse to *habeas corpus* was not available to him;
>
> Art.14(1), because he had no fair and public hearing and because the judgment rendered against him was not made public;
>
> Art.14(3), because he did not have access to legal assistance during the first 10 months of his detention and was tried in his absence;
>
> Art.15(1), because the penal law was applied retroactively against him;
>
> Art.19(2), because he was detained for having disseminated information relating to trade-union activities;
>
> Art.25, because he was barred from taking part in the conduct of public affairs and from being elected for 15 years in accordance with Acta Institucional No.4 of September 1, 1976.

The Committee expressed the opinion that Uruguay was under an obligation to provide Mr Weinberger with effective remedies, including his immediate release as well as compensation in respect of the violations suffered. No.28/1978: Uruguay. 29/10/80. CCPR/C/11/D/28/1978.

Commentary
The Committee's treatment of this communication shows the non-production of documents and evidence by the party, i.e. the state that would have access to such evidence will be taken as an inference of guilt.

Key Principles: **Membership of a minority; States cannot restrict definition of particular minorities, nor define membership of a minority.**

Lovelace v Canada (1981)

Facts: The author of the communication had been born and registered as a Maliseet Indian. Since she married a non Indian, she lost her rights and status as an Indian pursuant to Canadian legislation, the Indian Act. The author's marriage broke down and she wished to return to live on the Maliseet Reserve but was denied this opportunity under the Indian Act.

The submission before the Human Rights Committee was whether the Indian Act, by denying the author access to her native culture and language, was contrary to Art.27 of the ICCPR.

Held: The Human Rights Committee expressed the view that the rights under Art.27 of the ICCPR had to be secured to "persons belonging" to the minority. It was noted however, that the Indian Act dealt primarily with a number of privileges which did not as such come within the scope of the ICCPR. Protection under the Indian Act and protection under Art.27 of the ICCPR had to be distinguished. Thus persons who were born and brought up on a reserve, who had kept ties with their community and wished to maintain these ties, should normally be considered as belonging to that minority within the meaning of the ICCPR. It was held that since Sandra Lovelace was ethnically a Maliseet Indian and had only been absent from her home reserve for a few years during the existence of her marriage, in the opinion of the Committee she was entitled to be regarded as "belonging" to this minority and to claim the benefits of Art.27 of the ICCPR.

The question whether these benefits had been denied to her in turn depended on the scope of Art.27. The Committee acknowledged the right to live on a reserve was not a right guaranteed by Art.27 of the ICCPR and nor did the Indian Act interfere directly with the functions expressly mentioned in Art.27.

However, the Committee's view was the right of Sandra Lovelace to access her native culture and language "in community with the other members" of her group, had in fact been, and continued to be, interfered with because there was no place outside her particular reserve where such a community existed.

The Committee expressed the view that statutory restrictions affecting the right to residence on a reserve of a person belonging to the minority concerned must have both a reasonable and objective justification and be consistent with the other provisions of the ICCPR, read as a whole. In the particular case before it, the Human Rights Committee said that cognisance should be given to the personal circumstances of the author. Regardless of the merits of the Indian Act in other respects, the Committee did not believe it reasonable to deny her the right to reside on the reserve. The Committee also maintained that such denial was unnecessary for the preservation of the tribe's identity. The Committee thus concluded the failure to recognize her as belonging to the tribe was an unjustifiable denial of her rights under Art.27 of the ICCPR. (1981) 2 Selected Decisions H.R.C. 28.

Commentary
The finding of the Committee in this case prompted the subsequent amendment of the Canadian Indian Act so as to allow women who had married non Indians before 1985 to rejoin their tribes. There was a subsequent application alleging the amendment restricted the right of the tribe to determine its own membership. This application (*RL et al v Canada* 358/89) was declared inadmissible because of a failure to exhaust local remedies.

Key Principles: **Article 6 of ICCPR, death penalty, extradition.**

Kindler v Canada (1993)

Facts: The author of the complaint, Mr Kindler, had been convicted in the State of Pennsylvania of first degree murder and kidnapping and the death penalty was recommended. However before he was sentenced, he escaped from custody, but was eventually arrested in Quebec Province in 1985. Later that year a request was made for his extradition to the US from Canada on the basis of an extradition treaty of 1976 between the two countries. The Supreme Court of Quebec ordered the extradition. Pursuant to the extradition treaty of 1976 existing between Canada and the US it was provided that:

> "when the offence for which extradition is requested is punishable by death under the laws of the requesting state and the laws of the requested state do not permit such punishment for that offence, extradition may be refused unless the requesting state provides such assurances as the requested state considers sufficient that the death penalty shall not be imposed or, if imposed, shall not be executed".

Although the death penalty had been abolished in Canada in 1976, the competent Minister nevertheless did not seek assurances that the death penalty imposed on Kindler would not be carried out. Subsequently, Kindler pursued local remedies and the Supreme Court of Canada decided that Kindler's extradition would not amount to a violation under the Canadian Charter of Human Rights and thus Kindler was extradited.

Kindler maintained that the decision to extradite him was in breach of Art.6 of ICCPR as he was now at risk of capital punishment.

It should be noted that at the time of the communication the US was not a party to the ICCPR.

Held: The Human Rights Committee crystallised the issue before it as being whether Canada, through the act of extradition, would be exposing Kindler to a real risk of a breach of his ICCPR rights. The Committee claimed that Art.2 of the ICCPR required states to guarantee the rights of persons within their jurisdiction. If a person is lawfully expelled or extradited, the state party concerned will not generally incur responsibility under the

ICCPR for any violations of that person's rights that may later occur in the other jurisdiction.

However, if a state party should take a decision relating to a person within its jurisdiction, and the necessary and foreseeable consequence is that a person's rights under the ICCPR will be violated in another jurisdiction, the state party itself may be in violation of the ICCPR. In other words, where a state hands over a person to another state in circumstances in which it was foreseeable that torture would take place, responsibility will be incurred.

The Committee looked at the Canadian law and found that it did not provide for the death penalty, except in military cases. The Committee noted that although Canada could, under the Extradition Treaty seek assurances from the other party, this was not required, and when done it would normally be because of the existence of exceptional circumstances.

The Committee further recognised that the method of execution could also be relevant. Regarding the abolition of the death penalty, the Human Rights Committee on the basis of the General Comment on Art.6 of the ICCPR noted what was called for was not a total ban on the death penalty but rather a limitation of its use. The Committee highlighted that Kindler was over 18 years of age when he committed the crime, he had been tried according to the due process of law and he had been the subject of lengthy proceedings within Canada.

On the basis of the evidence before it the Human Rights Committee, in this particular case, found there was no violation of Art.6 ICCPR. (1993) 1–2 I.H.R.R.98.

Commentary
There were however five dissenting opinions.

Opinions similar to that in *Kindler* were expressed in subsequent applications regarding the death penalty and Art.6, see *Ng v Canada* (below). This position of the Committee however should be contrasted to that which it adopted in the case of *Judge* (see below).

Key Principles: Article 7 of ICCPR (prohibition on torture);
death penalty; extradition; method of execution.

Ng v Canada Human Rights (1994)

Facts: Ng claimed that if extradited from Canada to the US for
trial and convicted of serial murder the likely sentence would be
the death penalty. This he maintained would be in violation of
Art.6 of the ICCPR. Ng also claimed that there would be a breach
to his Art.7 rights by virtue of the method of execution which
would most probably be used, namely gas asphyxiation.

Held: The Human Rights Committee did not find that extradition would amount to a violation of Art.6. However, the
Committee did find that gas asphyxiation would not meet the
test established by the Committee in its General Comment No.20
on Art.7, in which the Committee has maintained that while
states parties are entitled to retain the death penalty, the method
of execution must be such as to inflict "least possible physical
and mental suffering" (para.6). In the view of the Committee, gas
asphyxiation would not meet this requirement and thus would
constitute cruel and inhuman treatment, which would be in
violation of Art.7 of the ICCPR. (1994) 1–2 I.H.R.R.161.

Commentary
This case illustrates that while the Human Rights Committee
strongly suggests abolition of the death penalty; it is per se not
prohibited by the provision of the ICCPR. However, as showed
by this case, the Committee will scrutinise the methods
employed for carrying out the death penalty so as to ensure that
these do not breach Art.7 of the ICCPR. Thus, in this case the
obligation incumbent on Canada was that required by Art.7: the
method of execution was required to comply with the prohibition on torture and inhuman treatment.

   An example of a method of execution compatible with the
ICCPR is that of lethal injection, see *Cox v Canada* (1994) 2
I.H.R.R. 307.

Key Principle: **The Human Rights Committee departs from** *Kindler* **position.**

Judge v Canada Human Rights (2004)

Facts: The author was convicted on two counts of first-degree murder and possession of an instrument of crime by a Philadelphian Court. He was sentenced to death, by electric chair, escaped from prison and fled to Canada. The author was then convicted of two robberies committed in Vancouver, Canada and sentenced to 10 years' imprisonment. He appealed his convictions but these were dismissed and his deportation to the US ordered.

His case was reviewed by the Canadian National Parole Board which ordered he be detained until the expiry of his sentence. In 1997 the author wrote to the Minister of Citizenship and Immigration requesting ministerial intervention with a view to stalling the deportation order against him, until such time as a request for extradition from the US might be sought and received in his case. If removed under the Extradition Treaty, Canada could have asked for assurances from the US that he would not be executed. The Minister refused his request. The author sought leave for judicial review of the Minister's refusal, but his application for leave was denied, no reasons were provided with no appeal possible from the refusal to grant leave.

The author claimed that Canada imposed mental suffering upon him amounting to cruel, inhuman and degrading treatment or punishment, having detained him for 10 years while the certainty of capital punishment was hanging over his head at the conclusion of his sentence, constituting a breach of Art.7 of the ICCPR. The author claimed Canada had no valid sentencing objective since he was sentenced to death, in another state party, and therefore Canada only prolonged the agony of his confinement. The author claimed he was not treated with humanity and respect for the inherent dignity of the human person, in violation of Art.10 of the ICCPR.

Held: The Human Rights Committee recalled its previous jurisprudence in *Kindler.* However, while recognising the value of consistency and coherence in its case law, it was noted there could be exceptional situations in which a review of the scope of application of the rights protected in the ICCPR is required, such as where an alleged violation involves that most fundamental of rights, like the right to life. It was said that this would be particularly true if there had been notable factual and legal developments and changes in international opinion. The Committee acknowledged the jurisprudence of *Kindler* was established some 10 years ago, and that since that time there had been a broadening international consensus in favour of abolition of the death penalty. In states which had retained the death penalty there was an emerging, broadening consensus not to implement the death penalty. Significantly, the Committee noted that since *Kindler* Canada itself had recognised the need to amend its own domestic law to secure the protection of those extradited under sentence of death in the receiving state. For example, assurances should be sought in all but exceptional circumstances that the death penalty would not be carried out. The Committee expressed the view the ICCPR should be interpreted as a living instrument and the rights protected under it applied in a contemporary context. Consequently, while recognising that Canada had not imposed the death penalty on Judge, the Committee held that by deporting him to the US, Canada established the crucial link in the causal chain that would make his execution possible. The Committee declared that Canada had breached its obligations under Art.6(1) of the ICCPR by extraditing the author to the US where he was under the death sentence. (2004) 11 I.H.R.R. 125, UN HRC.

Commentary
The importance of this opinion is the Committee recognised the ICCPR as a living instrument and human rights as evolving and developing. What may be regarded as compatible with the ICCPR may change with the passage of time and changing attitudes as to what is acceptable.

Key Principles: **The supremacy of the right to life and obligations incumbent on state authorities.**

de Guerrero v Colombia Human Rights (1982)

Facts: The Columbian police raided a house in the belief that a kidnap victim was detained there. Not finding the victim the police lay in wait for the suspected kidnappers. Seven individuals, none of whom were ever shown to have any connection with the kidnappers, were fatally shot as they arrived at the house. The police action was justified on the basis of domestic law Legislative Decree No.0070 which provided the police with a defence in respect of any criminal charge arising out of acts committed "in the course of operations planned with the object of preventing and curbing kidnapping".

Held: The Committee initially noted that the deprivation of life by the authorities of the state is a matter of the utmost gravity. The requirements that the right to life shall be protected by law and that no one shall be arbitrarily deprived of his life mean that the law must strictly control and limit the circumstances in which a person may be deprived of his life by the authorities of a state.

In the present case the Human Rights Committee maintained that the fact seven persons lost their lives as a result of the deliberate action of the police showed that the deprivation of life was intentional. The police action was apparently taken without warning to the victims and without giving them any opportunity to surrender or to offer any explanation of their presence or intentions. There was no evidence the police action was necessary either in self defence, or the defence of others. Such action was not necessary to affect the arrest or prevent the escape of the persons concerned. Moreover, the victims were no more than suspects of the kidnapping and their killing by the police deprived them of all the protection of due process of law as laid down by the ICCPR.

Consequently, the Committee held that the police action resulting in the deaths was disproportionate to the requirements of law enforcement in the circumstances. The deaths were an arbitrary deprivation of life contrary to Art.6(1) ICCPR and the right to life was not adequately protected as required by the law of Colombia. (1982) 1 Selected Decisions 112.

Commentary

The Committee's view in the instant case highlights the primary importance of the right to life and the taking of life by the state is legitimate only in very strict circumstances. The Committee's findings shed some light on what would be understood as arbitrary and in breach of Art.6(1). It may also be noted that an act may be legitimate under domestic law but may, in the international forum, be held "arbitrary" and thus constitute a breach of state party's obligations under the ICCPR.

Key Principles: **Interpretation of the notion of arbitrariness within the context of Art.9(1) ICCPR and Art.9(4) of the ICCPR; means of challenging arbitrariness.**

A v Australia (1998)

Facts: The claimant was one of 25 Cambodians ("boat people") who arrived illegally in Australia by boat, code-named "Pender Bay", and sought refugee status. Mr A and the others were detained in various detention camps and Mr A's complaint was that he had been detained arbitrarily and was eligible for compensation under Art.9(5) of the ICCPR. The so-called boat people were at the time the only group of unauthorised people who were mandatorily detained on arrival in Australia.

Three questions confronted the Committee, namely:

(a) whether the prolonged detention of the author, pending determination of his entitlement to refugee status, was "arbitrary" within the meaning of art.9, para.1;

(b) whether the alleged impossibility to challenge the lawfulness of the author's detention and his alleged lack of access to legal advice was in violation of art.9, para.4; and

(c) whether the proceedings concerning his application for refugee status fell within the scope of the application of art.14, para.1 and whether, in the affirmative, there had been a violation of art.14, para.1. The question before the Committee was whether Mr A's unlawful entry to Australia and the risk of his absconding if not held were sufficient to justify his indefinite and prolonged detention.

Held: The Human Rights Committee noted that arbitrariness should not be equated with "against the law" but should be broadly interpreted to encompass inappropriateness and injustice. The Committee acknowledged that remand in custody could be considered arbitrary if it were not necessary in a particular instance to prevent escape or interference with evidence. The Committee refuted Mr A's claim that it was per se arbitrary to detain those individuals requesting asylum. The Committee also refuted the contention under customary international law all such detention were regarded as arbitrary.

However the Committee observed that keeping a person in detention should be reviewed on a regular basis and in all instances detention should not continue beyond a certain period without appropriate justification. In examining the particular case of Mr A, the Committee concluded that Australia had failed to provide good reason for justifying Mr A's continued detention over a four year period.

The Committee therefore concluded that the Mr A's detention was arbitrary within the meaning of Art.9, para.1.

Regarding a court's review of the lawfulness of detention, the Committee expressed the view that this had to include the possibility of ordering release and should not be limited to mere compliance of the detention with domestic law. What the Committee found as decisive for the purposes of Art.9(4) was that such review be in its effects, real and not merely formal.

Regarding a right to legal assistance, so as to have access to the Courts, the Committee noted Mr A was entitled to legal assistance from the outset of his request for asylum and he would have had such access had he requested it.

Mr A's repeated moves between detention centres obliging him to change his legal representatives did not, in the Committee's view, detract from the fact that he retained access to legal advisors. The fact that geographical remoteness made such access inconvenient did not engage Art.9(4) of the ICCPR. (1998) 5 I.H.R.R.78.

Commentary
The Committee's views in this complaint underscores the obligations undertaken pursuant to human rights instruments are not to be assumed in name only, but must be effective and real. In other words, human rights demand more than mere lip service. Obligations incumbent on Contracting Parties to international human rights instruments are to be realised and if they are to be meaningful for those for whom they are intended the necessary implementing steps must be taken. The Committee did not, in this instance, consider whether any issue arose under Art.14(1) of the ICCPR, namely equality for all before courts and tribunals.

Key Principle: The notion of "arbitrariness" under Art.9 of
the ICCPR.

Mukong v Cameroon (1994)

Facts: The author, a Cameroonian journalist and a long-standing advocate of multi-party democracy in the one party state of
Cameroon, was arrested following his broadcast on the BBC in
1998 in which he criticised the President and the government of
Cameroon. It was contended that one of the reasons for his arrest
was that his remarks were subversive and in breach of an
Ordinance, under which he was later charged with an offence.
The author was re-arrested in 1990 after a public meeting in
which he advocated multi-party democracy.

   He alleged breaches of his rights under Arts 7, 19 and the
Committee agreed with him. The breach of Art.9(1) was also
alleged and so the Committee had to consider the notion of
"arbitrary detention".

Held: The Human Rights Committee reiterated that the "arbitrariness" as expressed in Art.9(1) of the ICCPR must not be
equated with "against the law", but rather must be interpreted
more broadly so as to include elements of inappropriateness,
injustice, lack of predictability and due process of law. The
Committee maintained that the mere fact that an arrest is carried
out pursuant to an existing law is insufficient, as remand in
custody must be also reasonable in all circumstances and further
must be also necessary to conform to the requirements of
Art.9(1). In the view of the Committee, the detention of the
author was neither reasonable nor necessary in the circumstances and thus Cameroon was also found to be in breach of its
obligations under Art.9(1). (1994) Communication 458/91.

Note: The Committee Against Torture was established pursuant to Art.17 of the Convention Against Torture and Other
Cruel and Inhuman or Degrading Treatment or Punishment
(CAT). A state can under Art.22 of CAT recognise the Committee's competence to receive individual communications from
alleged victims of torture.

Key Principles: The principle of *non refoulement* as reflected in Art.3 UN Convention Against Torture and Other Cruel, Inhuman or Degrading Treatment or Punishment.

Khan v Canada (1995)

Facts: The author of the communication, Tahir Khan, arrived in Canada in August 1990 having left Pakistan in fear for his personal security. Mr Khan applied for refugee status but this was refused by the Canadian Immigration and Refugee Board in January 1992 and he sought leave for judicial review. However, this was refused by a Federal Court Judge. Mr Khan then sought permission to stay in Canada for humanitarian reasons but this was also refused and his removal to Pakistan was ordered.

Mr Khan claimed that he would be at risk if returned to Pakistan from Islamic fundamentalists, the Pakistan Inter Service Intelligence and the Government of Pakistan because of his membership in the Baltistan Student Federation (BSF).

In his communication against Canada, Mr Khan submitted the Canadian authorities had failed to address the core issues of his case in not recognising him as a refugee. Mr Khan maintained that as he was in charge of the BSF overseas he was still at risk of persecution if returned to Pakistan.

The case was brought under the provisions of the UN Convention Against Torture and was considered by the Committee Against Torture.

Held: The Committee Against Torture initially noted that Canada had not raised any objections to the admissibility of the communication and thus the Committee could proceed to examine the communication on its merits. The task before the Committee was whether there were substantial grounds for believing Mr Khan would be at real danger of being tortured. Both parties made extensive submissions with respect to the fairness of the refugee determination process and the post claim risk assessment procedures. The Committee, however, emphasised that it was only called upon to review whether or not Canada, in the instant case, was complying with its obligations under the Torture Convention. It was not called upon to make any assessment of the existing system in Canada nor was it called upon to determine whether Mr Khan's rights under the Torture Convention had been breached by Pakistan (not a party to the Torture Convention).

Thus, having identified its task, the Committee made reference to Art.3(2) as to how it would determine whether Mr Khan would be personally at risk of being subjected to torture. The Committee noted that the existence of a consistent pattern of gross flagrant or mass violations of human rights in a country does not, as such, constitute a sufficient ground for determining that a person would be in danger of being tortured upon his return to that country. Additional grounds were required. Likewise the absence of a consistent pattern of gross violations of human rights does not mean a person may not be at risk of torture given his specific circumstances.

The Committee then turned to look at the specifics of Mr Khan's claim and highlighted a medical report which did not contradict Mr Khan's allegations. The Committee recognised some of Mr Khan's claims and supporting evidence had been submitted subsequent to his refugee claim being dismissed. However, the Committee also recognised that such conduct was not uncommon for victims of torture. The Committee also observed that even in the event of some doubts about the facts as put forward by Mr Khan the task of the Committee must be to ensure his security. The Committee noted the objective evidence narrating that torture was widely practised against political dissenters in Pakistan. The Committee then looked at Mr Khan's claim against the background of objective evidence and considered there were substantial grounds for believing that a political activist like Mr Khan would be in danger of being subjected to torture. Furthermore Pakistan, not being a party to the Torture Convention, meant if Mr Khan were returned he would no longer have the possibility of availing himself of the Committee for protection.

The Committee was of the view that the forcible return of Mr Khan to Pakistan would constitute a violation of Art.3 of the Torture Convention. Accordingly Canada was under an obligation to refrain from forcibly returning Mr Khan to Pakistan. (1995) 2 I.H.R.R. 337.

Ismail Alan v Switzerland (1997)

Facts: Essentially this case was similar to the above, although the parties were of course different; the case was examined once again by the Committee Against Torture.

Held: The Committee concluded that the expulsion or return of Mr Alan to Turkey, in the light of the objective evidence and the specifics of his case, would constitute a violation of Art.3 of the Torture Convention. Accordingly Switzerland was under an obligation to refrain from forcibly returning Mr Alan to Turkey. 4 I.H.R.R. 97. UN CAT.

Commentary

What is interesting and distinguishes this from the case of Mr Khan is that Turkey was a party to the UN Convention Against Torture and had also accepted the right of individual petition.

Mutombo v Switzerland (1993)

Facts: Mr Mutombo, a Zairean citizen, had claimed refugee status in Switzerland which had been refused. Mr Mutombo submitted that there was evidence of a consistent pattern of gross and massive violations of human rights in Zaire which, pursuant to Art.3(2) of the Torture Convention, are circumstances which a state party should take into account when deciding on expulsion.

Switzerland however maintained that the mere existence of a consistent pattern of gross flagrant or mass violations of human rights in a country should only be taken as an indication when examining all the circumstances and when determining whether a person would be in concrete danger of being tortured. The existence of the substantial grounds of Art.3(1) should be determined in the light of all the circumstances of a particular case. Switzerland invoked the jurisprudence of the European Commission of Human Rights in support of its contention that the general situation in a country is not sufficient to preclude the return of an individual. Switzerland also made reference to the case law of the European Court of Human Rights to emphasise that a mere possibility of ill treatment because of a general situation in a country was not in itself sufficient to transgress Art.3 of the European Convention on Human Rights and Fundamental Freedoms. Switzerland argued that Art.3 of the UN Convention Against Torture did not afford a wider protection than Art.3 of European Convention on Human Rights and Fundamental Freedoms.

Held: The Committee Against Torture initially observed that it was not called upon to determine whether Mr Mutombo's rights ler the UN Convention Against Torture had been violated by re, which was not party to it. Rather, the issue before the Committee was whether his expulsion or return to Zaire would violate Switzerland's obligation under Art.3 of the Convention Against Torture. The Committee endorsed Switzerland's view that a particular risk to an individual could not be adduced from a general situation prevailing in the country concerned. The belief that substantial grounds exist within the meaning of Art.3(1) can, as it was in this case, be strengthened by "the existence in the state concerned of a consistent pattern of gross flagrant or mass violations of human rights" within the meaning of Art.3(2). The Committee also highlighted that as Zaire was not a party to the Convention Against Torture, Mr Mutombo, if returned to Zaire, would no longer have the legal possibility of applying to the Committee for protection.

The Committee acknowledged that the concerns of Switzerland, namely the implementation of Art.3 might be abused by asylum seekers. However, it considered even if certain facts were doubtful, it was incumbent upon the Committee to ensure Mr Mutombo's security was not endangered. Therefore the Committee concluded that Mr Mutombo would be at risk and to return him would constitute a violation of Art.3 of the Torture Convention. 1–3 I.H.R.R. 122.

Note: The Committee on the Elimination of Racial Discrimination was established pursuant to Art.8 Convention on the Elimination of Racial Discrimination (CERD); Art.14 provides for states to accept the competence of the Committee to receive individual communications.

Key Principles: **State's obligations under CERD; a state's discretion to prosecute criminal offences remains governed by considerations of public policy and is not denied by CERD.**

Yilmaz-Dogan v the Netherlands (1988)

Facts: The principal issues confronting the Committee were whether a state party (the Netherlands) had failed to meet its obligation, under Art.5(e)(i) of CERD, namely that of guaranteeing equality before the law in respect of the right to work, and protection against unemployment. The question was also posed as to whether Arts 4 and 6 of CERD require a state to initiate criminal proceedings in instances of alleged racial discrimination and to provide for an appeal mechanism in cases of such discrimination.

Mrs Yilamz-Dogan, a Turkish national living in the Netherlands had been employed since 1979 in the textile industry. However, following a road accident in 1981 she was unable to work until 1982 when she resumed part-time employment of her own accord. In August 1981 she married and in June 1982, by which time she was pregnant, her employer sought to terminate her contract. That permission to terminate her contract was refused on the grounds that Dutch legislation prohibited the termination of employment contracts during the pregnancy of the employee.

However, a request was made by the employer to the appropriate Cantonal Court. The employer in his request stated;

"When a Netherlands girl marries and has a baby, she stops working. Our foreign women workers, on the other hand, take the child to neighbours or family and at the slightest set-back disappear on sick-leave under the terms of the Sickness Act. They repeat that endlessly. Since we all must do our utmost to avoid going under, we cannot afford such goings-on."

The employer's request was subsequently then granted.

Mrs Yilamz-Dogan then sought various domestic remedies culminating in a decision from the Dutch Court of Appeal in November 1983 stating, inter alia, it could not be determined that the defendant, by raising the issue of differences in absenteeism owing to childbirth and illness between foreign and Dutch female workers, intended to discriminate by race, or that his actions resulted in race discrimination. Although acknowledging the employer's remarks in the letter of July 19, 1982 as "unfortunate and objectionable", it was decided that the institution of criminal proceedings was neither in the public interest nor in the interest of Mrs Yilamz-Dogan. There existed no right of appeal to the Supreme Court.

Held: The Committee concluded that Mrs Yilamz-Dogan's dismissal was the consequence of a failure to take into account all the circumstances of the case and accordingly her right to work had not been protected.

Turning to the issue of a contracting party's obligation to prosecute cases of alleged racial discrimination and to provide

\ctims of racial discrimination with the opportunity of
l review, the Committee observed that that obligation still
took account of considerations of public policy. The Committee
recognised the existence of the "expediency principle" and held
in the instant case that the prosecutor acted appropriately. The
Committee also noted in the instant case the decision not to
prosecute had been reviewed by the Dutch Court of Appeal and
the Committee expressed the view this judicial review mechanism was compatible with Art.4 of CERD.

The Committee observed that the terms of Art.6 of CERD did
not impose upon state parties the duty to institute a mechanism
of sequential remedies, up to and including the Dutch Supreme
Court level, in cases of alleged racial discrimination. Communication No.1/1984, August 10, 1988, CERD Reports GAOR 43rd
Session Supp.18 p.59 (1988).

Commentary
This decision highlights how CERD may be used by an indivi-
dual but also demonstrates the discretion which Contracting
Parties still enjoy under the CERD.

Key Principles: **Interpretation of discrimination in terms of
CERD; the scope of Art.1(2) of CERD; obligation on states that
are Contracting Parties to CERD; competence of Committee.**

Diop v France 1991

Facts: Mr Diop maintained that his right to work had been
denied on the basis of national origin, and the French judicial
authorities had breached the principle of equality, enshrined in
Art.5 of the CERD. Mr Diop, a Senegalese citizen married to a
French citizen, had been denied membership by the Nice Bar
Council. Mr Diop invoked domestic appeal remedies and the
Court of Cassation determined that he fulfilled all statutory
requirements for the exercise of the legal profession except one,
namely French nationality. According to Mr Diop his right to
equal treatment had been breached in two respects. Although he
was denied the right to practise law in Nice, six lawyers of
Senegalese nationality had been admitted to the Paris Bar. Mr
Diop maintained that it was unacceptable that France should
allow such differences of treatment within the national territory.

It was also maintained that his refusal breached bilateral instruments existing between France and Senegal, whereby on the basis of reciprocity French lawyers could exercise their profession in Senegal and vice versa.

Held: Initially, the Committee considered France's contention that the communication was inadmissible. France's claim was based on Mr Diop's alleged failure to exhaust local remedies through his not invoking discriminatory treatment based on national origin before the domestic courts. However, the Committee noted that the Court of Cassation had in its decision addressed the issue of national origin and furthermore France had not indicated to Mr Diop that any other remedies were available.

Finding the communication admissible the Committee turned to consider whether Art.5(e) of CERD had been breached, whether Mr Diop's right to family life had been violated (Mr Diop maintained he had to leave his home and pursue his legal profession in Dakar in order to be able to provide for his family), and whether his refusal by the Bar Council was contrary to the bilateral treaty between France and Senegal, namely the Franco-Senegalese Convention on Movement of Persons.

Regarding the latter, the Committee concluded that it was not within its remit to consider bilateral Conventions, unless that is, the application of these Conventions resulted in manifestly discriminatory or arbitrary treatment of individuals under the jurisdiction of states parties to CERD which had made a declaration under Art.14 of CERD. In this particular instance the Committee expressed the view that there was no evidence that either the application or non-application of the Franco-Senegalese Convention had produced manifest discrimination.

In respect of Art.5(e) and the right to family life the Committee observed that the rights protected were:

" … subject to progressive implementation. It is not within the Committee's mandate to see to it that these rights are established; rather, it is the Committee's task to monitor the implementation of these rights, once they have been granted on equal terms. In so far as the author's complaint is based on article 5(e) of the Convention, the Committee considers it to be ill-founded." (para.6.4).

The Committee emphasised it was not for it to see these rights were established, rather it was its task to monitor the

nentation of these rights once they had been granted on
erms.

Accordingly the Committee found Mr Diop's complaint
unfounded.

As to the allegation of racial discrimination within the meaning of Art.1 para.1 of CERD the Committee noted that the relevant domestic provision operated as a preference or distinction
between citizens and non-citizens within the meaning of Art.1,
para.2, of CERD and therefore was compatible with CERD.

The Committee concluded that the allegation made by Mr
Diop related to a situation which did not violate Art.1 para.1 of
CERD. Communication No.2/1989, March 18, 1991, CERD/C/
39/D/2/1989/Rev.2.

Commentary

This case highlights that the rights protected under the CERD
Convention are not absolute and Contracting Parties still enjoy
discretion within fixedstated limits.

Note: The Committee on the Elimination of all Forms of Discrimination against Women was established pursuant to Art.17
of Convention on the Elimination of Discrimination against
Women (CEDAW); an Optional Protocol to CEDAW acknowledging the competence of the Committee to receive communications from or on behalf of individuals or groups of
individuals entered into force in 2001.

Key Principles: **Right of individual communication under
Optional Protocol to CEDAW; accountability of states for lack
of due diligence in affording protection from non-state actors;
obligations on Contracting Parties to CEDAW.**

Ms A. T. v Hungary 2003

Facts: Ms AT alleged violations by Hungary of Arts 2(a), (b)
and (e), 5(a) and 16 of the CEDAW for its failure to provide
effective protection from her former common law husband (LF).
Ms AT maintained that Hungary passively neglected its "positive" obligations under CEDAW and thereby allowed the
domestic violence against her to continue.

She contended the criminal procedures invoked against LF

were neither effective nor afforded immediate protection. Ms AT maintained that as one of her children is severely disabled she could not go to a women's refuge as they are not equipped to take in a fully disabled child together with his mother and sister. Ms AT had exhausted local remedies and although a pending petition for review had been submitted to the Hungarian Supreme Court Ms AT believed it would be very unlikely that she would get any satisfaction there as Hungarian Courts allegedly did not consider CEDAW as law to be applied by them.

Although Ms AT acknowledged most of the incidents against her took place prior to the date the Optional Protocol to CEDAW entered into force, these incidents constituted elements of a clear continuum of regular domestic violence and that her life continued to be threatened.

Held: The Committee recalled General Recommendation No.19 on Violence Against Women reinforcing that the definition of discrimination includes gender based violence and gender based violence may breach specific provisions of " ... regardless of whether those provisions expressly mention violence".

On the issue of states being held accountable for the conduct of non-state actors the Committee again invoked General Recommendation No.19, namely:

> "[U]nder general international law and specific human rights covenants, States may also be responsible for private acts if they fail to act with due diligence to prevent violations of rights or to investigate and punish acts of violence, and for providing compensation".

The Committee took into account that Hungary acknowledged that the remedies pursued by Ms AT were not capable of affording her immediate protection from LF and the legal and institutional arrangements within Hungary were not yet able to ensure the internationally expected level of protection for victims of domestic violence. The Committee highlighted that neither Hungarian civil or criminal proceedings afforded high priority to domestic violence cases. Additionally Hungary did not provide information as to alternate avenues that Ms AT might have pursued.

The Committee concluded that under CEDAW states are required to take preventative steps and afford protection to women in Ms AT's situation. Hungary, the Committee held, had failed to fulfil this particular obligation.

Committee also made reference to the traditional attitudes referred to in its 3rd and 4th periodic reports of Hungary in 2002, still persisted. Accordingly the Committee urged the expeditious introduction of a specific law prohibiting domestic violence against women and providing for protection and exclusion orders as well as support services including shelters. Communication No.2/2003.

Commentary

Although not binding, this decision demonstrates a recognition that states may be held accountable for failing to take preventative steps against, or providing remedies against, violence perpetrated by non-state actors. This is particularly relevant in the context of violence against women as that most frequently occurs in the domestic forum and the perpetrators are often other family members.

INDEX

LEGAL TAXONOMY
FROM SWEET & MAXWELL

This index has been prepared using Sweet and Maxwell's Legal Taxonomy. Main index entries conform to keywords provided by the Legal Taxonomy except where references to specific documents or non-standard terms (denoted by quotation marks) have been included. These keywords provide a means of identifying similar concepts in other Sweet & Maxwell publications and online services to which keywords from the Legal Taxonomy have been applied. Readers may find some minor differences between terms used in the text and those which appear in the index. Suggestions to *sweetandmaxwell.taxonomy@thomson.com.*

(all references are to page number)

Index